A MINISTER'S OPPORTUNITIES

RALPH G. TURNBULL

BAKER BOOK HOUSE
Grand Rapids, Michigan

To Honor
E. Joe Gilliam
Mark O. Hatfield
Earl J. McGrath
Paul S. Rees
D. Elton Trueblood
Lowell J. Williamson
Advisors of
Excellence
who have
"often refreshed me"
(II TIMOTHY 1:16)

Copyright 1979 by
Baker Book House Company
Grand Rapids, Michigan 49506

ISBN: 0-8010-8846-1

Printed in the United States of America

THE RECEPTION GIVEN to *A Minister's Obstacles* has led to this sequel and complement. In the earlier work there are intimate and personal matters which deal with the perils and pitfalls of the ministry. Some of my fellow ministers shared the inner struggles which they waged against trials and temptations common to all. Over the years the subject called for further investigation and five chapters were added. We are tested by temptation, and obstacles can be overcome by the grace of God.

From personal experience and the confidences of fellow servants, the theme is now expanded to set forth the opportunities open to us in the providence of God. Gleanings have come from the full spectrum of life; once again biographies and autobiographies give us glimpses of the inner tensions and triumphs of our common life.

What is shared is not advice, but musings from notes and scribblings. The minister is beset by a sense of unreality and lack of naturalness. He waits for popular approval and is the prey of every evil wind that blows. The servant of God today carries an awful sense of responsibility; he cannot escape sharing the burdens of others. This is the minister's opportunity, to "bear . . . one another's burdens. . . . For every man shall bear his own burden" (Gal. 6:2, 5).

Except where indicated, all Scripture quotations are from the King James Version.

At this milestone we thank God and take courage.

Ralph G. Turnbull
Warner Pacific College
Portland, Oregon
1977

CONTENTS

1

The Certitude of Vocation

"Of this gospel I was made a minister according to the gift of God's grace which was given me by the working of his power. To me, though I am the very least of all the saints, this grace was given, to preach to the Gentiles the unsearchable riches of Christ." (EPH. 3:7, 8, RSV)

"The office does not sanctify the man; the man sanctifies the office."
(A MINISTER'S OBSTACLES)

"Function and not status is of the essence of the Christian ministry."
(T. W. MANSON)

"If you are to get the preaching that you need, you must think highly, and you must teach your minister to think highly of his sacred office."
(BERNARD LORD MANNING)

THE MINISTRY IS a calling set apart from other tasks. In the divine providence there is an unfolding of a design and destiny for our lives. The Spanish thinker, Miguel de Unamuno (1864-1936), testified:

> There is a certain characteristic common to all those whom we call geniuses or great men and other heroes. Each of them has a consciousness of being a man apart, chosen very expressly by God for the performance of a certain work.

Men and women of destiny near the end of life have left on record words which indicate their convictions that the whole of their life had meaning. They were conscious of a divine providence which shaped and molded their lives for a definite goal.

Horace Bushnell (1802-1876), in his sermon "Every Man's Life a Plan of God," stated that "God has a definite life plan for each one, girding him visibly and invisibly for some exact thing which it will be the true significance and glory of his life to have accomplished." The thought reflects Isaiah 45:5: "I am the Lord, and there is none else, there is no God beside me: I girded thee, though thou hast not known me." The Gentile King Cyrus is here spoken of as in the hands of God. Here are plan and purpose, design and destiny. The writer remembers well that at the age of sixteen he read this sermon and was convinced that if God had a plan for his life, then it was right to seek that plan out and pursue it with modesty and an open mind.

For those who may not be familiar with Bushnell's remarkable sermon, it is well to recall its basic structure. In the first part he notes (1) that the Scriptures show the course of individual lives to be part of God's plan and (2) that in the works of God we trace design and not chance. In this part of the sermon, Bushnell expounds these truths with fitting illustrations. He also allows the possibility of the individual's missing God's plan: "God has, then, a definite life-plan set for every man; one that, being accepted and followed, will conduct him to the best and noblest end possible. No qualification of this doctrine is needed, save the fearful one just named; that we, by our perversity, so often refuse to take the place and do the work he gives us."

In the second part of the sermon, Bushnell raises the question: "How can we ever get hold of this life-plan God has made for us, or find our way into it?" He then gives practical answers to this question, the first of which are negative: (1) you will never come into God's plan if you study singularity; (2) you should not seek to copy the life of another; (3) you are never to complain of your birth, your training, your employments, your hardships; nor should you fancy that you could be something if only you had a different lot and sphere assigned to you; (4) you should not expect that God will set you in a scheme of life, the whole course of which you will know beforehand.

Following the negative, the positive note is sounded with the question: "How, then, can a man, who really desires to do so, discern the plan God has for him, so as to live it?" One may be on the point of choosing this or that calling, wanting to know where duty lies and what course God Himself would have him take. Bushnell's directions begin at a point most remote, where the generality of truth is widest: (1) consider the character of God, and you will draw a significant deduction from that, for all that God designs for you is in harmony with His character; (2) consider your creaturely relationship to Him; (3) remember you have a conscience; (4) regard God's law and His written Word as guides to present duty; (5) be an observer of God's providence; (6) consult your friends, especially those who hold to the teaching of God; (7) go to God Himself, and ask for His help; for as certainly as He has a plan or calling for you, He will somehow guide you into it. This is the proper office and work of His Spirit.

In the third and final section of the sermon, Bushnell discusses objections to and problems raised by his thesis, and in ten paragraphs (not unlike the Puritan structure) he makes the application pertinent and personal without dubiety. Prosperity and adversity, knowledge and ignorance, success and failure, young and old—all are brought under review. His conclusion sounds the conviction that it is never too late to seek and find God's plan. A condition is that

> there must be a complete renunciation of self-will. God and religion must be practically first. . . . Take your duty, and be strong in it, as God will make you strong. . . . Understand, also, that the great question here is, *not what you will get*, but *what you will become*. Take your burdens, and troubles, and losses, and wrongs, if come they must and will, and your opportunities, *knowing that God has girded you* for greater things than these. O, to live out such a life as God appoints, how great a thing it is!—to do the duties, make the sacrifices, bear the adversities, finish the plan, and then to say, with Christ (who of us will be able?)—"It is finished!"

This sermon has a timeless quality, a magnificent simple theme. The profound conviction of a divine life-plan catches the imagination, fires the mind, and challenges the will. Bushnell has outlined and elucidated in this sermon God's providential caring for those who seek His mind and will. In this sense the sermon is timeless in its application and influence.

Bushnell surely and wisely outlined practical steps to follow in seeking to know the will of God. Man experiences a growing consciousness of inner awakening when such steps are taken. Bushnell took his examples from Scripture and history. There were others who also discerned the same providence at work in molding the destinies of mankind. Shakespeare has it:

> There's a divinity that shapes our ends,
> Rough-hew them how we will.

Similar convictions were voiced by Alfred, Lord Tennyson:

> And out of darkness came the hands
> That reach thro' nature, moulding men;

and by Robert Browning:

> But I need, now as then,
> Thee, God, who mouldest men.

For a number of years, Robert Browning has been out of favor, as if he had nothing to say to our tempestuous age. But for those of us who were once exposed to his insights, there is satisfaction in rereading Browning. Who can deny the strength and vigor of those poems which treat of biblical subjects? Recall, for example, the memorable "Rabbi Ben Ezra" with its wrestling concerning doubt and the question of purpose and destiny. Borrowing Jeremiah's metaphor of the potter's wheel, Browning states:

> He fixed thee 'mid this dance
> Of plastic circumstance,
> This present, thou, forsooth, wouldest fain arrest;
> Machinery just meant
> To give thy soul its bent,
> Try thee and turn thee forth, sufficiently impressed.

Heart and head, love and reason, were intertwined as the poet shared the fruit of his faith and passion for righteousness. Browning has that robust spirit which does not play with lesser loyalties but encircles the highest and the best. His incurable optimism is not a passing and ephemeral mood of the moment, but finds its roots in eternal truth. His interpretation of truth is realistically linked to divine revelation.

Constructive critics of Browning include Welshman Henry Jones (1852-1922), professor of philosophy at Glasgow University, who issued a small book of selections entitled *Browning as a Religious and Philosophical Teacher* (Philadelphia: Richard West, 1973 reprint of 1891 edition). Jones claimed that in Browning we have seminal ideas which not only are profound, but are expressed in simple terms where ordinary people live.

Linked with Jones is the Scottish preacher John A. Hutton (1868-1947), whose ministry utilized the major poets of his generation to illustrate and interpret eternal truths. Fascinated with Browning, he wrote *Guidance from Robert Browning in Matters of Faith* (Philadelphia: Richard West, 1930 reprint). He, too, paid tribute to the enduring worth of Browning's poetry. Imagination played a major part in Browning's insights and the down-to-earth language which is not out of alignment with our realistic generation. "Rabbi Ben Ezra" is a sample of biblical realism regarding the plan and purpose of God in shaping human lives which have discerned and accepted the divine will.

There are rich deposits of truth to be mined from the major poets in every generation. The poets are helpers of the preacher who obeys the call of God to minister. In preparation of the mind and spirit in study and reflection he ponders the deep things of life and nature which are dealt with by those who have given us music and mystery in unison. That opportunity to work with our minds—minds filled with knowledge concerning God and man; salvation and sin; Christ and providence; faith, hope, love; suffering, death, and life beyond—opens unexplored realms of truth; and we discover through meditating on the Bible that the poets are channels of imaginative reason.

In unexpected places we learn of those whose lives are not lived in a vacuum but who achieve the ideal of accomplishing something worthwhile. John Reith became the first chief of the BBC (British Broadcasting Corporation) and was eventually honored as Lord Reith. He never forgot the heritage he received from his father (a Presbyterian minister) and mother, who gave him a foundation of devotion and rugged strength of character. John Reith set high standards for the BBC and maintained them throughout his leadership, though they were to prove controversial to secular society. This story has been told in his autobiography *Into the Wind* (1949).

In another book, *Wearing Spurs* (1966), Reith presents the portrait of a strong man bent upon maintaining the highest ideals he cherished from youth. As an officer leading his men during World War I, he was in regular correspondence—almost daily—with his parents in Scotland; in letters from home he found great comfort. In answer to Reith's anxieties as to what he wanted to do after the war, and his doubts as to whether he would get where he wanted with an engineer's training, his father wrote:

> We have to believe that the call of the present, and its work, are the most important things to think of, and not some happy

future which may never come. To be happy where we are in
the present duty, and to feel that Christ is with us in that, is all
we need. What God sends will be best.

Our daily prayer is that you may feel the presence of Christ
with you, and be a help in that way to other fellows around
you. You won't perhaps have much time, but a glance at your
Bible will set you up; and a heart lifted in prayer to God can
bring down His peace into it in a moment.

But John Reith records in his diary that he did more than
glance at his Bible; he read it every night, and every night and
morning he studied a little book called *Daily Light* which his
mother gave him when he was a boy and which he supposed he
would continue to use until he was no longer able to turn the
page. As a young man uncertain about the future because of the
carnage of war and possible death, John Reith reflected on the
plan of God for his life. Such reflections were obviously a major
contributing factor to the greatness he eventually achieved.

Men of destiny in all walks of life have confirmed the truth
that life has meaning. The minister of the Word of God whose
calling is clear and sure will find that he is not alone in saying
that God has summoned him to minister. Winston Churchill suggested he was a man of destiny. His life story reviews the shaping and molding of a personality of unusual possibilities. At this
point the ordinary person in the ministry protests, "But not
everyone is a Churchill!" True enough. But we who are in the
majority and must work the daily round of duty and drudgery
without any glamour or publicity are invited to believe that
there is a blueprint of life known to the Divine Architect.

When William Robertson Nicoll (1851-1923) went to the
Presbyterian (North) Church at Kelso on the borders of Scotland,
his pastorate was cut short through illness which forced him to
give up the ministry of that congregation and seek to begin life
over again in London. He founded the *British Weekly*, which became the foremost Christian paper of Great Britain during the
first half of this century. Nicoll remembered a young lady who
had been influenced by him in that border kirk. Under his tute-
lage and encouragement Jane T. Stoddart had begun to train
herself in religious journalism. Now she became his associate
and helper in the production of that paper, writing her own ar-

ticles and later publishing several books. To read her account, *My Harvest of the Years* (1938), is to see how God providentially prepared her for her life task. Everything she wrote about a design in human life, especially in her own life and work, might well be entitled *I Remember*. Meeting people in all walks of life she wrote down her reactions. She recorded impressions and conversations which dealt with the deeper realities of life. Over her years as a journalist and an editor she surveyed many professions and became firmly convinced that there were an obvious plan and purpose in the lives of countless numbers. *Great Lives Divinely Planned* (1930) gathers up a representative and select group of those whose stories support the thesis that "human life is a plan of God." With authority and persistency the roster of names and the galaxy of invested lives cry out that no minister worthy of his vocation should at any time by-pass this truth, but should wrestle with it in mind and heart. For without assurance that God plans lives the ministry may become empty and without meaning.

Significantly, the "gloomy Dane," Sören Aabye Kierkegaard (1813-1855), has a secure niche in church history as the thinker who prodded the complacent church of our modern era out of its softness and tragic casualness in dealing with the dynamic realities of the Christian faith.

He came, as others have done, to the fork in the road when decision was called for concerning his life and work. In a letter, he wrote about choice of a profession. Law seemed to beckon as something formal, but he realized there was a deeper question to be faced. As he himself said, "What I really need is to become clear in my own mind *what I must do*, not what I must know— except in so far as a knowing must precede every action. The important thing is to understand what I am destined for, to perceive what the Deity wants *me* to do; the point is to find the truth which is truth for me, to find *that idea for which I am ready to live and die*."

A young person who engages in a service for God and for the church of God has before him a lifetime of unparalleled opportunity to fulfill high ideals and express his gifts and abilities. Does life have meaning for the individual? Indeed it does, according to Viktor Frankl, who survived the concentration camps

of Hitler in World War II and returned to begin a new life in
Vienna as a psychotherapist, not only for his patients, but for
himself as well. He had found a secret in those dark days when
he found *the will to live* because God in Christ had indicated
that life has meaning. In this light we may trace the opportunities of the minister.

By way of definition we are thinking especially of the man
who has been called of God into the pastoral ministry as known
traditionally. Recognizing the new demands that the church
open the pulpit to our sisters in Christ, we include them wherever applicable. Moreover, the ministry is wider than the pastorate and this we recognize. Other opportunities to serve are
manifold today. Teaching, preaching, and healing immediately
come to mind. Whether professor or teacher, pastor or
evangelist, doctor or nurse, there are basic principles to be followed in each ministry. Diversity does not preclude what this
book lifts up as an ideal and goal. Regent College of the University of British Columbia (Vancouver) offers courses in theology
and biblical knowledge aimed not at those who wish theological
training for pastoral ministries, but at established professional
people who already have a university or college degree in
another vocation. Thus a nurse, a doctor, a lawyer, a business
executive, a politician, a government servant, or any lay person
can avail himself of such education to supplement his capabilities and return to his professional career better equipped to
serve his day and generation. This is the holy ideal of the members of the body of Christ. All the members of the whole church,
then, are in service wherever they are placed. This is in addition
to those who have been called to special ministries utilizing the
gifts of the risen Christ. "He gave some, apostles; and some,
prophets; and some, evangelists; and some, pastors and teachers;
for the perfecting of the saints, for the work of the ministry, for
the edifying of the body of Christ" (Eph. 4:11, 12).

A number of other scriptural references deserve mention at
this point:

> For we are his workmanship, created in Christ Jesus unto good
> works, which God hath before ordained that we should walk
> in them. (Eph. 2:10)

Whereof *I was made a minister*, according to the gift of the grace of God given unto me by the effectual working of his power. Unto me, who am less than the least of all saints, is this grace given, that I should preach. . . . (Eph. 3:7, 8)

. . .the gospel, which ye have heard, and which was preached to every creature which is under heaven; whereof *I Paul am made a minister*; who now rejoice in my suffering for you, and fill up that which is behind of the afflictions of Christ in my flesh for his body's sake, which is the church; whereof *I am made a minister* . . . Christ in you, the hope of glory: whom we preach, warning every man, and teaching every man in all wisdom; that we may present every man perfect in Christ Jesus, whereunto I also labour, striving according to his working, which worketh in me mightily. (Col. 1:23-29)

Tychicus . . . beloved brother and a faithful *minister [dia-konos]*. . . . Epaphras . . . a servant of Christ. . . . Luke, the beloved physician. . . . And say to Archippus, Take heed to the ministry *[diakonia]* which thou hast received. (Col. 4:7-17)

In the church there are many servants with diverse ministries. Colossians 4 gives a sample of those who are given to the *diakonos* ministry while Luke has his special ministry of *healing* and *writing*. His medical allusions are clear. (W. K. Hobart's *Medical Language of Luke's Writings* [Grand Rapids: Baker Book House, 1954] pinpoints much that might easily be overlooked in this connection.) The "we" sections in Acts draw attention to Luke's partnership with the apostle Paul in travel across the Roman Empire. The presence of Doctor Luke was a great asset to Paul on his missionary journeys. Luke was also a historian (witness his Gospel and the Acts). Sir William M. Ramsay of Aberdeen University has put us in his debt by his researches into the background of that period and especially Pauline and Lucan studies.

In the modern era the winds of change swirled around from time to time, especially after the ministry became a full-time involvement apart from the world of business. On one occasion there was a difference in judgment among many in Scotland about a minister's place in the church and in the social and political affairs of the land. I recall the genuine contributions of two prominent men. E. Rosslyn Mitchell, lawyer, was the member of parliament for Paisley: he had defeated Winston Churchill at the election. James Barr was a Presbyterian minister second to none in passionate speech and oratory, both in pulpit and on platform. Deciding to enter the political arena, he won a place in the House of Commons.

No one then could say that the needs of the underprivileged, the lowly in the land, and the poor were forgotten. The ranks of the Labour Party found in James Barr and in Rosslyn Mitchell two advocates for social justice and the application of Christian principles through legislation and statute. They were also the leaders against the proposed revisions in the Book of Common Prayer, when a bill which advocated compromising tendencies for the Church of England was defeated. That night in the British Parliament, the spirit of John Knox was still alive in the rhetoric of Barr and Mitchell along with that of Lord Inskip of the Church of England.

However, there were those who questioned James Barr's action in leaving the church pastorate for the political sphere. No doubt he wielded a strong influence among the parliamentarians and much good was accomplished. The same was true of C. Sylvester Horne of Whitefield's Chapel, London, who as a Congregational pastor stood for Parliament and for a while in that august body let his voice plead the case of the people. As we think of others in later and more recent days leaving the pastoral ministry for business, education, and the political arena, no one can judge their motives; time will tell what has been accomplished. Nevertheless, let this minister and a host of others testify that there is nothing higher than and no other opportunity quite like the *call* of the pastor-teacher-preacher.

When in Edinburgh for a political rally, Winston Churchill met a Presbyterian pastor who was a guest at the same home after the work of the day was over. In conversation, Mr. Churchill inquired about the services and the attendances at the minister's church. On the basis of two services each Sunday and a pastorate of many years, it was evident that all in all more people had heard the minister than had heard the statesman. In fact Churchill asserted that people would not turn out night after night or week after week to listen to a politician!

The unique potential of the ministry is also apparent in an episode involving Andrew Herron, moderator of the General Assembly of the Church of Scotland in 1971-1972. He was faced with the temptation to become involved in politics and counsel from the pulpit how the question of Northern Ireland should be resolved. He concluded that there were many Christian agencies and people already involved in that arena and that he could best serve by continuing in his present role. To fortify the faith of the people, to assist others to find God in Christ and to engage in worship, and to present the good news of the gospel had a priority for him and the church.

Another example is Bernard Lord Manning (1892-1941), a devoted son of Congregationalism and an exponent of Reformed and biblical truth. As professor and fellow of Jesus College, Cambridge University, he accepted many invitations extended to him to occupy pulpits throughout England. To read some of his sermons as found in *A Layman in the Ministry* or *More Lay Sermons* is to be introduced to a master of English prose who was capable of preaching at its highest level. Style and content blend with intense interest and appeal. He was a workman who did not need to be ashamed! All through his life he was conscious of his physical limitations and weaknesses, yet by dint of concentrated investment of time, he managed an extraordinary amount of writing and preaching alongside of his academic load. Through his interpretations of the hymns of Charles Wesley and Isaac Watts, he supplemented the light and life brought by the spoken Word.

William E. Sangster (1905-1960) was an English Methodist who was tested and tried before he gave himself to the gospel ministry. At the last moment other pressing demands forced him to pass up taking his examinations for an academic degree in the arts. In a biography his son tells how this became a severe testing area for Sangster, who had an instinct to study and achieve a university degree. But in the hour of God's dealings with him, Sangster came to realize that there was a fierce struggle being waged inside himself between academic reputation, prestige, and success on the one hand, and the spiritual character and ministry God intended for him on the other. In silence and prayer in an attic room he surrendered his will to God in the beginning of something deeper and more enduring. Later, during

World War II, in his Westminster pastorate Sangster was able to earn a Ph.D. from London University, publishing a thesis dealing with the doctrine of holiness.

In similar ways W. Graham Scroggie (1877-1958), a Scottish Baptist, struggled with crisis in the early days of his pastorate. He was tested and tried in faith. In an address to ministers at New College, Edinburgh University, he confessed that while seeking to be a preacher he had been merely a middleman between his people and his books. Then he learned to become a messenger for God, with a master passion for the will of God whatever the cost, and a love for others. He, too, magnified the grace of God and knew the mercy of God in his vocation.

Alexander Whyte (1836-1931) knew poverty, ostracism, and hard work in his struggle to become a minister, but that call of the Spirit was never stilled after he shared in the revival in the northeast of Scotland.

If the ministry degenerates to a "job" with demands of monetary returns for services rendered and a tendency to unionize conditions and terms, then the peril of being the hireling and not the shepherd is obvious. The call to service has usually been associated with a call to sacrifice. In the business world financial terms can be bargained, but in the ministry commitment implies service without reference to the financial return. We salute those servants of God who serve sacrificially and whose dedication is marked with the sign of the cross. Their numbers are many. The opportunity is there to exercise faith and courage in service by the grace of God. The Lord of the harvest (Matt. 9:38) who calls laborers supplies for our needs if not always for our wants. There are other compensations in Christian service.

A good definition of waste of life is the service we have not rendered, the love we have not given, and the sacrifice from which we have drawn back. The lure of success measured in terms of Madison Avenue standards can be a snare to entrap the unwary. The New Testament ideals of ministry lie on a higher plane.

David Daiches, professor of English at the University of Sussex, has called attention to the Scottish poet and interpreter of human nature, Robert Burns, who was never a man to suffer fools gladly. So if he paraded himself as an uneducated plowman in Edinburgh, it was not out of humility, but a stamp of his poetic genius and inspiration. He knew that formal education was no guarantee of wisdom:

> What's a' your jargon o' your schools,
> Your Latin names for horns an' stools;
> If honest nature made you fools,
>   What sairs your grammars?
> Y'd better ta'en up spades and shools,
>   Or knappin'-hammers.

The insight of the Scottish poet reminds us that when God's call comes to us we are usually counseled to obtain the best education possible. However, we should not forget that there are some ministers of God who do not have that privilege or opportunity. They are not thereby deprived of a ministry. Amos was called from the sheepfold; Moody from being a shoe salesman; Bunyan from being a tinker; Billy Sunday from baseball; like many others of limited education they exercised significant ministries. The church should ever have an open mind to recognize the exceptional person with the seals of divine anointing. God plans for and prepares His servants in strange surroundings for special tasks.

2

The Stewardship of Time

"Redeeming the time. . . ." (EPH. 5:16; COL. 4:5)

"Making the most of the time. . . ." (RSV)

"Use the present opportunity. . . ." (NEB)

"We must work the works of him that sent me, while it is day: the night cometh, when no man can work." (JOHN 9:4, RV)

TIME TO BE USED and invested is not a tyranny but an opportunity. Many and varied are the uses of time by those who have utilized it fully and realistically. Each day in a pastor's life and work he is faced with preparing for weekly services and speaking engagements. Sunday after Sunday with unfailing regularity comes that opportunity to lead a congregation in public worship. He finds he must prepare himself first of all. Then the congregation expects his leadership to be such that he is always prepared and ready. No slipshod methods are sufficient; no casual or careless efforts will suffice. "Busyness" is no excuse for failure to accomplish the "business" which is his. "Wist ye not that I must be about my Father's business?" (Luke 2:49), asked the Son of God in an hour of growth. The things of God demand the highest respect and the honest devotion of our wills to seek the best.

There are those who plead the lack of talent or ability when seeking an excuse for poor performance in the hour of testing. The parable of the talents (Matt. 25:14-30) is sometimes quoted in this connection, especially when coupled with the contemporary interpretation that "talented" people may possess five or ten special abilities, while others may have only one. But the hermeneutics of this parable should be restudied. The key point is that "to every man was given talents *according to his ability.*"

In this light we discern the significance to be that God has given to each of His servants one, or five, or ten "talents" (meaning, "opportunities of service"); and these one, or five, or ten opportunities are matched according to our endowed "ability" or "abilities" (the equivalent of our modern idea of having a "talent" or "talents"). In this revised view the meaning of a disciplined use of time becomes clear and plain. God gives to each one of us the *opportunities to use our abilities*; no one has an excuse to be lazy or indolent or to say he is not equipped for the situation when actually he may have frittered away the time with trivia.

Anthony Trollope (1815-1882) in his *Autobiography* (New York: Oxford University Press, n.d.) laid bare part of his early struggle after a youth of restricted education. Entering the postal service in England he worked diligently, reading and studying at odd times of the day and night when free from his employment. Gradually he became a self-educated man and his sense of responsibility and diligence in business gained him promotion. During that time he began to write novels, although he had no reason to believe at the outset that a publisher would be interested in his manuscripts. However, he was surprised and delighted when his books were issued and the public eagerly received his lucid interpretations of character and social life in the Victorian era.

As a young man Trollope had been urged by his father to enter either Oxford or Cambridge University, but this had depended on his ability to get a scholarship. He tried several times but failed. The idea of a university career was abandoned. He entered the world of business and routine postal work without formal university training in language and arts. With this discouraging background, we may well ask how Trollope managed to invest so heavily in time and pen when the regular stint of employment ended for the day.

Believing that a man can exert himself and find enough strength to do an extra amount of work, Trollope set himself *a system of task-work:* he set himself an obligation to accomplish a certain amount of writing each day; writing was not allowed to become spasmodic. He found it expedient to bind himself by a few self-imposed laws.

> When I have commenced a new book, I have always prepared
> a diary, divided it into weeks, and carried it on for the period
> which I have allowed myself for the completion of the work.
> In this I have entered, day by day, the number of pages I have
> written, so that if at any time I have slipped into idleness for a
> day or two, the record of that idleness has been there, staring
> me in the face, and demanding of me increased labour, so that
> the deficiency might be supplied. According to the circum-
> stances of the time—whether my other business might be then
> heavy or light, or whether the book which I was writing was
> 'or was not wanted with speed,—I have allotted myself *so many
> pages a week*. The average number has been about 40. It has
> been placed as low as 20, and has risen to 112. And as a page
> is an ambiguous term, my page has been made to contain 250
> words; and as words, if not watched, will have a tendency to
> straggle, I have had every word counted as I went. . . . I have
> prided my self especially in completing a book within the pro-
> posed time,—and I have always done so.

Trollope anticipated those who would find fault with his system and his self-discipline.

> There are those who would be ashamed to subject themselves
> to such a taskmaster, and who think that the man who works
> with his imagination should allow himself to wait till inspira-
> tion moves him. . . . To me it would not be more absurd if the
> shoemaker were to wait for inspiration, or the tallow-chandler
> for the divine moment of melting. . . . The author wants that
> as does every other workman,—that and a habit of industry. I
> was once told that *the surest aid to the writing of a book was a
> piece of cobbler's wax on my chair*. I certainly believe in the
> cobbler's wax much more than the inspiration.
>
> I am ready to admit the variations in brain power which are
> exhibited by the products of different men, and am not dis-
> posed to rank my own very high; but my own experience tells
> me that *a man can always do the work for which his brain is
> fitted* if he will *give himself the habit* of regarding his work as
> a normal condition of his life. I therefore venture to advise
> young men who look forward to authorship as the business of
> their lives, to avoid enthusiastic rushes with their pens, and to
> seat themselves at their desks day by day as though they were
> lawyers' clerks;—and so let them sit until the allotted task shall
> be accomplished.

Others have told of how they have set apart one day each

week when they could write without interruption. A busy pastor, a diligent executive in business, an educator find there is no easy way to authorship. It takes certain blocks of time and a pen or typewriter to record thought and word. Some moderns find they can dictate their thoughts and ideas into the tape recorder to be reproduced again in transcription. While Trollope set himself to goals and evidently reached them in an age which lacked the competition of radio, television, automobile, and telephone, yet in this age of rush and strain there are those who set their goals in similar vein.

F. F. Bruce, professor of biblical literature, languages, and history at the University of Manchester, shares his method, which is not unlike that of Trollope. The material gathered in research for teaching and courses of study has been recycled and later become a foundation for manuscript and book. Bruce testifies that when invited to write something, be it a book or an article, he fixes a realistic deadline and tries to meet it. He tells of an aid to his self-discipline: "I like to carry around in my pocketbook a sheet of paper with a list of literary projects which I have undertaken and a note of their respective deadlines, ticking off each as I finish it. From time to time I take it out to refresh my memory on the situation. . . ." As we are not all cast in the same mold, we must allow that each would-be writer must work out his own method by which he can engage in the ministry of writing.

Matthew Henry (1662-1714) the commentator has a timeless word which has pointed application for all ministers. This concerns a fixedness of thought, and a close application of mind, to the duty of prayer. We must go about it solemnly, as those who have something of moment much at heart, something in which we dare not trifle.

In Psalm 5:3 the psalmist pledges: "My voice shalt thou hear in the morning, O Lord; in the morning will I direct my prayer unto thee." This speaks of sincerity and steadiness in prayer. (When we pray, we should give God His titles, just as when we address a person of honor. We should address Him as the great Jehovah; God "over all, blessed for evermore"; the "King of kings, and Lord of lords"; "the Lord God, gracious and merciful." Our hearts and mouths should be filled with holy adorings and admirings of Him. We should fasten upon those titles of His which strike a holy awe of Him upon our minds, that we may worship with reverence and godly fear. Our prayers should be directed to Him as the God of glory, with whom is terrible majesty and whose greatness is unsearchable. We must not trifle with Him or mock Him in what we say to Him.)

In the morning we should pray to the Lord. We find that under the law every morning there was a lamb offered in sacrifice (Exod. 29:39), every morning the priests burned incense (Exod. 30:7), and the singers stood every morning to thank the Lord (I Chron. 23:30). And so were offerings appointed in Ezekiel's temple (Ezek. 46:13-15). Note also the following considerations:

1. It is fitting that He who is first should have the first part of our day, the morning.

2. In the morning we are fresh and lively, and in the best frame of mind.

3. In the morning we are most free from company and business, and ordinarily have the best opportunity for solitude and retirement.

4. In the morning we have received fresh mercies from God, which we are concerned to acknowledge with thankfulness to His praise.

5. In the morning we have fresh matter ministered to us for the adoration of the greatness and glory of God.

6. In the morning we have, or should have, fresh thoughts of God, and sweet meditations on His name; these we ought to offer up to Him in prayer.

7. In the morning, it is to be feared, we find cause to reflect upon any vain thoughts that have been in our minds in the night; on that account it is necessary to address ourselves to God in prayer for the pardon of them.

8. In the morning we are addressing ourselves to the work of the day, and therefore are concerned to seek unto God by prayer for His presence and blessing.

We are going about the business of our calling. Let us first look up to God for wisdom and grace to manage it well, in the fear of God, and to abide with Him. Then we may in faith beg of Him to prosper us in our calling, to strengthen us for its duties, to support us under the fatigues of our calling, to direct its designs, and to give us comfort in its gains.

Prayer is intimate communion with God. In the secret place of the Most High we are silent because we do not come primarily with our demands, but we listen and wait for that which God would say to us. The Quaker view of silence in worship is a profound and practical aid to us for they have engaged in a spiritual discipline which has been given little place in our services of worship. In this activist age we are prone to imagine that nothing happens unless there is a voice or music or some activity. It seems the contemporary worshiper is afraid of silence. "Be still, and know that I am God . . ." (Ps. 46:10). Elijah in that traumatic experience in the cave found that God's presence and power came not in the earthquake nor in the wind nor in the fire, but in "a still small voice" (I Kings 19:11, 12). The Hebrew allows as a translation "the sound of a great silence." In that silence was the awesome power of almighty God. God's transcendent presence which had been manifested in wind, earthquake, and fire was now manifested in silence.

The minister has an opportunity to find out that prayer is a means of grace by which his inner bent of worship is lifted to new heights of devotion. There are no limits to this. The man of God, whether he be highly learned or limited in endowment and gifts, must never assume his worship to be at maximum peak. There are the lower levels of prayer as a beginning (as suggested by George S. Stewart in *The Lower Levels of Prayer* [Nashville: Abingdon, 1939], but the higher levels beckon every minister without exception or distinction. We have everything to learn. The school of Christ continues throughout the whole of life. We engage in it every day of our ministry.

The value of meditation has been cited, for prayer does not come easily to those who must lead a congregation hundreds of times throughout the years of service. Those who use the Book of Common Prayer have a safeguard against clichés and banal repetitions of personal idiosyncrasies as well as crude and displeasing phrases. At once we may be open to the criticism that the freer prayer is preferable, for prayers read or recited from a book of orders and worship fall into repetition. This we admit, but what is used again and again over a period of time from a book of prayers is the legacy of spiritual minds from the church

of the ages. We are in that succession of faith and devotion. At
the same time there is a place for the repeated prayer when it is
used in spirit and in truth and we by the Holy Spirit engage in it
as an act of worship. The minister prepares a sermon to deliver
to a congregation as an act of worship before God. There is
nothing objectionable in preparation to pray on behalf of a congregation. There must be preparation in our own life before we
engage in that public act.

The Scriptures afford a means of grace in learning to pray.
The early disciples asked our Lord, "Lord, teach us to pray,"
and He replied, "After this manner, pray . . ." (Luke 11:1-13).
He gave them and us a model prayer, a guide, a method in
prayer.

The important position which the minister should ascribe to
prayer is given expression by George Herbert (1593-1633) in
"Public Worship":

>   Restore to God His due in tithe and time;
>   A tithe purloined, cankers the whole state.
>   Sundays observe: think when the bells do chime,
>   'Tis angels' music; therefore come not late.
>   God then deals blessings; if a king did so,
>   Who would not haste, nay give, to see the show? . . .
>
>   Resort to sermons, but to prayers most:
>   *Praying's the end of preaching. . . .*
>
>   Judge not the preacher, for he is thy judge:
>   If thou mislike him, thou conceiv'st him not.
>   God calleth preaching folly. Do not grudge
>   To pick out treasures from an earthen pot.
>   The worst speak something good: if all want sense,
>   God takes a text, and preacheth patience.
>
>   He that gets patience, and the blessing which
>   Preachers conclude with, hath not lost his pains. . . .
>
>   Jest not at preachers' language or expression:
>   How knowest thou but thy sins made him miscarry?
>   Then turn thy faults and his into confession:
>   God sent him whatsoe'er he be: O tarry,
>   And love him for his Master: his condition,
>   Though he be ill, makes him no ill physician. . . .

At this point it is appropriate to cite several books which can help the minister grasp the opportunity to grow and mature in spiritual leadership and prayer.

In *Lord, Teach Us to Pray* (Grand Rapids: Baker Book House, 1976) Alexander Whyte correlates Luke 11:1 with several other passages. Sermons included in this volume include "The Magnificence of Prayer" and "Imagination in Prayer." In other books illumining the spiritual life Whyte treats such topics as the intricacies of the heart, John Bunyan, the Puritans, and Bible characters.

Andrew Murray's messages on prayer, holiness, and power go right to the heart of things. There is always more to the Christian life than we have yet experienced.

The incisive writings of A. W. Tozer (1897-1963) bring fresh insights into the ways of God and the work of the Holy Spirit. Tozer was an evangelical mystic whose thought was permeated with the sovereignty of God. His *Pursuit of God* (Harrisburg, PA: Christian Publications, n.d.) and *The Knowledge of the Holy* (New York: Harper and Row, 1975) as well as selections of his mystical verse open up a treasury of spirituality.

Samuel Chadwick (1860-1932) said that "a sharp spear needs no polish" and his books confirm this aphorism. *The Path of Prayer* (Fort Washington, PA: Christian Literature Crusade, 1963), *The Way to Pentecost* (Fort Washington, PA: Christian Literature Crusade, 1960), and *The Call to Perfection* are a noteworthy trilogy of this Methodist master of writing.

The opportunity to husband our time and use it wisely is not easy to grasp. We have many demands made upon us. Turn to Austin Phelps's small volume *The Still Hour* and learn afresh that no one is exempt from testing. "A consciousness of the absence of God is one of the standard incidents of religious life." Few of us will challenge that statement. Drought and lack will come to us. After the altitude of the hill will come the depths of the valley. Even in the secret place of the Most High we will find testing.

Lancelot Andrewes (1555-1626) was a leader in the translation of the King James Version of the Bible (1611). As a preacher he influenced his period, but is known chiefly for his unusual book on cultivation of the devout life. From his classic writing *The*

Private Devotions of Lancelot Andrewes (Nashville: Abingdon, n.d.) we can learn how to invest our time and how to be a good steward of time for prayer. The richness of this book is that the prayers written therein are couched in biblical language. This becomes a thesaurus to the learner in prayer. Inspired by the biblical English of that time, he is led each day, each week, and on special occasions, to reach hidden depths of meaning and application in prayer.

The stewardship of time requires an order and plan. In addition are those moments which come on the wing of inspiration. The set of the mainsail and the lifting of that smaller sail are one way of using time aright, for then comes the breeze and wind of the Spirit.

In *A Minister's Obstacles* a chapter was given to one of the temptations of the Christian life and ministry—"The Vice of Sloth." The tendency to delay, procrastinate, or put off to a more convenient season may be nothing less than the desire to take things with ease. Ease can degenerate to evil. The lazy student readying for his life's work is in danger for all time. He may be cultivating habits which will lead to lack of discipline in character and conduct. The pastor does not have any clock to punch as do other workers who have to check in and out in relation to their time spent in the factory or store. Offices have means of checking the work-time of those who are engaged in business pursuits. But the man of God is a privileged person concerning his hours. He may be busy many hours of the day and the week, and yet fritter away precious periods. Busyness is not necessarily the business of the kingdom.

At this point there arises another problem or temptation. The temptation lies not in laziness, but in overwork. The workaholic is not a new phenomenon. Certainly he has been known in other times without the new label. He is the pastor or the servant of God who so works that he is led on to excess in giving of his strength and spirit until he is worn out physically, mentally, and spiritually. His so-called zeal is not tempered with knowledge and judgment; he knows no bounds in service for God. We admire the man who wears out and does not rust out; nevertheless, we can be so busy that we are prone to become failures. Dr. Edward H. Roberts, dean of Princeton Theological Seminary, told on one occasion of attending a public worship service in which the pastor seemed to boast in his remarks that even though it was summer, he would not take any holiday or vacation. To support his position he noted that the devil never takes a vacation. As Dean Roberts commented afterwards, "The devil was a bad model to shape the preacher's ideals and actions!"

Our Lord and Master counseled His apostles and followers to "come apart and rest a while" (Mark 6:31). Sometimes a pastor has been so caught in the manifold duties of the church that he has neglected his family. His wife and children are normal people like any other family in the congregation, but pastors have been known to pay more attention to others than to their own family. Often the cost of that devotion and neglect has been scars and wounds on those whom the pastor loves yet unwittingly hurts.

William Robertson Nicoll (1851-1923) said it well in *Letters on Life* (Philadelphia: Richard West, n.d.): "It may be doubted whether we have a right to sacrifice life to the work of life. Life, it has been said, is not for working, neither is life for learning, but learning and working are for life." The goal of a minister's sacrificing life to the work of life is unrealistic. But many a conscientious man is tempted by the fact that there are those who unwittingly carve out that goal. The balanced life and the fourfold development of our Lord when a lad in Nazareth are surely a much better and more realistic aspiration. "Jesus increased in wisdom and stature, and in favour with God and man" (cf. Luke 2:39, 40, 51, 52). The mental and physical, the spiritual and social, are interrelated in the wholeness of the person. Each part is God-given and each requires the others. Service in dedication to God is best achieved when there is coordination. Dedication becomes concentration. The pressures build and suddenly the man who thinks he is doing most for God finds he is ineffective when disorder and imbalance strike. Instead of pressing his work and seeking to accomplish the multiplied commitments, he finds that *they have pressured him* and now he cannot function.

The medical profession has talked about depressive illness. Psychiatrists have found this a mark of the overworked minister as well as other vocations. Persistent depression is an emotional disorder that needs recognition and treatment. We may have boasted about "pushing our work" and working the plan to squeeze that extra out of the minister's week. Now it is time to learn wisdom in not allowing our work to push us to a sense of frustration and despair. Like the actor of the ancient world we may deceive ourselves that it cannot happen to us when we are actually wearing the "masks" which cover the true person within.

The workaholic pastor is in peril when he sets goals and builds up pressures which will erupt like volcanic lava unless he finds a rhythm and balance of service in proportion to his strength, ability, and commitments. Priorities are sure to be found after heart-searching. The Ministers' Life Insurance Company of Minneapolis some years ago engaged in a poll to find out how many hours the average pastor worked during a week. Members of the congregations involved were asked to state what they believed were the priorities of a minister's life and work and how many hours he should give in a week to each of these demands. When results were tabulated it was found that the congregational view was that the pastor should work eighty hours each week! It was only after this poll that the absurdity of the demands placed on the average minister was seen. Sermon preparation, visitation of families in the congregation, hospital calls, worship services, Bible classes, funerals, weddings, committees of the church and those of the presbytery or association, besides innumerable calls from other sources in the community—add all these together and there is no time for the minister to spend with his family! The so-called forty-hour week demanded of the ordinary worker or the longer workweek expected of executives or doctors pales into insignificance alongside the eighty hours of the minister.

God's order in creation is that we cooperate with Him in resting one day of the week, even as we set aside eight hours each night for rest, and take an annual vacation or holiday. There are several practical suggestions which can assist us. One which worked for the writer at a critical period of his life was to take his weekly calendar and enter for Friday evenings that he had an important engagement—the family. Unless an emergency disrupted the weekly routine, his family knew that he would be there for dinner and the rest of the evening. Record player, singing around the piano, games, conversation, fun, reading—in season the fire burning—and each one sharing. The two older children knew that although the two younger children were told they could stay up as late as they wished, sleep would soon overtake them and the older ones would then have the quietness of the later hours with their parents as companions. Thus the family was nurtured and shared together in common goals and aspirations.

There are other ways in which the minister's life can be geared to recreation. An annual vacation should be entered into with zest and gladness. A change of scene and a relaxing of the bow are necessary to renewal of strength and vocation. Alexander Whyte of Scotland counseled in his day to take as long a holiday as possible. Not every congregation can allow their pastor what he received, but the principle is sound if the pastor takes part of those weeks for meditation and study away from home. A faithful minister who invests part of the hours of his vacation in study returns ready to resume the long year's ministry with resources already garnered for the enrichment of the congregation. John Ruskin said, "There is no music in the rest but there is the making of music."

To conclude, the admonition of Proverbs 6:6 to note the work of the ant is a reminder that one of our perils is sloth. That temptation was considered in *A Minister's Obstacles* and now there has arisen in our jet age another temptation—to so toil that a minister works excessively and beyond what is balanced and normal. In a word—there is the danger of becoming a workaholic.

When Ian Ramsay (1915-1972), philosopher, theologian, and bishop of Durham died, the Christian church learned a costly lesson. This gifted leader and writer in the Anglican communion died prematurely because he could not resist the exciting possibilities of ever new demands made upon his time and strength.

There is great opportunity in the ministry for service, but Ramsay took part in national affairs in addition to pastoral work in the community, study, reading, thought, and teaching. As he poured out his energies in multiple interests, it became impossible to discipline himself to banish the secondary claims.

He had reached the stage when in his spirit *he could not say no.* Pastoral service requires discrimination and the wise use of mind, body, and time.

The opportunity to be a steward of time is a reminder of our mortality as well as of what God has set as the boundaries of our earthly life and work. The Bible has special words concerning *time* and *eternity.* If there is anything in our human experience more embracing than love it is time. There is no escape from its encircling coils. We are caught in its tendrils at the beginning, and we are still its captives at the end, for our beginning and our ending are dated events. Our little systems have their day, and cease to be. The promising morning is there and the rest of noonday. Then come the arduous afternoon and the swift advance of eventide. Our life circle has rounded itself in God. "Thou sendest forth thy Spirit, they are created. . . . Thou takest away their breath, they die, and return to their dust" (Ps. 104:30, 29).

The stewardship of time is our opportunity to live fully and wisely, to invest our days for the highest and the holiest of occupations possible to man. Thus the hours, the days, the weeks, the months, the years—and then time is swallowed up in eternity, for God has set the eternal in our hearts.

3

The Satisfaction of Study

"Study to shew thyself approved unto God, a workman that needeth not to be ashamed, rightly dividing the word of truth." (II TIM. 2:15)

"The fire shall ever be burning upon the altar; it shall never go out." (LEV. 6:13)

"Every man's work shall be made manifest: for the day shall declare it, because it shall be revealed by fire; and the fire shall try every man's work of what sort it is." (I COR. 3:13)

WE KNOW FROM Deuteronomy 6 that already in the early days of the Hebrew nation the children were instructed in the Sacred Scriptures as the foundation of religious and ethical life. The *Shema* stressed the monotheism of the Mosaic law, and in that sovereign and eternal truth concerning the nature and being of God came the injunction to love and reverence God with heart and soul and strength.

> These words, which I command thee this day, shall be in thine heart: And thou shalt teach them diligently unto thy children, and shalt talk of them when thou sittest in thine house, and when thou walkest by the way, and when thou liest down, and when thou risest up. And thou shalt bind them for a sign upon thine hand, and they shall be as frontlets between thine eyes. And thou shalt write them upon the posts of thy house, and on thy gates. (Deut. 6:6-9)

Given instruction within the family and the pronouncements of seers and national leaders, Israel became involved in reading and studying. The nation developed a great love of learning. In like manner Paul enjoins his protégé Timothy to study. Christians have always emphasized the privilege of learning and study.

Theological college or seminary is a necessary preparation for the ministry. The cloistered life is a prelude to the contest in the arena. Lawyers testify that their cases are won in their offices and chambers before they plead in court before jury and judge. Patient preparation means permanent power. Think of the minister's privilege. He is given time to invest in studies. While others have limited periods for study dependent upon their employment, free hours, and other commitments, the minister ideally is set free during the days of the week to engage in study which is directly in line with his occupation. At least five days each week ministers can invest their morning hours in that which they enjoy.

Study varies among ministers: because of different gifts and personalities some are slow while others find a quick way of absorbing what is before them. Subject matter, the tools of learning, and creative imagination all play a part. Francis Bacon (1561-1626) in his *Advancement of Learning* (1605) rendered his judgment that "reading makes a full man; conference a ready man; writing an exact man" (with variations, of course, according to capacity and skill). "Studies serve for delight, for ornament, and for ability. . . . Crafty men condemn studies; simple men admire them; and wise men use them, for they teach not their own use."

A wise pastor who knows that he has to face a congregation with two separate sermons each Sunday, lead a midweek service, and (in the Scottish tradition) teach a Bible class of adults or young people each week will plan his studies accordingly. For daily use he should keep at hand as tools of learning whatever preaching-teaching resources are available to him. Happy the minister who never grows tired of his involvement in this task. Only by carefully following a daily schedule and a plan of working ahead will he come to his most important tasks ready to minister.

The wise pastor studies the best books. What an honor to keep company with the best minds of the ages! Here there is contact with the best in literature and in theology. The Bible, a library in itself, calls for mastery and familiarity. We must become thoroughly acquainted with the outstanding tool of our vocation. We should learn the art of selection. As our own library begins to grow, we discover that a library is the true university for education and life. This is not a call for every minister to be a technical scholar, although there will be many in that category. The regular parish minister has many demands made upon him in the areas of pastoral oversight, administration, counseling, and visitation. According to his gifts and ability he will find his major field of service. However, the first priority remains preaching-teaching along with its demands of study and preparation.

A number of prominent authors have commented on the importance of books. For example, Thomas Carlyle (1795-1881) said, "The true university is a library of books." John Milton (1608-1674) said, "A book is the precious life-blood of a master spirit." Contrast Lord Rosebery's dictum that "a library is a cemetery of dead books." The point relates to the use made of a library: if it is not used, the treasures are neglected and beget no more life.

Think of the fields of interest open to the minister. Among the classifications in ministers' libraries are biography, history, theology, literature, preaching and homiletics, counseling, Christian education, missions and evangelism, commentaries, dictionaries, encyclopedias, science and philosophy, devotional works, classics, Bible studies and hermeneutics, as well as special areas of personal interest.

We will all have our personal preferences wherein we cultivate our taste for concentrated studies through books gathered for that end. This could be in a realm removed from the theological needs and afford change and balance as well as fruitful enrichment in mind and heart. To read systematically in theological subjects needs to be balanced by outside reading in another field. The particular field would depend upon personal interest and inclination, whether in science, history, or literature.

Puritan literature has enlarged the horizon of my mind. Through Alexander Whyte and others, I explored, as time permitted, an inexhaustible mine of knowledge. Reading in Thomas Goodwin, Richard Sibbes, Thomas Preston, Richard Baxter, and John Bunyan opened the door to other treasures. A few friends who had similar tastes shared their rare items and thus enabled me to delve into books and authors that might have escaped my attention. Books about the rise of Puritanism, its history and personalities, their writings and heritage, are available. For

many years these books were scarce, but now they have been re-
discovered and reprinting is taking place. If reprints are un-
available, old copies can often be located in libraries.

The Puritans, who lived "under their Taskmaster's eye" (Milton's phrase in *Paradise Lost*), have been widely caricatured and
criticized. Some of this criticism is justifiable in the light of
some excesses which reflected the need to make decisions under
pressure and persecution. However, we owe an incalculable debt
to them for their stand in righteousness of life and their committal to truth as found in Jesus Christ. Puritanism in both Old
England and New England gave to the church and society standards which we do well to recognize as a God-given heritage.

During the Bicentennial celebrations of the United States of
America much was written and spoken concerning our national
heritage. Unfortunately, there was little recognition that the
birth of "this nation under God" was no accident. Remember
the Pilgrim Fathers and the Puritans who a century earlier had
laid the religious foundations of the American republic.

A study of New England Puritanism is not to be overlooked.
Among the prominent names are the Mathers (Richard, Cotton,
and Increase), Thomas Shepard, John Cotton, John Winthrop,
Thomas Hooker, and Jonathan Edwards. There are others who
cry out for attention and interpretation to our age. Mention
should be made of the English Puritan William Perkins whose
writings were the texts for his brethren who sought training for
the ministry. *The Art of Prophesying* (1611) was especially significant. On the flyleaf of the books in his library Perkins wrote
these words:

> Thou art a minister of the Word;
> Mind thy business.

When college and seminary days are over and we are in our
manse or parsonage, a timetable should be made out for each
week. Some churches provide a study at the church, but in the
morning hours I prefer to study at home without interruption
(except, of course, in cases of emergency). By using a timetable
or schedule the morning hours can be restricted to devotions, Bible study, theological reading, and sermon writing. A similar
pattern should be followed each day, allowing, of course, for
variations according to personal preference and interest as well

as the amount of time needed for the work to be done.

A proven technique is to select one major book from a different field of study each month. Thus in the course of a year a pastor might have covered Bible study, apologetics, theology, Christology, pneumatology, history, philosophy, biography, missions, doctrine, literature, and a special field. These books should in no way be light or surface reading, nor should they already have been used as texts in theological college or seminary. They should require careful thought and also the taking of notes.

To someone who has never tried this method of study I would suggest a sample package something like the following: in the field of biography, *Autobiography with Letters* by William Phelps (New York: AMS Press, 1977 reprint); in literature, *The Idea of a University* by John H. Newman (Westminster, MD: Christian Classics, 1976 reprint), or *The Arts and the Art of Criticism* by Theodore M. Greene (Staten Island, NY: Gordian Press, 1973 reprint); in history, *A History of the Reformation* by Thomas M. Lindsay (Naperville, IL: Allenson, 1907); in preaching, *A History of Preaching* by Edwin C. Dargan (New York: Burt Franklin, 1965); in doctrine, *Doctrine of the Atonement* by John K. Mozley (Naperville, IL: Allenson, 1915); in a special field, *The Training of the Twelve* by Alexander B. Bruce (Grand Rapids: Kregel, 1971 reprint).

As an alternative, the pastor might prefer not to read in different fields each month, but to concentrate in one area. He might choose to study Christology for three months. I would suggest, for example, that he read *The Person of Jesus Christ* by Hugh R. Mackintosh (Naperville, IL: Allenson, 1912); *The Finality of Jesus Christ* by Robert E. Speer (Grand Rapids: Zondervan, 1968); and *The Mediator* by Emil Brunner (Philadelphia: Westminster Press, 1947).

Another suggestion is to study the writings of Vincent Taylor, the Methodist scholar. Over the years he produced eight volumes on the doctrine of the atonement as displayed by our Lord's death and sacrifice on the cross. Every year I turn again to these writings before I attempt to preach about the sufferings and passion of Christ. These are but samples of what is possible in the pastor's study, if he uses the hours wisely and well.

Many ministers might find it beneficial to select one book of

the Bible for special study each year. For example, during vacation one might read the Acts of the Apostles. It is a good practice to begin by reading familiar versions and then to turn to
other translations in order to gain the sweep of the whole before
coming to analytical study. After detailed studies involving the
language, geography, customs, special texts, and so on, the minister is prepared to preach and teach from the book. This practice can be followed with Old Testament books also, for example, Genesis or Nehemiah.

John Henry Jowett testified that he followed a plan of this
kind, taking a book of the Bible and dwelling on its contents for
a long period of time before expounding on it. Many of his
books of devotional studies as well as his expositions reflect this
method. We might mention his *Epistles of St. Peter* (Grand Rapids: Kregel, 1970 reprint), *Life in the Heights* (Grand Rapids:
Baker Book House, 1973), and *Springs in the Desert* (Grand
Rapids: Baker Book House, 1976). Andrew W. Blackwood's
Preaching from Samuel (Grand Rapids: Baker Book House,
1975) is another example of the preaching which can be accomplished by concentrating on individual books of the Bible. In
every case the method to be followed is clear: from synthesis (acquiring a coherent view of the whole book) to analysis to exegesis and finally to exposition.

In addition to devotional aids the wise pastor during the
course of a year will concentrate upon an author of English literature. James Stalker, Scottish pastor and then professor and
author of many stimulating books (including the invaluable
handbooks *The Life of Jesus Christ* [Westwood, NJ: Fleming H.
Revell, n.d.] and *The Life of the Apostle Paul* [Grand Rapids:
Zondervan, n.d.]), aimed to read all of William Shakespeare's
works once each year. This practice balanced his theological and
biblical studies and at the same time enriched his vocabulary.

Instead of casual reading for relaxation, a minister and his
wife might well agree to read through the complete works of an
author. It has been done! There is a thrill to reading George
Eliot, the Bronte novels, or James M. Barrie in their entirety. We
could also call attention to Robert Louis Stevenson, Charles
Dickens, Sir Walter Scott, or poets like Robert Browning and
T. S. Eliot. To live for a long time with the writings of a single

author is to widen one's horizon. Other names will leap to mind: C. S. Lewis and even the novels of certain modern American authors. The selection will be a matter of individual taste. Indeed, to read for pleasure is one of life's opportunities and privileges. The much needed unbending of the bow or the pause in the music has its place in the stress and strain of our accelerated life in the Space Age. Moreover, the material read will over the years work its way into the minister's sermons and writings.

It is imperative to have a program for study. The hours must be planned. It is a wise course to safeguard especially the morning hours. This is the freshest part of the day. It is sad that some people do not go to their studies with eagerness and perhaps do not even enjoy reading to enrich their knowledge. But a minister must have knowledge in his special subject, and the only way to get it is to study in depth. There is a need to exercise discipline and to grasp the fleeting moments. We may utilize odd times while we are traveling or waiting for appointments. To economize our time is to invest for the best ends of the ministry. We remember the words of Paul, "The fire shall try every man's work of what sort it is" (I Cor. 3:13). And the servants of God earlier had been advised, "The fire shall ever be burning upon the altar; it shall never go out" (Lev. 6:13). The opportunity to study is ever before us and no one can make excuse that he cannot find time to study or that he lacks the tools of learning, for there are countless resources available.

During my ministry I was able to devote a year to reading all of Alexander Whyte. Other years were given to W. Graham Scroggie, G. Campbell Morgan, Samuel Chadwick, J. H. Jowett, and G. H. Morrison. A winter apiece was spent with the works of C. H. Spurgeon, Jonathan Edwards, and Phillips Brooks. I read selections from the last three to gain a feel for their preaching styles, whereas the works of the others mentioned were read in their entirety. Biographical studies of each were part of the investment.

During summer vacations I took up other kinds of reading; for example, *The Rockefellers: An American Dynasty* by Peter Collier and David Horowitz; Robert Lacey's *Majesty: Elizabeth II and the House of Windsor*; Solzhenitsyn's *Gulag Archipelago*; Constantine FitzGibbons's *Life of Dylan Thomas.* I also found refreshment in historical novels and lighter, relaxing reading, such as Arthur Conan Doyle and Agatha Christie.

Dale Oldham, former pastor and radio preacher of the Church of God, Anderson, Indiana, in his book *Giants Along My Path* (Anderson, IN: Warner Press, 1973) shares the struggles and opportunities of his fifty-year ministry. He tells of the tests and trials of the ministry and how the man of God longs for a closer walk with God and hungers for spiritual renewal. He relates that in his pushing ahead as a leader he became so overly aggressive that people resented him. He tells of his struggles to find a new birth of spiritual power at the height of his ministry. Every year he read the Bible through once and dipped into devotional books, but something else was needed. He resolved to depart from his usual pattern and give himself to the serious study of the Book of Romans for a year. Early every morning he took an hour to read slowly and thoughtfully a critical commentary, including the footnotes and the notes in the back of the book. He carefully read seven commentaries on Romans in seventeen months, and later added another to the list. Listen to his own words:

> It was during this study of Romans that I began to change. It had not come about through prayer, the reading of the Bible, or my attendance in retreats. But, as I began to realize afresh the deeper meanings of Paul's teachings regarding justification by faith and what the love of God really means to a Christian, the change began. It seems to me that a great many "perfectionist" people, although they *teach* justification by faith, actually *practice* justification by works. They seem to be saying, "If I can be good enough, if I can toe the line and make no infringement of the rules, if I can guard my tongue and never talk out of turn, I will be saved." Paul did not teach this. He taught that none of us merits salvation. None can earn or deserve it. It is the gift of God, not of works, lest any man should boast.
>
> This is almost too good to be true, but I decided to trust Paul and try him out. So I ceased my struggling. I ceased my everlasting straining to be good and began to relax in the arms of a loving God. To my great relief and satisfaction it "worked."

Oldham's experience is reminiscent of the crisis which John Wesley's religious background of "works" underwent on May

24, 1738. On that date Wesley came to feel the full *assurance* of what Christ had done for him. He came to see justification as the initiation by faith into a life of sanctification in which works express the inner reality of a renewed person. All this is in Christ alone. Not unlike others, Wesley's mind was opened after hearing the preface to Martin Luther's commentary on Romans.

In his inaugural address as rector of Edinburgh University, Thomas Carlyle recalled his own entry into those halls of learning when a callow youth from Ecclefechan. He counseled the students concerning what he termed the golden season of life. He told them they were in the seed time of life; if they did not sow, or if they sowed tares instead of wheat, they could not expect to reap well afterwards. "The habits of study," he admonished, "acquired at universities are of the highest importance in afterlife." He then stressed diligence, honesty, and studying according to conscience. Morality as regards study is, as in all other things, the primary consideration, and overrules all others. The doctrine is old, but a true one and confirmed by those who engage in the Christian ministry. The habits of study begun in college or seminary continue in the privacy of the pastor's preparation for a task which is never ending.

No man can be expert in all realms of knowledge. The minister should know the basic areas of Christian experience and be able to lead his people in understanding and development with growth in discipleship. As he is built up in his faith and devotion, so he will assist in the upbuilding of his officers and congregation. This is the true way to build the church in our day.

Among the fields of study at least ten subjects touch the pastor's life and work in practical dimensions. These are listed in *Baker's Dictionary of Practical Theology* (Grand Rapids: Baker Book House, 1967): preaching, homiletics, hermeneutics, evangelism-missions, counseling, administration, pastoral, stewardship, worship, and education.

The preacher could begin a series of studies in practical theology and in the process add to his knowledge, increase his faith and devotion, and better serve the Head of the church. Of course there are other books calling for attention. We could mention volumes on Christian ethics and theology, concordances, Bible dictionaries, encyclopedias, histories, biographies and autobiographies, studies in the person and work of the Holy Spirit, devotional guides, and commentaries.

One of the abiding satisfactions of a teaching-preaching ministry is experienced when God calls out from the congregation young people who are trained as doctors, nurses, engineers, social workers, teachers, and even as evangelists to work at home or overseas. That is the seal of God's approval on the ministry which is *based upon study*. The satisfaction in study issues in tokens of this kind. The divine Word has been received and obedience in the faith follows.

Indeed, satisfaction was found by the early church in sending out young men and women into other agencies of service. In Acts 13:1-3 there is the record of how God called during an hour of worship at Antioch. Some of the leaders of that congregation are named. As they ministered *(leitourgounton;* i.e., worshiped or carried through the liturgical order of the service), the Holy Spirit said, "Separate me Barnabas and Saul for the work whereunto I have called them." That call came during a session of public worship which included reading of the Scriptures, prayers, and exhortation and teaching. Something exciting was taking place in public worship—not the earthquake, nor the wind or fire, but the still small voice—the sound of a great silence in which the divine Spirit applied the divine Word and called the new servants.

God commissioned the best of that congregation to leave and pioneer in other regions of the Roman world. After the ritual of prayer and fasting, the hands of ordination were laid on Barnabas and Saul as missionary agents. We read further: "So they, being sent forth by the Holy Spirit, departed . . . they sailed. . . . They preached the word of God in synagogues of the Jews: and they had also John [Mark] to assist them." And what the congregation did the Holy Spirit did.

When a pastor continues to use what he has learned in college or seminary he becomes a good steward of what God has given him. We are privileged who are called to the ministry of the Word of God. James D. Smart, pastor of the Rosedale Presbyterian Church in Toronto, spent part of his life as professor at Union Theological Seminary in New York. In both positions he found great need to teach the Scriptures, for the biblical knowledge of thousands is severely limited. His book *The Strange Silence of the Bible in the Church* (Philadelphia: Westminster Press, 1970) addresses this problem. If would-be preachers graduate without the enthusiasm to teach people and if pastors have forgotten their supreme task, then it is time to transform the nature of education in congregations. Instead of mere lip service, each church could become a genuine Christian school with classes for adults as well as youth and children. The pulpit especially should be the leader in this. Sermons would no longer recite trite generalities and moralisms, but, instead, would become systematic expositions of the Bible with all the knowledge now available to us. A study in hermeneutics is urgent. Did not the Reformation open the Bible to the people?

When one is involved in a continuing ministry which views the congregation as a Bible school, ever learning, study is no drudgery but a delight. The teaching pulpit gives strength and vitality to both church officers and lay people. No longer spoonfed on simple, superficial addresses, the congregation feeds on strong meat and matures. Many of them will become teachers of others and worthy pillars of the church.

The life and work of the apostle Paul can afford a most satisfying study to the pastor-preacher. Among the best monographs in the field are the writings of William M. Ramsay. These include *The Cities of St. Paul, Pauline and Other Studies in Early Christian History*, and *St. Paul the Traveller and Roman Citizen*. Ramsay gives a great deal of geographical and historical background not readily available elsewhere. Happily, these volumes have recently been reprinted (in the William M. Ramsay Library—Baker Book House).

There are many other volumes on Paul which the minister can use with profit. Among them are James Stalker's brief but stimulating *Life of St. Paul* (Old Tappan, NJ: Fleming H. Revell, n.d.); David Smith's *The Life and Letters of St. Paul* (New York: Gordon Press, 1977); the standard work of W. J. Conybeare and J. S. Howson, *The Life and Epistles of St. Paul* (Grand Rapids: William B. Eerdmans, 1949); and James S. Stewart's *A Man in Christ* (Grand Rapids: Baker Book House, 1975). The works of A. M. Hunter, F. F. Bruce, and Herman N. Ridderbos are also to be recommended. For challenge and stimulus one might try Albert Schweitzer's *The Mysticism of Paul the Apostle* (New York: Seabury Press, 1968). Not to be overlooked are background books covering the geography, archaeology, social customs, and religion of Bible lands and peoples.

In *The Reformed Pastor* (Richmond: John Knox Press, 1963 reprint of 1656 edition) Richard Baxter shared an abiding testimony about the satisfactions of the ministry. When asked, "What is to be gained from it?" Baxter responded, "I'll tell you but the truth: *constant study*, preaching, and all other labours; yet though I am day and night full of pain, *study I must*, preach I must, instruct the ignorant, resolve the doubting, comfort the dejected and disquieted, admonish the scandalous and relapsed."

For those who find it difficult to study continuously, the best advice is to take heart. When others began, it was not easy. It is wise to begin gradually but persistently. Outlining a schedule can be helpful. Charles Haddon Spurgeon studied daily; so did Alexander McLaren. John Henry Jowett invested the morning hours in personal study as did George H. Morrison. G. Campbell Morgan and W. Graham Scroggie captured the best hours of the day in study. In fact, any preacher of great influence—in spite of his fallible ways—is known also for his investment of time in study. Preparation is but the prelude to power. Knowledge thus acquired in study is forever a part of the mind and heart. The wise man finds abiding satisfaction in his enlarged vision, strengthened will, enthusiastic devotion, and the service he is ready to render as the calendar notes his commitments.

The names of Donald Grey Barnhouse, Henry A. Ironside, Harold J. Ockenga, Clarence E. Macartney, Henry Sloane Coffin, Harry Emerson Fosdick, David H. C. Read, Harold E. Luccock, and a host of others have been enshrined in memory because they found satisfaction in study. Without it they would have beaten the air and become superficial in what they presented. By diligent study they not only found a satisfaction for themselves, but they brought to others the fruits of their labors.

Jonathan Edwards summed up his method: "My method of study, from my first beginning the work of the ministry, has been very much by writing." To be exact in study habits he cultivated writing out notes; this exercise helped him advance and mature. In addition to making notes from his reading, he wrote down for his own benefit what appeared to him to be the best thought on countless subjects. The more he used this method, the more habitual it became, and the more profitable and pleasant he found it. He testified: "So far as I myself am able to judge of what talents I have, for benefiting my fellow creatures by word, I think I can write better than I can speak." From some of his miscellaneous notebooks in the Yale collection we find examples of his habits of study. We shall know much more when the full manuscripts are deciphered and edited.

Throughout the centuries there has been continual stress upon ministerial study. In the furtherance of the gospel or the teaching and upbuilding of the church universal, God has been pleased to call and equip people who continued to study. The models are there and today's leaders find encouragement and inspiration to follow their steps. Each develops personal habits in study. Taking notes, writing reflections on material read, marking the texts with personal insights, and creative writing are among the methods used to accumulate knowledge. Moderns may have typewriters, index cards, filing and duplicating systems to ease their labors. But the principle and the goal are still the same—"a workman needing not to be ashamed in the pursuit of truth," and all this through hours and years of constant study.

4

The Tools of Learning

"And even things without life giving sound, whether pipe or harp, except they give a distinction in the sounds, how shall it be known what is piped or harped? For if the trumpet give an uncertain sound, who shall prepare himself to the battle? So likewise ye, except ye utter by the tongue words easy to be understood, how shall it be known what is spoken? for ye shall speak into the air." (I COR. 14:7-9)

"So with yourselves; if you in a tongue utter speech that is not intelligible, how will anyone know what is said? For you will be speaking into the air." (I COR. 14:9, RSV)

"And he [Jesus] goeth up into a mountain, and calleth unto him whom he would: and they came unto him. And he ordained twelve, that they should be with him, and that he might send them forth to preach."

(MARK 3:13, 14)

WHEN THE LORD of the harvest calls men to serve Him, He does not send out novices. Notice that in the account of the calling of the apostles (Mark 3:13, 14), a principle is clearly indicated.

First, there is the call to service.

Second, there is the response of the will.

Third, there is the ordination to special tasks.

Fourth, there is the training required before being sent out.

Fifth, there is a statement of the task: preaching.

The key factor here is that these apostles were to be "with him" for a period of three to three-and-a-half years. During that time they were under instruction by the Master Teacher. They witnessed His miracles and heard His talks and messages. They were with Him at the festivals and the feasts of Judaism. They followed Him to the Mount of Transfiguration. They heard words of conflict as He was criticized and opposed by Roman authorities and Hebrew leaders of religion. They shared in the experience of the upper room. They were near to Him in the Garden of Gethsemane. They saw Him taken and tried as a criminal. They witnessed the crucifixion, although from afar off (except John). They later were eyewitnesses of the resurrected Lord and kept company with Him during forty days until He ascended in glory. They heard His promise that the Father would send the Holy Spirit, and they received their marching orders in the Great Commission and again in the command of Acts 1:8 to be witnesses unto Him throughout the world.

Being with Him was the essence of the apostles' training and education. That school of the cross tested and tried the apostles as well whenever He faced temptations and trials. While Judas betrayed Him and Peter denied Him and the rest of the apostolic band forsook Him and fled (with the exception of John), they rallied by Pentecost and became witnesses to their generation. The examinations at the conclusion of that three-year course of instruction and practical experience left some doubt as to their fitness and qualifications for service. However, the gifts of the risen Lord, the Head of the church, inspired them and empowered them for the work to which God had called them.

We, too, are called to be with Him. The years of preparation for our lifework require an attentive mind and listening ear as we translate His teaching and doctrine into practical ends. We, too, are sharers in His hours of temptation; and the obstacles which confront us are overcome by the same grace and Holy Spirit. We are also given opportunities to serve in our day and generation by the will of God.

Opportunity to use the tools of learning is given to those who are themselves the gifts of God to the church. Many and varied are the tools of learning which can be used in preparation for and during the ministry of the servant of God. Among the most valuable are books. Geoffrey Chaucer (1342-1400) noted the important role of old books:

> Out of the old fieldes, as men saithe,
>   Cometh al this new corne from yere to yere,
> An out of old bookes, in good faithe,
>   Cometh al this new science that men lere.

New books continue to come from publishers and constant appeals are made to read the latest. But we can afford to leave the most recent books for a while, even a year or more. Time will judge the inherent value of a book. The books of yesterday and of other ages are not necessarily out of date, but may be a means to mental and spiritual strength. Those that have endured to become classics have done so after much testing and sifting. Selection of the best books requires familiarity in the chosen field of study and a knowledge of the literature available.

The problem of discipline arises constantly with college and seminary students as they wrestle with time and its demands upon reading and study. Unless the battle is won early, there will abide for the minister a similar struggle. Thus the need for discipline must be faced early in one's vocation. F. M. Powicke in *The Legacy of the Middle Ages* (1926) refers to the so-called pagan as one who is destitute of inward discipline. The Christian, on the other hand, knows the reality of a "code" and "self-discipline." But here a question arises—is not Christianity regulated not by rules but by a spontaneous spirit? Kenneth E. Kirk, in *The Vision of God* (Greenwood, SC: Attic Press, 1978 edition), has pointed out that Christianity does not involve legalism but a free spirit; it is not the living of a life by a code, but dedication to God and penetration by His grace. "What else is the message of Christ, the promise of the Spirit? What other meaning can we attach to Paul's indictment of the law?"

The modern mind is perhaps partisan in this matter. It welcomes spontaneity, and rejects suggestions of discipline and regulation. Yet it would be absurd to maintain that the ideal of ordered self-discipline has no place in the Christian life. There are dangers in rigorism and formalism and these we must know. We do well in our Protestant and evangelical context to decide what is proper and what form the discipline shall take. Certainly, the minister cannot escape the call to live "under orders" and there is the daily call to accept the cross. This affects our studies, our pastoral work, and all our public life as well as our private.

"Blessed are the pure in heart: for they shall see God" (Matt. 5:8). Beyond this word of our Lord we cannot go. This is the absolute, the highest, the ultimate. This should be our goal as we discipline our character and make it ready for the final virtue. Christian character is the goal of all self-discipline, service, and worship. The active life in the world, whether in office, factory, or wherever, is a means of growth and maturity. God's calling is not limited to the pastoral office or ministerial life, but is also fulfilled in any other sphere of human endeavor. The highest format of Christian character demands, not merely that intellect, emotion, and will shall be *rightly directed*, but also that they shall be *highly developed*. Excellence and moral righteousness meet one another. The Christian should be a man not merely of good will, but of strong will too; a man not merely of *right desires*, but of *strong right desires*.

The tools in the school of Christ include nature. Many lessons can be learned from the out-of-doors. In Bible days devotion of life was cultivated in the secret place as well as in the synagogue or temple. Sometimes by a lake or on a hillside there was instruction. A garden could become both oratory and study. But always of greater importance were the tools of literature and history as the rolls of Scripture were read, memorized, exegeted, and interpreted. Example came from the Model Teacher Himself, whose parabolic stories and sermons brought new knowledge and instruction.

Ivor Brown has said that "the craftsman is proud of his tools; the surgeon does not operate with an old razor-blade; the sportsman fusses happily and long over the choice of rod, gun, club or racquet. But the man who is working in words, unless he is a professional writer (and not always then), is singularly neglectful of his instruments." While the tools are abundant today, using them is a never-ending apprenticeship. As Chaucer put it:

> The lyfe so short,
> The craft so long to learn.

Or, in the words of John Ruskin (1819-1900):

> No book is worth anything which is not worth MUCH, nor is it serviceable until it has been read and re-read, and loved, and loved again; and marked so that you can refer to the passages you want in it, as a soldier can seize the weapons he needs in an armoury, or a housewife bring the spice she needs from her store.

If ever a man used the tools of learning, it was John Wesley. He was steeped in the church fathers; the breadth of his reading led him to become an evangelist to his age. His amazing versatility and his adaptability to new situations in preaching enabled him to disciple others and gather them into societies for their growth and moral welfare. Inward conviction was linked with outward expression as he became God's agent to lead his generation into the knowledge of the Christian faith. Conversion of the individual was stressed as "he shewed people Christ" in his preaching everywhere. He also stressed corporate worship and the social fellowship of praise and prayer and preaching (which emphasized to the new converts the doctrines of faith and salvation).

Augustine Birrell in one of his essays wrote, "No man can understand the history of his own country [England] unless he knows Fox's *Journals* for the seventeenth century and Wesley's for the eighteenth." Historians may overlook these dynamic men of faith, but they cannot adequately explain the moral and spiritual power, the upsurge of new life and character, at that period of history apart from the life and work of these Christian men.

Linked with these two examples of practical Christianity there is also William Booth in the nineteenth century. With him we must recognize Catherine his wife. She, too, equally shared and ministered with her illustrious husband in becoming all things to all people in the Victorian period. The pawnbroker's assistant and part-time Methodist churchman moved out from the church into the marketplace, the theater, the prison, and the highway. Novel in their method, the Booths introduced the Salvation Army as an arm of the whole church to bring the gospel to the outcast and downtrodden in society. They discovered that however important political and economic questions might be, the religious question is ultimately the most fundamental of all. The Booths worked deliberately for the salvation of people and society.

Near the close of his life William Booth reviewed his life's work:

> I might have chosen as my life's work the housing of the poor. . . . I might have given myself up to the material benefit of the working classes. . . . I might have given myself to temperance reform. . . . I might have given my life to the physical improvement of the people. . . . I might have formed another political party. [But] the object I chose all these years ago embraced every effort containing in its heart the remedy (that is

the point) for every form of misery and sin and wrong to be found on the earth and every method of reclamation needed by human nature.

In the L. P. Stone Lectures to seminarians at Princeton Theological Seminary (1940), which were later published as *Poetry as a Means of Grace* (Staten Island, NY: Gordian Press, 1965 reprint), Charles G. Osgood, professor of belles-lettres at Princeton University, expressed his view of literature:

> For a genuine sense of literature I would insist upon a man's passionate interests in the human individual, on his passionate concern in the spiritual life of men, and the issue between failure and success, between perdition and salvation. . . . Such is the indispensable basis of a full, true and responsive sense of values in literature: For literature is life, with the same scale of values, the same ineluctable laws, the same unerring and beautiful justice.

After a lifetime of study and teaching, Osgood shared his judgment that only by reading could he keep himself fit for his high calling. But how, then, shall we read? How economize time and energy, how keep the head above the deluge of books that now overflow the world? To avoid dependence on the opinion of others, we must practice to become our own judge and critic. A critic in this context is one who is in search of permanent values, and who develops a power to recognize them—and the ultimate reasons for believing in them.

To judge a work of art—a poem or a picture—one must examine characteristics within the work itself. Is it technically good or unusual? Is it what the author set out to make it? Does it cause us to respond emotionally or to take some action? Above all, if we are to invest our time wisely, we must distinguish between good and bad, right and wrong, sacred and secular.

Osgood was afraid that ministers did not grasp opportunities to read. He recognized that the Bible contains a living literature which in manifold forms interprets life in the light of moral values. He concluded that sacred literature thus transcends but embraces the secular. "By this means secular literature is not humiliated but exalted, not dimmed but illuminated, not defaced but glorified, not sterilized but fertilized, to the infinite increase and enrichment of the world's language and letters." His plea is that the minister should keep in touch with current literature, but chiefly with the perennial and dateless. The best poetry can survive the test of time because its truth is not abstract or filled with platitudes. It has an eternal quality which speaks to man's condition in every generation. Osgood advises selecting one poet (not to the exclusion of the rest) and learning to live with his spirit and writings.

Robert Browning can be a source of great strength, for his poems express rich and deep insights into Scripture. His "Rabbi Ben Ezra" puts Jeremiah's symbolism of the potter and the clay in a new light. Man is upon the wheels of circumstance, yet in the hands of God. Browning also graphically portrays the life of Saul, the king of Israel, as a morning of promise, an afternoon of indolence, and a night of disaster.

Steeping ourselves in such poetry helps us to see what is really important, though the world call it a trifle, and to see trifles as trifles, though the world call them important. Like Lazarus in Browning's "Epistle of Karshish," we become newly aware of "the spiritual life around the earthly life." Or take Browning's dramatic poem "Ned Bratts," which revolves around John Bunyan's blind daughter, who was employed at an inn while he was in prison for the preaching of the gospel. Bratts is the innkeeper. With his wife he exposes Bunyan's daughter to moral risks. Finally he is converted. When charged before judge and jury, he gives crucial testimony to a changed life. Or consider the poem "Easter Day" with its opening line, " 'Tis very hard to be a Christian!" Browning's "Death in the Desert" furnishes much to ponder as we trace the story of John the Apostle and his remarkable long life.

If our choice of concentration be Robert Browning, we will find a robustness and masculinity in the language which bring strength and power to elucidate much of Scripture. In "Bishop Bloughram's Apology" is presented a defense of the Christian faith. "A Grammarian's Funeral" has some pointed things to say to those who regard the Scriptures as the basis of truth.

If not Robert Browning, why not John Milton as guide? Or is William Shakespeare beyond us today? As we have already seen, James Stalker endeavored to read Shakespeare's works once each year. Of course, Shakespeare is a master writer who stimulates, enlivens, and opens windows of understanding concerning human nature and man's relation to the world and his Creator. He was steeped in the language of the English Bible and drew deeply from that well. Many today will select the Bard of Stratford to be their guide in their reading outside of theology. The choice of one poet must be an individual matter.

Things have not changed much with the majority of people since Shakespeare wrote in *Love's Labour's Lost*:

> He hath not fed of the dainties that are bred in
> a book; he hath not eat paper as it were;
> he hath not drunk ink.

However, today it is much easier to correct the situation. There are so many good books on the market. The most basic tools of learning are books—old and tried books and books of more recent vintage.

We learn how best to use tools by experience. We learn how best to use books by simply reading. We acquire general knowledge from dictionaries, encyclopedias, and lexicons. These are indispensable tools ready at hand for immediate reference and consultation. Happy is the person who has some items of ready reference close to his own desk in his study or den and doesn't have to make a trip to a library.

In addition there are the volumes we need to guide us in specialized subjects. We should have a volume on hermeneutics, another on geography, certainly one on archaeology, as well as on the background of our Lord's parabolic teaching, the life and work of Paul, homiletics and preaching. All subjects of a biblical nature require books. A library grows gradually as we experience need for more and more tools. For those without opportunity to gather certain tools of learning, there is always the open door of libraries. We might also do well to share some of our rare treasures with others.

What a wealth of information there is in the three-volume *Cambridge History of American Literature* (New York: Macmillan, 1943)! Here are essays on and critical appraisals of the best in American writing. The same is true of the fifteen-volume *Cambridge History of English Literature* (New York: Cambridge University Press). Since its first issue it has been revised to bring the saga of literature up to the end of the Second World War, with its final chapter given the intriguing title of "The Age of T. S. Eliot." Regular reference to these tools will open up a post-graduate course in literature to supplement our Bible studies and enable us to engage in our culture with relevance and reality.

In *The Five Hundred Best English Letters* and *The Hundred Best English Essays* (Norwood, PA: Norwood Editions, 1929), both compiled and edited by F. E. Smith, Lord Birkenhead, we are exposed to the best thought across the centuries. One of the benefits derived is that we become familiar with the various strands of literature and the endless uncertainties of human nature. The passions which men and women experience are dealt with in these storehouses of letters and essays. These passions which sweep human nature—involving failure, anger, jealousy, pride, lust, hatred, greed, murder, and also those occasions of rising above and not yielding to nature and the self because of moral and spiritual power—are also depicted in pictorial realism in the Bible. We find we are able to demonstrate that Christianity can transform human nature by the eternal gospel. By studying the Bible, the greatest masterpiece of literature, we learn to use whatever tools of learning are available to us.

Although youth is the best time to acquire a taste for reading and a love for books, there is no period of life when a beginning may not be made. The slower reader or the handicapped scholar may find in later life a spur and a rebirth of desire and opportunity to engage in this delightful task. Thus a new world is born and the horizons of the mind are pushed back without limit. Lord Macaulay said: "I would rather be a poor man in a garret with a love for books, than a king on a throne without that love." Edward Gibbon, historian of the Roman Empire, declared that a taste for books was the pleasure and the glory of his life, and that he would not part with it for the riches of the Indies. William Robertson Nicoll toward the close of his life remarked: "Reading has given me such pleasure that I am in danger of falling into extravagance when I speak of it. That pleasure has gone on and is now stronger than ever." "The purest pleasures I have ever known, are those accessible to all," says Richard Cobden. "It is the calm intercourse with intelligent minds, and in communion with the departed great, through books, by our own firesides."

The wise man will see to it that he is not without basic tools for his task. Some of these are with us from early years in the aptitudes we already possess for the divine vocation in which we serve. Fortunate is the person whose early schooling gave him a foundation of language facility. Many are now grateful for the Latin, Greek, or other language which gave them a start later in biblical and theological studies. Those not so blessed can still acquire some degree of language facility for the special needs of the ministry.

Thankful are those whose background instilled a love for books and reading. In early life they may have started a small library of sorts which they used in the growing days of youth. To build a rich library and thus to become familiar with standard works afforded enrichment and a cause for thanksgiving. With the accumulation of thousands of books over the years, these friends and companions now speak from the shelves and remind their owners of their abiding contribution.

Our Lord spoke of disciples coming under His yoke (Matt. 11:28-30). The central symbol of this favorite text calls for comment. The yoke not only was the means for controlling oxen, but it suggests a teacher gathering a class for instruction. Disciples came under the yoke of the teacher and this implied discipline in learning. Christ's yoke is "easy" but that does not imply a slack way of life. The Scottish version indicates this to mean that the yoke "fits exactly and does not chafe." Thus the disciple is under the yoke of his teacher.

Those who, unlike Christian disciples, seek to be "free" from their yoke find that in the free state they are enslaved. Philosophers have noted, "Man was born free, but he is everywhere in chains." They have counseled that man should get rid of all his chains, including Christ's yoke, in order to be himself and live as he pleases! *That* is the way of loss of discipline, disintegration of life, and ultimately the death of freedom.

Among the tools handed to the disciple is a disciplined life. This does not mean regimentation of a time or of personal progress. There is a burden to carry and we are in the yoke with Christ our Lord and Teacher. Our "burden" involves responsible tasks and a life full of duties. We are not free from the pathway of duty for on that pathway we discern the will of God. The spirit of our Lord was one of humility, and we learn from Him that pride is our bane.

Pride leads to self-will and self-love. Pride seeks the first place and recognition. Pride is the spirit of self dominating a life or a congregation. Diotrephes loved to have the preeminence (III John 9) and that congregation had trouble.

Humility is the grace and gift of a spirit which is willing to give others the first place and to be content that God's work is done. It does not matter who (if anyone) receives credit for it! The humble mind is like to that of our Lord, who, "when he was reviled, reviled not again" (I Peter 2:23).

Salvation cannot be by the self-efforts of a sinful man who thinks he can achieve it in his pride. Salvation is only a grace and gift of God. In humility we must accept His invitation to be under His yoke (which has a cross-shaped tree as its base).

The tools of learning are a must, for no one of us in the ministry can live to himself. Others have labored and we enter into their labors. When we think of the wealth of the past and how the church of God has stored up that knowledge from every age, we are in debt to those who have gone before. The whole church throughout all the centuries has learned through testing and trial, through discipline and devotion, how to select the tools for those who serve.

Think of the plodding, patient toil of Alexander Cruden in compiling his concordance and then imagine what a loss to us if we lacked the concordances of Young and of Strong. There are dictionaries with learned articles throwing light upon subject after subject. The Bible may mention a place or a name or an event in history, but not give us any details. Where to find that background but in books like Bible encyclopedias? William Thomson was a missionary in the biblical lands. The majority of ministers have never been to Israel, but with a book like Thomson's *The Land and the Book* he can be their eyes and guide, for he spent a lifetime absorbing the land, the life, and the customs of the people of former centuries. Older books like Thomson's pinpoint the manners and customs of Israel before modernization. Here is a practical tool for the preacher to use.

In acquiring the tools of learning much will depend upon the particular emphasis to be given by the servant of God. A pastor-teacher with a regular congregation and constant output of sermons and lectures each week will certainly need the major reference books. Important dictionaries for biblical and theological consultation should be at hand. Special commentaries are necessary to check his own work on the Scripture text. Several sets are on the market. The whole Bible is covered by a variety of expositors whose contributions are invaluable. A solid way in which to build a theological library is to secure a major work on each book of the Bible. It is wise to procure the most critical commentaries, for they treat in detail the precise meaning of Scripture.

No one can prescribe for another; only by testing and trial is a pastor led to what he deems best for himself. But I would like to mention a few titles at random among the hundreds which await use:

W. H. Griffith Thomas. *Genesis: A Devotional Commentary.* Grand Rapids: William B. Eerdmans, 1946.

G. Campbell Morgan. *Studies of the Four Gospels.* Four volumes. Old Tappan, NJ: Fleming H. Revell, n.d.

W. Graham Scroggie. *A Guide to the Gospels.* Old Tappan, NJ: Fleming H. Revell, 1975.

Charles H. Dodd. *Interpretation of the Fourth Gospel.* New York: Cambridge University Press, n.d.

Charles K. Barrett. *The Gospel According to St. John.* Naperville, IL: Allenson, 1955.

F. F. Bruce. *The Book of the Acts.* Grand Rapids: William B. Eerdmans, 1954.

Karl Barth. *Epistle to the Romans.* New York: Oxford University Press, 1968.

J. B. Lightfoot. *Commentary on St. Paul's Epistle to the Galatians.* Grand Rapids: Zondervan, 1957.

_____. *Commentary on St. Paul's Epistle to the Philippians.* Grand Rapids: Zondervan, 1957.

Brooke F. Westcott. *Commentary on the Epistle to the Hebrews.* Grand Rapids: William B. Eerdmans, 1950.

Joseph B. Mayor. *The Epistle of St. James.* Saint Clare Shores, MI: Scholarly Press, 1976 reprint.

Robert H. Charles. *Revelation of St. John.* Naperville, IL: Allenson, 1920.

Henry B. Swete. *The Apocalypse of John.* Grand Rapids: Kregel, 1977 reprint.

Among recent releases are Ronald A. Ward's *Commentary on First and Second Timothy and Titus* (Waco, TX: Word Books, 1974) and *The Pattern of Our Salvation* (Waco, TX: Word Books, 1977). The latter is a study of New Testament unity dealing with the nature and character of God. All of this Canadian scholar's works are incisive, yet down-to-earth exegetical writings.

Mention has been made of John Baillie, whose spiritual life was reflected in all he wrote and did as teacher of theology and philosophy. His books have been cited as deposits of deep thought yet simple expression. What was his secret? He never repudiated the evangelical faith of his early boyhood. His cousin described his study during his busy years in Edinburgh:

> It was *a quiet room*, with noises kept out—no telephone, no radio, no typewriter. There were three focal points: the big uncluttered desk by the window where he sat hours of the day writing, in clear handwriting, the sermons, letters, and manuscripts, etc.; the big leather chair, where he often sat into the night reading books and theology and philosophy, novels, poetry—all seasoned [like the reading of many theologians] with a reasonable sprinkling of good "detectives"; the prayer-desk by the window with its little pile of well-worn versions of the Scriptures and of devotional books. There, at the time when he was sure to be alone, John Baillie read and thought and worshipped. And through that daily, faithful discipline of the will and mind and soul, it became true that the great theologian and church-statesman was first and foremost *a man holy and humble of heart*.

James Murray devoted his whole life to the *Oxford English Dictionary*. This achievement in Victorian scholarship is a monument of painstaking plodding and persistence. Assumption of the task condemned him to problems of money, time, and space, from which he was never to escape for the rest of his life. But he never doubted the importance of the work; he believed it was *his destiny*. His favorite text, a saying of Charles Kingsley, hung in his bedroom:

> Have thy tools ready;
> God will find thee work.

Whenever tools of learning are required, an abundance can be found. The servant of God with pen and paper can go far in using tools simple and yet indispensable.

We now see how valuable are those books which grace our shelves and which we use daily. Thanksgiving should be offered for all the gifts and virtues of this life. We offer prayers of thanks and a grace for our daily bread and life and health. It was Charles Lamb who reminded us: "I own that I am disposed to say grace upon twenty other occasions in the course of the day besides my dinner. . . . Why have we none for books?" Let us give thanks graciously to God for His gifts of *The Book* and all good books.

5

The Devotion of the Heart

"God is a Spirit; and they that worship him must worship him in spirit and in truth." (JOHN 4:24)

"I exhort therefore, that, first of all, supplications, prayers, intercessions, and giving of thanks, be made for all men." (I TIM. 2:1)

"Ye have not, because ye ask not." (JAMES 4:2)

"Ask, and it shall be given you." (MATT. 7:7)

OPPORTUNITY IS GIVEN to the man of God to give himself "to prayer and to the ministry of the word" (Acts 6:4). The daily and continuous nature of this task is obvious. It is easier to be diligent in delivering the spoken word to men, than to learn the secret of speaking to God.

Worship is primary if our hearts are to be set in the right frame and spirit. True devotion is the test of our commitment. Confession never occurs apart from prayer. Who are we that we should have this freedom of access to the throne of God? We are beset by temptation so that we become casual and careless. We confess there are times of barrenness and periods of dryness. This is a puzzle to some and a problem to others. Nevertheless, the pastor carries in his heart the congregation he serves. He cannot be free from the cares and anxieties of his people. Thus there is intercession continually. Because the pastor must pray hundreds of times in a year, he finds he must find help primarily from the Scriptures, and then from books of devotion. This is a regular discipline of the mind and heart.

A minister's devotions, his interior communion with God, his prayers and cries of intercession, and growth in grace and in spiritual wisdom do not come easily. From the beginning there is a struggle. The chief enemy of the minister may be competing interests which erode time. Or it may be a dryness of spirit and lethargy of will which steal the best moments and reduce the man of God to a man of words without the Word from God.

The youthful aspirant to the ministry may center his daily devotions in reading the Psalms and other familiar parts of the Bible. These lead to the first stumbling steps on the long road of the pilgrimage. Over the years he meets teachers and examples who have left their footprints. Among these are some well-known names whose words often stab afresh and prod the minister. Some hymn writers and poets are among the best teachers of the devotional life.

James Montgomery (1771-1854), a Moravian of Scottish birth, gave us a vivid description of the life of prayer in his hymn, "Prayer Is the Soul's Sincere Desire":

> Prayer is the soul's sincere desire,
> Unuttered or expressed;
> The motion of a hidden fire
> That trembles in the breast.
>
> Prayer is the burden of a sigh,
> The falling of a tear,
> The upward glancing of an eye,
> When none but God is near.
>
> Prayer is the contrite sinner's voice,
> Returning from his ways,
> While angels in their songs rejoice
> And cry, "Behold, he prays!
>
> Prayer is the Christian's vital breath,
> The Christian's native air,
> His watchword at the gates of death;
> He enters heaven with prayer.
>
> O Thou by whom we come to God,
> The Life, the Truth, the Way;
> The path of prayer Thyself hast trod:
> Lord, teach us how to pray!

The Book of Common Prayer helped to unite the Church of England when Thomas Cranmer (1489-1556) was Archbishop of Canterbury. Along with the King James Version of the Bible

(1611) it later served to help unify the nation. It also gave to the English-speaking world a standard of excellence in prayer which is still recognized today. Wherever men gather to worship in the tradition of the Anglican communion throughout the world (and some 65 million people claim some association), the cadences of those prayers arise as music. In reciting these prayers in unison there is an awareness of the communion of saints before the throne of God. I treasure a copy I received in 1954 from Bishop Chirakarotto K. Jacob of the Church of South India, which combines Anglican, Methodist, Presbyterian, and Congregational elements. A national of India, living at Kittayam, Jacob patterned himself after his Lord and Master in humility of spirit and deed.

The preface to the revised edition of 1662 recognized the sublimity of the Book of Common Prayer:

> It has been the wisdom of the Church to keep the mean between the two extremes, of too much stiffness in refusing, and of too much easiness in admitting any variation from it.... It is, we believe that it will always be, one of the great books of the world. Nothing save the English version of the Holy Scriptures is enwoven so closely in the language and the deepest thoughts of our people at home and beyond the seas.

Based as it is upon the Scriptures and the beauty of the English language of the sixteenth century, the Book of Common Prayer is an unsurpassed devotional manual. One might dare to call it the Bible in devotional form. It is for everyone and deeply moves the congregation that uses it for public worship. If the minister uses it as his own private guide and mentor, he will find strength to meet his own personal needs. As a part of public worship, the Book of Common Prayer enriches the worshipers in offering prayer together, just as our Lord taught His disciples, "After this manner therefore pray ye ..." (Matt. 6:9). The unity of the group in speaking the same words is a symphony of thanksgiving, petition, intercession, and adoration before God. The congregation is also joined with all the saints of all the ages. In literature of this nature all the members of the body of Christ find joy and strength. From Catholic to Protestant, from Quaker to Pentecostal, all are built up in faith.

There are many other books available to us today which can

aid the inner life of devotion. One might mention *The Inward Pilgrimage* by Bernhard Christensen (Minneapolis: Augsburg, 1976). Or take the anthology of prayers and meditations from Scripture and devotional books edited by John W. Doberstein and entitled *Lutheran Prayer Book* (Philadelphia: Fortress Press, 1960). For the minister seeking a guide to the devout and holy life, this will occupy a preeminent place. A list of other contemporary masters of the inner life would include A. W. Tozer (1897-1963), whose *The Knowledge of the Holy* (New York: Harper and Row, 1975) interprets the deep things of the spirit. Tozer's reflections stretch the mind to kindle the heart.

Robert E. Speer (1867-1947), Presbyterian missionary-statesman, has given us *Five Minutes a Day* (Philadelphia: Westminster Press, 1977), a compact coverage of the days of the year. By sharing Scripture, hymns, poetry, prayers, and choice findings in literature, this volume assists the moods of the soul in devotion.

John Baillie (1886-1960), a theologian and philosopher who kept a prayer bench in his study, has left a self-revealing testament of truth for us in *Invitation to Pilgrimage* (Grand Rapids: Baker Book House, 1976). His *Diary of Readings* (New York: Scribner's, 1955) is a thesaurus of spiritual insight. His *Diary of Private Prayer* (New York: Scribner's, 1949) has become a tested and tried classic to help us meet our contemporary needs.

How is it possible to advance in the Christian life? Part of the answer is evident in John the Baptist's witness to his Lord and Master. He said, "He must increase, but I must decrease" (John 3:30). John was a burning and a shining light, great in the sight of the Lord, the last of the prophets, cousin of Jesus, forerunner of the Messiah, the friend of the Bridegroom, a man sent from God. His ministry was honored by God; crowds flocked to hear him while he spoke in passionate judgment. Later, when our Lord began to draw people, John the Baptist found himself in prison and near death. A small man would have been jealous of Jesus. John, however, was not hurt or humiliated, but humble in spirit. He rejoiced in what Jesus was doing. He was not a rival but a friend.

Church history offers us examples of sterility and barrenness resulting from the fact that Christ was not uplifted and the church did not decrease. In A.D. 325 Constantine embraced

Christianity and the church increased in pomp and pride. The Christian life became easy because of the encouragement of the state. Ecclesiastical pride increased. The clergy dominated the laity and prepared the way for the Dark Ages. Only in the Reformation did Christ again increase and churchmen decrease. Martin Luther said, "Martin Luther is dead; Christ lives here." John Wesley broke with convention and diminished his own reputation in order to preach the evangel in the open air: "I made myself more vile." Recall that Paul said, "Not I, but Christ." When John on the isle of Patmos saw a vision of Christ, he "fell at his feet as dead." Doubting but confessing Thomas said, "My Lord and my God!" Recall also that the New Testament speaks of losing life to find it, denying self to enrich it, pressing toward the mark for the prize of the upward calling of God in Christ Jesus.

Does our advance then depend upon our humility? Yes. Progress is by decrease; gain is by loss. A subtle danger in the minister's life is self-sufficiency—to be self-centered, self-seeking, self-opinionated. We may indicate this by talking too much or seeking in subtle ways to be heard and have the last word! The deadliness of Pharisaism lurks in our blind spot of egotism, conceit, and lack of poverty of spirit. With a clenched fist we speak of the love of God as though we were in a boxing ring. Our telling of correct doctrine is without love. When William Booth was asked the secret of his life, he replied: "If there is any, it is that Christ has had all that there is of me to have."

To reckon ourselves dead to sin and to mortify the deeds of the body (Romans 6) is no easy procedure. To regard ourselves of lesser account is difficult. Note how the composer Gounod compared himself with Mozart:

> When I was twenty, it was all Gounod,
> When I was forty, it was some of Gounod and some of Mozart,
> Now I am turned sixty, it is all Mozart,
> Gounod does not count.

Similar expression is found in the hymn of Theodore Monod:

> All of self, and none of Thee!
> Some of self, and some of Thee!
> Less of self, and more of Thee!
> None of self, and all of Thee!

A mountain climber recalled his reaction on gazing at the Alpine peaks: "I stood there, getting smaller and smaller, and happier and happier, as I realized my own place in that great world of beauty and wonder." Thus the cry of the poet,

O Jesus Christ, grow Thou in me,
In all things else recede.

As the patron is greater than the protégé, and the head than the hand, so Christ is greater than the Christian, and we advance only as He increases and we decrease.

There are different schools of thought as to the meaning of terms such as holiness of life, sanctification of spirit, and sinless perfection. The New Testament speaks of sainthood. There is need in our day for a balanced interpretation which avoids lopsided views which divide God's people, for in deed and in truth the whole church is *one* under the Head of the body. Doctrine and deed, teaching and experience, are wedded when the unity of the Spirit as described in Ephesians 4:1-16 is caught. There is a "speaking the truth in love" (v. 15).

It is in this connection that we mention Keswick. In 1875 in the Lake District of northwest England, the poets' corner, Anglican pastors came together to seek a deeper experience of God and power to overcome temptation and sin. For a hundred years a convention has been held in the little town of Keswick. Those who have taught at this convention have not only testified to their own experience of the Holy Spirit, but have dealt with sin in the believer, God's remedy for sin, consecration, and the Spirit-filled life. Bible readings have been the foundation. Life, and life abounding, has been stressed for the deepening of the spiritual experience. Sainthood and holiness have been taken seriously. The convention stresses that the pious are to be practical, the godly are to be gracious, and the separated are to be sent into society and into all walks of life. As W. Graham Scroggie summed it up in his interpretation of the distinctive message of the movement: "Conference has a subject, but a convention has an object." As applied to Keswick, that is not a mere epigram, but a profound truth. The object is the life more abundant and out of that quality of character comes a witness.

There is another emphasis in Methodist circles and also in pietistic groups who revere the name of the Wesleys. John Wesley spoke of his experience at Aldersgate on May 24, 1738, when "he felt his heart strangely warmed." Some biographers see this as his conversion hour, yet others, relying in part on the testimony of his mother, think that he was a true Christian believer before. More recent studies see in this experience of Wesley a rebirth of *assurance* of his salvation. Beyond that they see in the Aldersgate experience his Spirit-filled commission to proclaim not only the message of salvation, but also the gospel for the saint as well as for the sinner. Out of that decisive hour came the Evangelical Revival of the eighteenth century, which was destined to shake the modern world and set in motion forces to transform social, political, industrial, and moral problems.

Others also testify to a personal experience of the divine Spirit subsequent to the transforming grace of God in Christ. If we regard this as an implication that all Christians must have a similar experience, then we would do well to read again about the varieties of Christian experience. God does not have an assembly-line production for saints! There are some who have told of the Spirit's power and grace since childhood and have never had any subsequent crisis experience. We must not think in terms of a standard pattern. Rather let all recognize that when we are in Christ we are then in unity with each other. At the circumference there are various types of experience, but the center is Christ.

We should bring our various experiences under the searchlight of truth and ever reexamine in the light of divine revelation what we claim to be valid. The New Testament does not urge union of all Christians into one monolithic structure. We are shown the oneness of all who believe and we are asked to "keep the unity of the Spirit in the bond of peace" (Eph. 4:3). All who are truly Christ's have been placed into the one body, the church: "For as the body is one, and hath many members, and all the members of that one body, being many, are one body: so also is Christ. For by one Spirit are we all baptized into one body, whether we be Jews or Gentiles, whether we be bond or free; and have been all made to drink into one Spirit. For the body is not one member but many" (I Cor. 12:12-14).

In the cultivation of the devotional life, the minister has a unique opportunity to spend time with the masters of the interior life. With meditation on the pages of the Bible will come an awareness of the majesty of God and the sinfulness of the heart. Then will come knowledge of how to rise to worship of God through confession and renewal. The minister will learn to pray from the Scriptures. Then he can turn to others who have left their imprint for us to follow. Admonitions to pray and to rise to the throne of God are before us in life and literature. Teaching about prayer and the prayer of those who have taught are everywhere. We can take these prayers and use them for ourselves and then proceed to voice other inner cries unspoken before.

In prayer there are moments of extempore expressions. Private prayer is a solitary hour. "Be still, and know that I am God" (Ps. 46:10). Then we pass from private and personal prayer to that communion with all the saints. Here we can employ that choice and abiding masterpiece, the Book of Common Prayer, used by the Anglican Church universally.

To cultivate the spiritual life, we might well use *The Private Devotions of Lancelot Andrewes* (Magnolia, MA: Peter Smith, n.d.). His "An Act of Praise" can profit and strengthen ministers who engage in prayer with thanksgiving:

> O Lord, my Lord, I bless Thee
> > For my being,
> > My life,
> > My endowment with reason;
> For my nourishment,
> > My preservation,
> > My guidance;
> For my education,
> > My civil government,
> > My religion;
> For the gifts of grace,
> > Of nature,
> > Of the world;
> For my redemption,
> > My regeneration,
> > My instruction in the truth;
> For the voice of Thy calling,
> > Repeated often,
> > Again and again;

For Thy patience,
    Thy long-suffering,
    Thy very long forbearance,
    Many a time and oft,
    And many a year, till now;
For all the benefits I have received,
For all my undertakings which have prospered;
For all the little good I may have done;
For the enjoyment of present good;
For Thy promise and my hope
    Of enjoying good to come:
For my kind and honest parents,
    My gentle teachers,
    My benefactors, never to be forgotten;
    My brethren, of one mind with me,
    My congregation, who listen to me;
    My relations, who are my friends,
    My faithful domestics;
For all who by their writings,
    By their sermons,
    By their discourses,
    By their prayers,
    By their examples,
    By their reproofs,
        Have done me good;
For all these, and for all others,
    Known or unknown,
    Open or concealed,
    Remembered or forgotten,
    Asked or unasked,
I praise Thee and will praise,
I bless Thee and will bless,
I thank Thee, and will give thanks.

According to Alexander Whyte, the *Seven Meditations on the Lord's Prayer* of Santa Teresa (1515-1582), the Spanish mystic, stands alone in its originality and suggestiveness. Her *Way of Perfection* has freshness and power. It is likely that when William Law (1686-1761) wrote his *Christian Perfection* (Carol Stream, IL: Creation House, 1975) he was indebted to Teresa. Consider, for example, some of her comments "On Learning and Intellect":

I always had a great respect and affection for intellectual and learned men. It is my experience that all who intend to be true Christians will do well to treat with men of mind and books about their souls. The more learning our preachers and pastors have the better. For if they have not much experience themselves, yet they know the Scriptures and the recorded experiences of the saints better than we do. The devil is exceedingly afraid of learning, especially where it is accompanied with humility and virtue. I bless God that there are some men in the world who take such great pains to attain to that knowledge which we need but do not possess. And it delights me to see men taking the immense trouble they do take to bring me so much profit, and that without any trouble to me. I have only to sit still and hear them. I have only to come and ask them a question. Let us pray for our teachers, for what would we do without them? I beseech the Lord to bless our teachers, that they may be more and more a blessing to us.

When I spoke of humility, it must not be understood as if I spoke against aspiring after the highest things that mind and heart and life can attain to. For though I have no ability for the wisdom and the knowledge of God myself, and am so miserable that God did me a great favour in teaching me the very lowliest truths: yet, in my judgment, learning and knowledge are very great possessions, and a great assistance in *the life of prayer*, if only they are always accompanied with humility. I have of late seen some very learned men become in addition very spiritual and prayerful men. And that makes me pray that all our men of mind and learning may soon become spiritual men and men of much prayer. . . .

For the most part they that are defective in mind ever think that they understand things better than their teachers. And ignorance and self-deceit is a disease that is incurable; and besides, it usually carries great malice along with it. Many speak much and understand little. Others, again, speak little and not very elegantly, and yet they have a sound understanding. There is such a thing as a holy simplicity that knows little of anything but of how to treat with God. At the same time commend me to holy people of good heads. From silly devotees, may God deliver us!. . .

Even for prayer, let those who have to teach and preach take full advantage of their learning, that they may help poor peo-

ple of little learning, of whom I am one. Ministering with all
learning and all intellectual ability to souls is a great thing,
when it is done unto God. . . . I love to converse with men of
mind as well as of heart. At the same time, my difficulties but
increase my devotion, and the greater my difficulty the greater
the increase of my devotion. Praise His name.

Or consider some of her comments "On Prayer":

The Price of Prayer. O Thou Lord of my soul, and my Eternal
Good, why is it that when a soul resolves to follow Thee, and
to do her best to forsake all for Thee, why is it that Thou dost
not instantly perfect Thy love and Thy peace within that soul?
But I have spoken unadvisedly and foolishly, for it is we who
are at fault in prayer, and never Thee. We are so long and so
slow in giving up our hearts to Thee. And then Thou wilt not
permit our enjoyment of Thee without our paying well for so
precious a possession. There is nothing in all the world wherewith to buy the shedding abroad of Thy love in our heart, but
our heart's love. If, however, we did what we could, not clinging with our hearts to anything whatsoever in this world, but
having our treasure and our conversation in heaven, then this
blessedness would soon be ours, as well Thy saints testify. God
never withholds Himself from him who pays this price and
who perseveres in seeking Him. He will, little by little, and
now and then, strengthen and restore that soul, till at last it is
victorious. If he who enters on this road only does violence
enough to himself, with the help of God, he will not only go to
heaven himself, but he will not go alone: he will take others
with him. God will give him, as to a good leader, those who
will go after him. Only let not any man of prayer ever expect
to enjoy his whole reward here. He must remain a man of faith
and prayer to the end. Let him resolve, then, that whatever his
aridity and sense of indevotion may be, he will never let
himself sink utterly under his cross. And the day will come
when he will receive all his petitions in one great answer, and
all his wages in one great reward. For he serves a good Master,
who stands over him, watching him. And let him never give
over because of evil thoughts, even if they are sprung upon
him in the middle of his prayer. But all these toils of soul have
their sure reward.

W. Graham Scroggie (1877-1958) gave to the church a legacy
of prayer discipleship in his book *Method in Prayer*. He surprised many devout people by calling for the discipline of

planned prayer. This would seem to be contrary to the *spirit* of prayer. The majority regard prayer as being led by the Holy Spirit and waiting for a moment of inspiration or prompting. However, Scroggie taught otherwise. He did not deny or discourage the extemporaneous prayer, but he counseled the wise discipline of regular praying *according to a pattern*. There is biblical warrant for this.

Jeremy Taylor (1613-1667) penned a summary portrait of men whose hearts are devoted to God:

> There is a sort of God's dear servants who walk in perfectness; who perfect holiness in the fear of God; and they have a degree of charity and divine knowledge more than we can discourse of, and more certain than the demonstrations of geometry. . . . But I shall say no more of this at this time, . . . and they who never touched it with their fingers may, secretly perhaps, laugh at it in their hearts and be never the wiser.

> All that I shall now say of it is, that a good man is united unto God. As a flame touches a flame and combines into splendour and glory, so is the spirit of a man united unto Christ by the spirit of God. These are the friends of God, and they best know God's mind; and they only that are so know how much such men do know.

Isaac Penington was a member of the Friends or Quakers, who have been quaintly described as "the Quiet in the Land." It was because he possessed life that his soul panted for "life more abundant." The goodness of God which leads man to repentance can in like manner lead him to present his body a living sacrifice.

In contemporary life there are not wanting those who have the same desire and earnest longing for more than the ordinary Christian life. As they read the Scriptures they find words of exhortation and goals worthy of achievement as examples in the lives of God's servants are noted. Moreover, across the centuries a voluminous literature has been compiled by the church universal, testifying to a deeper and richer life in the spirit of the Christ of God. All branches of the church have their "saints" or those whose lives and characters have stood the test of temptation and trial.

Prayer is a spiritual sacrifice, and through it the instincts that were expressed in the ancient sacrificial system find utterance. Like sacrifice, therefore, prayer in corporate worship is a public matter and cannot be the same in language and atmosphere as private devotion.

There are three conditions to effective prayer: (1) a sense of the divine presence; (2) a personal experience of the Eternal; (3) communion with God. Likewise, as the essence of worship, prayer has three functions. (1) Prayer is educative. We learn as we corporately recite the classic prayers of the past, especially the Lord's Prayer. We gain a sense of feeling for our heritage and the beauties of language. (2) Prayer grants experiences available nowhere else. Apart from prayer the mystery and wonder, the directness and immediacy, of God's relation to us are only abstractions. Portions of the Christian life find expression only in an "I-Thou" experience. What we say to God is always deeper than what we say about God. (3) Prayer mediates between the finite and infinite; prayer links the past and the future. Public prayer recalls the heritage of the past, offers up present wills and lives, and anticipates the hope and promise of the future. Communion of the saints and pleas for the coming of the kingdom are part of the province of public prayer as the offering of the church militant.

There are four types of prayers corresponding to man's needs: (1) a cry for either material or spiritual help; (2) contemplation—an emotional experience which may involve mysticism or the aesthetic part of one's personality; (3) an instinct to seek knowledge of God (noetic); (4) spiritual communion—the human will meets the will of God. The marks of prayer include adoration (exaltation of God), confession, petition, supplication, intercession, thanksgiving, and a final blessing.

The life of our Lord was a life of prayer. It is well to recall the crises of our Lord's life and how prayer entered in.

(1) During the silent years of preparation at Nazareth Jesus was under the influence of Mary and Joseph and the teaching of the synagogue school. He must have been instructed in the Torah and undoubtedly memorized many of the prayers of the Old Testament. Personal prayer was a part of His growth. "And Jesus increased in wisdom and stature, and in favour with God and man" (Luke 2:52).

(2) At Christ's baptism the Holy Spirit in the form of a dove descended upon Him (Mark 1:9, 10). The Father expressed His pleasure in His Son, endorsing the thirty years of preparation (Matt. 3:17). All this occurred as Jesus was being baptized and *praying* (Luke 3:21). And being full of the Spirit, Jesus returned from the Jordan (Luke 4:1).

(3) Driven by the Spirit (Mark 1:12), Jesus endured forty days of fasting and testing in the wilderness (Luke 4:2). During the threefold temptation (God testing; Satan tempting), Jesus was sustained by the Word of God and *prayer.*

(4) During the course of His ministry of preaching, teaching, and healing, Jesus often withdrew from the crowds for the purpose of prayer (see, e.g., Luke 5:16; 6:12).

(5) At the time of the transfiguration Jesus had taken Peter, James, and John up into a mountain to pray (Luke 9:28).

(6) After His farewell discourse to the disciples in the upper room, Jesus prayed (John 14-17).

(7) In Gethsemane Jesus uttered prayers of intense agony. "O my Father, if it be possible, let this cup pass from me" (Matt. 26:39).

(8) Jesus prayed while suffering on the cross.

(9) Since His resurrection and ascension Jesus has served as our High Priest, interceding on our behalf before the throne of grace (Heb. 2:14-18; 4:14-16).

Our Lord's teaching concerning prayer is probably most evident in the Sermon on the Mount (Matt. 5-7). This sermon is bathed in prayer; more than that, it contains the model prayer (6:5-14). In this section Christ explains the proper attitude of prayer. It should not be hypocritical. This is not easy, for men love to be seen while they pray. But they have received their full reward. Prayer should be private. Go alone into your closet. Prayer should be cultivated; vain repetitions must be avoided. In this we can learn from the Bible: our prayers should not be mere words, but reflections of the Word. Finally, we must have confidence in God the Father. We must not try to cajole Him to get our way; rather, we should seek out and enter into His plan.

Note the various types of prayer which are contained in the Lord's Prayer:

Adoration . . . . Our Father
                                        Hallowed be thy name
Intercession. . . . . Thy kingdom come
                                        Thy will be done
Petition . . . . Bread for the day
Confession. . . . . Forgive us our debts
Guidance . . . . Lead us not into temptation
                                        Deliver us from evil
Ascription . . . . For thine is the kingdom
Amen . . . . So let it be

Here is my life in the prayer.

Our Lord's teaching on prayer can also be found in some of
His parables (e.g., Luke 18:1-14). "Men ought always to pray,
and not to faint" (v. 1). Life offers an alternative between faint-
ing, collapsing, becoming discouraged, losing spirit due to physical handicaps, illness, or mental problems, and being re-created
in spirit. "For which cause we faint not . . ." (II Cor. 4:16-18).
As the scientist can break the atom for energy, so prayer can
harness divine energy. But we must beware of wrong attitudes.
We must not be more conscious of the thing we desire than of
Him from whom we ask. We must lose all consciousness of self.
We must not make prayer an end in itself. Rather, the end of
prayer should be fellowship and communion with God.

God is not like the unjust judge in the parable of the judge
and the woman (Luke 18:2-8). Note the qualities of prayer that
are emphasized in this parable: the importance of being persistent and the necessity of setting proper priorities.

In the parable of the Pharisee and the tax-collector (Luke
18:9-14), the prayer of the Pharisee is really a soliloquy. He
prays with himself. The word *I* appears five times; God is addressed but once. Emphasis on self is clearly a wrong attitude.
Though it is good to tithe and fast, the Pharisee's motives are
impure. The tax-collector, on the other hand, in humility confesses his need. He is justified by grace and God's benefits follow. It
is evident that God *denies* some prayers, *delays* answers to
others, but ultimately *delivers* His will to those who have the
proper attitude. Think of Abraham, Isaac, Jacob, the psalmist,
Elijah and the other prophets. The application is self-evident: if

we faint, it is because we do not pray; if we are praying, we should not lose heart.

There is also much to be learned from the high-priestly prayer of John 17. The words of this prayer could be uttered only by Christ Himself. He includes special petition for the apostles (vv. 9-19) and intercession for the world (vv. 20, 21).

In this connection the prayers of Paul for the church of God are also to be mentioned. Paramount among them are the prayer for spiritual knowledge (Eph. 1:15-23), the prayer for spiritual strength (Eph. 3:14-21), the prayer for discriminating love (Phil. 1:9-14), and the prayer for fullness of spiritual life (Col. 1:9-11).

Opportunity is given the minister to cultivate prayer as a means of grace. The teaching of and the examples given by our Lord and by the apostle Paul afford a wealth of inspiration to us. A busy pastor can take these prayers and not only pray them for himself, but then pray them for his congregation. In addition he has all the other prayers throughout the Scriptures. These, like the Psalms, reflect the manifold desires and needs of the individual and the congregation.

There is no moment when we are without prayer as a means of grace. The throne of God is just where we are at any hour. Direct access to the High Priest who ever lives to make intercession for us is the strategy of divine unfoldings. Within us the Holy Spirit assists us in our prayers and on high the Son of God prays for us to interpret before God what we cannot express in words. The eternal God thus bends down to our need and we are caught up to His heart of grace.

6

The Beauty of Holiness

"Blessed is the man [whose] delight is in the law of the Lord; and in his law doth he meditate day and night. And he shall be like a tree planted by the rivers of water, that bringeth forth his fruit in his season; his leaf also shall not wither; and whatsoever he doeth shall prosper." (PS. 1:1-3)

"I am the true vine. . . . Every branch that beareth fruit, he purgeth it, that it may bring forth more fruit. . . . I am the vine, ye are the branches: he that abideth in me, and I in him, the same bringeth forth much fruit: for without me ye can do nothing." (JOHN 15:1-5)

THE SERVANT OF GOD discovers that his growth and development in the Christian life do not simply happen. Public worship, prayer, and Bible reading are useful avenues of encouragement by which people of all levels of Christian experience are aided. But he who would be a pastor or engage in other special ministries requiring leadership finds that something more is needed.

The word *culture* brings to mind the act of cultivating the soil. Agriculture and horticulture are words which suggest the farmer cultivating the land and the gardener cultivating a bed of flowers. If these actions are not carried out with regularity and plan, then the weeds bloom, development is arrested, and the harvest of grain or of flowers is limited. What is involved in nature is also true in the spiritual life of the Christian.

Speaking the word *Christian* does not produce one. There is an assumption by some that if we have the word, we have the reality. If we have the word for faith, we have faith. If we have the word for repentance, we have repented. If we know the words for "born again," we have experienced that new birth.

As well might we say that if we have the word for food, we have food. A person could starve to death with his mouth full of words, even if the words described every kind of bread or food.

The body does not derive its strength from the name of things, but from the things themselves. It lives on substance, not names.

Thomas à Kempis in *The Imitation of Christ* said, "Surely great words do not make a man holy and just, but a virtuous life maketh him dear to God. I had rather *feel* compunction than know the definition thereof."

If words are not enough and Christian vocabulary does not guarantee the substance and reality of what is professed, then this matter of *the culture of the Christian life* is significant. That the servant of God lives in a general culture or social environment is obvious. In certain respects we are influenced by and have become part of the result of that culture. H. Richard Niebuhr in *Christ and Culture* (New York: Harper and Row, 1951) has shared his insights into various aspects of this subject. When the Christian faith is related to our civilization, what results? Is Christ *against* culture? Is Christ *above* culture? Is there a Christ *of* culture? Is Christ the *transformer of* culture?

There are professing Christians who talk in terms of abandoning culture because of a coming judgment. There are others who are engulfed in culture and squeezed into its mold, losing their influence upon it. Our Lord enjoined upon His followers to "render unto Caesar the things which are Caesar's; and unto God the things that are God's" (Matt. 22:21), surely an admonition to the disciples to be part of the culture and witness in it to the things of God.

An article of our belief, then, is the conviction that *Christ is the living Lord.* As such He answers all the questions of history and life in a fashion which transcends the wisdom of all His interpreters. Yet, at the same time, we can make use of their partial insights.

We notice that God's leaders across the ages of the advancing church of God were "cultured" people: Moses in Egypt, Daniel in Babylon, Isaiah in Israel, Luke in companionship with Paul within the Roman Empire, Augustine, Luther, Calvin, Pascal, Wesley, Edwards, as well as countless numbers of other dedicated people since, have had the marks of culture in that special sense of knowledge both of society and also of the church. Spiritual affluence and power have characterized these people. Yet God has "chosen the foolish things of the world to

confound the wise; and God hath chosen the weak things of the
world to confound the things which are mighty; and base things
of the world, and things which are despised, hath God chosen,
and things which are not, to bring to nought things that are:
that no flesh should glory in his presence" (I Cor. 1:27-29).
When the glory of the gifts of culture is returned to the Lord,
then God sanctions and uses those who possess them.

Spiritual culture is abetted by all the means of grace common
to God's people in their worship and fellowship. To cultivate
holiness (sanctification) is a priority of the servant of God. To be
able to choose the best books—next to the Bible—is a valuable
asset. It will bring us to the spiritual classics of the ages. Invitation to learning is part of the ongoing life of the preacher and
pastor. The great books instruct us in the subject of life and their
authors are friends who abide.

John Ruskin, in *The Seven Lamps of Architecture*, interprets
the laws of life and studies the principles of building character.
Christ is the *character* of God (Heb. 1:3). Inasmuch as we are involved in shaping the characters of others for good or ill, we
ought to learn from the supreme demonstration of character.

From the description of human psychology in many of the
world's great novels, we gain an appreciation of the effects of
sin. In George Eliot's *Romola* we find in the person of Tito a
tampering with conscience and gradual deterioration of character. Judas comes to mind. Nathaniel Hawthorne's *The Scarlet
Letter* unveils the tragedy of a pastor in New England who experiences retribution in the working of his conscience and the necessity to repent and confess his sin. Victor Hugo's *Les Mis-
erables* depicts the struggle within the soul where good and evil
are in conflict for mastery. One is reminded of the conflict between flesh and spirit described in Romans 6-8.

Shakespeare's tragedies set forth in dramatic form the passions
and turbulence of the inner life of sinful man. Especially noteworthy are *Hamlet*, *Macbeth*, *Lear*, and *Richard III*. William
Hazlitt's *Table Talk* essays (e.g., "Great Little Things," "Knowledge of Character," "On the Fear of Death," and "People of
One Idea") stimulate the open mind questing after truth.

Classics dealing with the spiritual life are legion, and the servant of God will find his own choices to minister to his hour of

dryness and blight. Among them might be Augustine, Pascal, Thomas à Kempis, Bunyan, Andrews, Luther, Newman, the Wesleys, and the hymn writers and poets.

We must not forget the Scriptures with their vivid word pictures. Take, for example, Revelation 3:4, in the letter of the Head of the church to the congregation at Sardis: "[There are] a few names even in Sardis which have not defiled their garments; and *they shall walk with me in white*; for they are worthy."

This is a salutary reminder in these days when the distinction between black and white is toned down, resulting in a gray area of uncertain moral distinctions. Today's ethics would deny absolutes in morals and allow deterioration of standards. The white garments of Sardis speak of sanctification or holiness of life. The sanctified life is separated to Christ and therefore a moral antiseptic in the community.

Paul wrote in somewhat the same vein to the Corinthians (II Cor. 10:12): "For we dare not make ourselves of the number, or compare ourselves with some that commend themselves: but they measuring themselves by themselves, and comparing themselves among themselves, are not wise."

Paul dared not venture to class himself with others—knowing he was the chief of sinners and less than the least of all saints. While others put themselves in a higher class and wrote their own testimonials, Paul knew that only God could give a true estimate of his character and service. No wild claims for Paul! He simply did his duty and let the results speak for themselves.

At the heart of Psalm 90, the prayer of Moses, is the realization of the searching light of the holy nature of God upon his life. Like Moses we are aware of the obvious sins and failures in our life. "Our secret sins [are] in the light of thy countenance" (v. 8). God probes the interior life of His servant. We have our own blind spots and excuses as to why we have allowed aspects of our moral life to go unjudged. Are we better than others? If the life of separation and holiness is to be realized, there is a ruthless surgery required when the blaze of divine purity unmasks us to ourselves. We know the difference between the truth and a lie. How is it that we allow for a half-truth? a fraud that has a semblance of honesty? and filth that may appear clean? The mirror of the Word of God shows us what we are.

John Whale wrote, "There is no sin so subtly dangerous as the self-sufficiency of the morally religious man." The servant of God who would aspire to the beauty of holiness has the task to read widely and deeply, to meditate where God has spoken, and to translate into life and deed the ideals conveyed to him. Holiness is a word which frightens many. However, we should be eager to qualify for sainthood, if that be the goal of Christian living.

We are enjoined to become holy or mature in Christ. "Be ye therefore perfect, even as your Father which is in heaven is perfect" (Matt. 5:48). Paul's goal was "that we may present every man perfect in Christ Jesus" (Col. 1:28). Maturity of faith and strength of character are the hallmark of the saint. From Old Testament days God's people had been chosen and set apart unto God as His treasured possession. The idea was carried forward into the New Testament and given new emphasis.

Significantly, the word *saint* in the singular seems to be absent; the plural *saints* is used throughout. In Romans 1, I Corinthians 1, II Corinthians 1, Ephesians 1, Philippians 1, and Colossians 1, the salutation is addressed to "the *saints* who are *in Christ* at _____." It was Adolf Deissmann who, from his archaeological research in the Middle East, established the formula. The word *saints* is used 62 times and the key phrase "in Christ" is used 164 times. When Paul writes of the saints *in Christ*, he is writing out of his own transforming experience with the risen and eternal living Lord of glory.

To be holy, then, is to be separated to God. Paul writes that "by one Spirit are we all baptized into one body . . . and have been all made to drink into one Spirit. For the body is not one member, but many" (I Cor. 12:13, 14). Members of the body of Christ, the church, are described as saints *(hagioi)*. They are so by virtue of the agency of the Holy Spirit and not human action. This baptism of or by the Holy Spirit is the one guarantee that they belong to Christ, whatever gifts He may have bestowed on them for ministries within the body. As Hebrews 10:10-15 puts it: "By the which will we are sanctified through the offering of the body of Jesus Christ once for all. . . . For by one offering he hath *perfected for ever them that are sanctified.* . . . Whereof the Holy Spirit bears witness to us."

In this paradoxical language the author of Hebrews gives us the heart of holiness. Because we are already sanctified, we go on to perfection. The tenses indicate that those who are in the process of being sanctified by that one offering of the great High Priest, even our Lord, are thereby now being perfected or brought to complete maturity through the agency of the Holy Spirit. This is the ultimate goal or end *(telos)* of Christ's sacrifice.

We learn then that holiness is viewed as a *standing* before God and that our present experience is a *state* which, after being initially introduced by grace, continues to deepen and mature in conformity to that standing. This view allows for a moment of crisis and a continuing development up to the final goal. The New Testament has a number of words to describe the ministry of the Holy Spirit: He baptizes, seals, gives the earnest, gives birth from above, fills, anoints, advocates, empowers to witness, adopts, and so on. The justified sinner is given status "in Christ" immediately and joins that church of which Paul said, "Ye are all one in Christ Jesus" (Gal. 3:28). That unity transcends any organizational union devised by men, for it is a unity already given and realized by all those who are "in Christ." Some Christians have a cataclysmic experience, while others, like Timothy, have known from childhood the truth of salvation. Still others, like Lydia, find that their hearts open quietly to the message of divine truth.

Variations of teaching found in Luther, Calvin, and the Wesleys should be interpreted as a result of their differing experiences. These experiences should be viewed in the light of divine revelation in Scripture. Words and vocabulary must never be allowed to separate those who are "in Christ." We are members one of another.

This chapter began with a description of the righteous and godly man (Ps. 1:1-3). The godly man—the man who pursues and observes the way of holiness—is blessed indeed. From a negative standpoint, he does not walk in the counsel of the ungodly; he does not stand in the way of sinners; and he does not sit in the seat of the scornful (v. 1). From a positive standpoint, he delights in the law of the Lord; and in His law he meditates day and night (v. 2). As a result, he is like a tree planted by the rivers of water, that brings forth his fruit in his season; his leaf also shall not wither; and whatsoever he does shall prosper (v. 3).

Life-giving streams are most important to the land of Israel with its sizable desert areas. Drought is commonplace. From Genesis to Revelation the imagery of life-giving water is abundant. Ezekiel 47:9 notes: "Every thing shall live whither the river cometh." The symbolism is self-evident: as deserts can be watered and made fruitful, so lives can be revived by the water of the Spirit to counteract the barrenness and aridity of much that passes for religious profession.

The beauty of holiness is linked with leadership rooted in fertile soil. That soil must be cleared of thistles, free from rocks, and broken up in order to receive the seed. The divine seed must get down beneath the surface, and the soil must be cultivated until harvest (Matt. 13).

At this point much that begins with hope and promise is stunted and lost to the Harvester. Only if the soil is cultivated can we grow and advance in spiritual knowledge. The ongoing of the spiritual life, the life of holiness, is the supreme aim of the Christian. To those who are pursuing their studies will come the insidious temptation to major in intellectual pursuits at the expense of the spiritual. Others, so-called pietists, would stress the devotional life and downgrade the intellectual. However, these are not in opposition, but are complementary. We are to love the Lord our God with all our heart, soul, strength, and *mind*. Note the summary of our Lord's development from childhood to manhood in Luke 2:52: "Jesus increased in wisdom and stature and in favour with God and man." The fourfold growth to maturity did not omit wisdom and the growing mind.

How, then, is holiness to be encouraged? Certainly the Bible should be preeminent in our reading and study, especially in what is called meditation. In this we do not aim to acquire knowledge of the text (that we have done previously in the educational process), but to apply the Scriptures to ourselves as persons. Though ever aware of the historical background of the books, we find in the substance and content a reflection of ourselves and by meditation relate the message to ourselves. We make it our own with the help of the Holy Spirit.

George Fox, guiding spirit behind the Quaker movement, said: "To such, and such only, as had attained the same Spirit which they were in who wrote the Scriptures, could the Scriptures be intelligible." Knowledge and obedience are one in the experience of meditation. It needs no elaboration to plead that Christian leaders should know the Bible better than any other book. Familiarity with the characters in the Bible will bring to light the secrets of the men and women whom God used as leaders. Their weaknesses will offer as much enlightenment as will their strengths. It will be apparent that within the sovereignty of God's will special gifts are granted to individuals for crises in history. Study of the leadership of those persons will make clear the qualities and principles which gave them spiritual influence.

To assist our meditation and study for personal growth, we have the examples of hundreds of lives over the centuries. A good rule to follow is to learn from them, but to avoid imitation. That is, we should learn what is relevant for us, but not attempt to become that person whom God fashioned exactly for some special task. Remember that our lives are like clay in the hands of the Potter who shapes and reshapes us on the wheel.

Moreover, we will develop through our prayer life a spirit yielded and obedient. Are we willing to be made willing? God has a definite plan for us; the fulfillment of that design depends on our willing obedience. Prayer consciously reaches up to the throne of God, yearning only to know and to do the will of God—nothing less, nothing more, nothing else. The measure of our Christian influence in service is the measure of our growth in holiness of life. The integrity of our character determines the service of our life. Industry is no substitute for integrity. Let integrity and industry intertwine and God will have a servant ready to use. It is vital to realize that education is not giving information through lectures or books. In the words of John Ruskin: "You do not educate a man by telling him what he knew not, but by making him what he was not, and what he will remain for ever." In the education of "a man in Christ," holiness is the standard because we have seen it displayed in the life of our Lord.

Reflecting upon our day and the need for dynamic spiritual leadership, we must encourage young people to obtain the best intellectual education possible. Alongside of this should be the cultivation of the inner life, that interior spirit wherein the mind and heart blend in a unity of purpose and aim. If the glory of God is the goal of endeavor, then the unity of mind and heart should not experience disruption or conflict of interest. The one complements the other.

The Christian believer lives not only for the present but for the future. He looks back in faith, upwards in love, yet forward in hope. In the past many in the body of Christ have led the way in witness and evangelism throughout the world. We are the heirs of that legacy in discipleship and also Christian nurture. We are indebted to those pioneers who have written about their experience in Christ and have shared the wealth of their learning concerning the devout life at all levels of faith and obedience. Our confidence is in the living God who has chosen us in Christ to be set apart unto Him and then within the universal church to be given opportunities of witness and ministry. Again, the stress here is upon the *character* of the one who finds an open door of service. The separated life, holy living and holy dying, sensitivity to the Spirit of God, will give us strength and prompt us to serve in humility.

The cultivation of the spiritual life involves ever drawing from the past, ever experiencing divine grace in the present, and ever knowing that the future is bright in the vision of the regnant Christ who is the Head of the church. He has destined us to be conformed to His image and likeness (Eph. 1:4, 5); at the second advent we shall not only see Him as He is, but we shall be made like to Him (I John 3:2). Then Ephesians 3:18, 19 will be fulfilled. We will "be able to comprehend *with all the saints* what is the breadth, and length, and depth, and height; And to know the love of Christ, which passeth knowledge, that [we] might be filled with all the fulness of God."

The beauty of holiness becomes very real to us as we reflect upon the truth purveyed in Scripture and confirmed in Christian literature. The saints have been caricatured, derided, and often persecuted because of their faith and (usually) purity of life. Such goodness of character is not for personal reward but solely for the sake of pleasing God. Some imagine that to be good or holy means a dull life; and that might be the case if by "holy" we mean a respectable way of life, a conventional code, and lack of touch with the struggles of life. In truth, contrary to popular opinion, wickedness is by nature dull. Not only is it easy to drift into wickedness, but it soon becomes monotonous. Psalm 1:4-6 depicts the way of the ungodly. Only saints in holiness can enjoy humor and fun in its pure form, which proves a puzzle to those who are not of the initiated. The end of holiness is not to be an average Christian, but rather to seek higher levels of life. Not that we can rise to perfection in our own strength, but that we should constantly seek to be dead unto sin and alive unto God as sons of light and not darkness.

The secret is that Christ should be the goal and center of all life. "By him all things consist" (Col. 1:17). Paul is here wrestling with the sublimest realities of our experience. He saw the vastness of the universe and man on the stage of history. He knew that man without redemption would slide into the abyss of wickedness and pollute his world. The Bible specifes that man must relate to several dimensions of experience—above, without, and within himself. But in self-will man ignores some of these levels. So Paul, the saint of God, relates himself to the mystery of the infinite above, to the outward world to explore its secret, and to the inward personal self to discern its God-given meaning and purpose. Paul regards Christ as the interpretive center of the vast universe—material, mental, and moral. The saints of God live alongside others in the same material order, but also witness to them concerning its spiritual cosmic purpose and their place under the divine plan. There is a Christian view of God and the world. There is a Christian interpretation of the universe, of personality, and of everything in history. Believing in the sovereignty of almighty God, the saints are not pessimists; they are optimists, the true realists.

That the Christian view is a practical creed can be demonstrated. John Wesley in the eighteenth century lived a long and arduous life and reached the ripe age of eighty-eight years. From his early years to maturity he lived simply and practically. He set the Lord always before him and served with a single view of pleasing God. Control of his thoughts disciplined his habits. The writings of Thomas à Kempis, Jeremy Taylor, and William Law brought a sense of order to his life; the *Book of Health and Long*

Life by John Cheyne served as a guide to his bodily needs.

John Wesley cultivated his devotional life in prayer, meditation, fasting, grace at meals, and worship. An early riser, he set himself a pattern of routine study and conducted services in jails, schools, workhouses, as well as more conventional religious settings. He found strength in temperate eating; a small, wiry man, he weighed less than 125 pounds at the age of eighty. He preached twice a day at that age. A man of vision and venture for the kingdom of God, he traveled across England during sixty years of ministry (3,000-4,500 miles a year) and preached 40,000 sermons in his lifetime. His prodigious writing included journals and tracts. He also issued a selection of books for his itinerant preachers. There was no time wasted by John Wesley. Many of his personal qualities reflected holiness of life: physical and mental health; devotion in ministry; avoidance of luxury, ostentation, and sensuality; outstanding dedication to the service of the gospel of Christ. Holiness depends in great measure on practical, down-to-earth living.

Admittedly there are failures in the ministry, but the general record of achievement is high. Let the critics vent their harsh judgment and spew out their invective as they will; the record of those who have stood across the years for truth and righteousness and godliness is unimpeachable. Thomas Fuller (1608-1661) highly esteemed the members of the clergy (at least of the Episcopal Church of England), noting that they "for their living, preaching and writing, have been the main champions of truth against error, of learning against ignorance, of piety against profaneness, of religion against superstition, of unity and order against faction and confusion."

Certainly the apostle Paul wrote with confidence in commending those who, like himself, were engaged in that highest of all vocations, the ministry of the good news concerning Jesus Christ, the Lord of glory and of all good life. In II Corinthians 4 there are directives concerning such a calling. The role of leaders in the early church can be traced clearly in the writings of Luke and in the letters of the apostle Paul. Our Lord's words and acts in the upper room at the celebration of the Passover and the inauguration of the sacrament of communion bring into focus the stress upon the role of the slave in relation to the Master and upon the need for the minister to function as a servant.

The opportunity to be a pastor and undershepherd to a congregation is a minister's highest privilege. To care for and love others in their need is his greatest service. By teaching and preaching, by leading in worship, the minister can draw near to others who look to him for help and strength, for guidance and courage. The pastor—whether he be ordinary or excellent in the pulpit—stands as one to whom others instinctively turn when they need assistance.

In *Shackleton's Boat Journey* (New York: W. W. Norton, 1977), which deals with Antarctic exploration, F. A. Worsley testifies to the strength of one absolutely committed to his task. "For scientific discovery, give me Scott; for speed and efficiency of travel, give me Amundsen; but when disaster strikes and all hope is gone, get down on your knees and pray for Shackleton." In 1907 Ernest Shackleton announced his intention of mounting an expedition to the South Pole. He did not have government backing, and the raising of finances proved an almost insuperable obstacle. He was forced to economize in every direction and make do with a tiny vessel—the 200-ton *Nimrod*. But despite the lack of support and finance, Shackleton's reputation was enough to gather a number of quality men around him.

Judged by the history of Antarctic explorations—if success is measured by the standard of whether a set goal has been achieved—Shackleton would probably be regarded as unsuccessful on all his major journeys! But it was as a leader, as a man who could overcome appalling obstacles, that Shackleton really excelled. "Not for him an easy task and a quick success—he was at his best when the going was toughest."

Here in a single sentence is distilled the quality of commitment and dedication which is called for by the Lord and Master who rallies round Him those of us who would be His slaves and servants in expeditions into the enemy's territory to raise the standard of the cross. Not for us a lowered standard and never a lost endeavor! We are not judged by the world's measure of success. Like Shackleton, our seeming failures may be filled with glory, for we have been tested by the fire as to the character we displayed throughout the long haul of our nonglamorous ministry and service. "Each man's work will become manifest; for the

Day will disclose it, because it will be revealed with fire, and the
fire will test what sort of work each one has done" (I Cor. 3:13,
RSV).

Paul's wise counsel comes to grip with a reality not always
touched upon when the ministry is discussed. What are the
characteristics of a true and tried minister? Do we estimate his
service by traditional standards of success? That is the way of
Mr. Worldly Wiseman. The story of Ernest Shackleton and his
failure to reach his goals points up the fact that failure can be
greater than success. The ordinary ministries of the vast majority
of those who serve God do not make headlines in the newspapers; such lives at the end receive but scant notice by the public. Only those close to the individual in church or family know
the service rendered. Above the ordinary, however, are the un-
swerving devotion and the patient endurance which such lives
have given to the community of the world church.

The pastoral leader is described in II Corinthians 4. At the
heart of this description lies the truth that "we have this treasure
[i.e., the light of life and the proclamation of Jesus Christ as
Lord; cf. vv. 4, 5] in earthen vessels" (v. 7). The clay of a man's
earthly nature is the container for the valuable riches of the gospel. At the beginning Paul says that "having this ministry by the
mercy of God, we do not lose heart" (v. 1, RSV). As he proceeds
to describe a minister's life and work, several items are
stressed—renunciation of underhanded ways; refusal to tamper
with the Word of God; commending ourselves to every man's
conscience in the sight of God; preaching not ourselves, but Jesus
Christ as Lord, with ourselves as servants (slaves) for Jesus' sake.

Having affirmed that we have the treasure in earthen vessels
to show that the power belongs to God and not to us, Paul
continues: "We are afflicted in every way, but not crushed;
perplexed, but not driven to despair; persecuted, but not forsaken; struck down, but not destroyed; always carrying in the
body the death of Jesus, so that the life of Jesus may also be
manifested in our bodies." After more in the same vein, verse 16
repeats the message of verse 1 as a refrain: "So we do not lose
heart." Then comes the climax: "Though our outer nature is
wasting away, our inner nature is being renewed every day. For
this slight momentary affliction is preparing for us an eternal

weight of glory beyond all comparison, because we look not to the things that are seen but to the things that are unseen; for the things that are seen are transient, but the things that are unseen are eternal" (RSV). This is the secret of that inner strength which enables the servant of God to accept opportunities to serve without fear or favor, without reference to reward or applause.

The ideal of excellence in service is well summed up in a hymn of the Welsh preacher John Elias (1774-1841):

> Jesus, I live to Thee,
> The Loveliest and Best;
> My life in Thee, Thy life in me,
> In Thy blest love I rest.
>
> Jesus, I die to Thee,
> Whenever death shall come;
> To die in Thee is life to me
> In my eternal home.
>
> Whether to live or die,
> I know not which is best;
> To live in Thee is bliss to me,
> To die is endless rest.
>
> Living or dying, Lord,
> I ask but to be Thine;
> My life in Thee, Thy life in me,
> Makes heaven forever mine!

We recognize beauty instinctively. It is unnecessary to analyze the component parts in architecture, art, music, or nature. We simply enjoy the beauty. J. F. Millet's picture *The Angelus*, with the workers in the field pausing to bow their heads and pray, captures a moment of beauty in which light bathes the scene in shadow. Likewise, the minister of God in his manifold service captures moments of similar spiritual exaltation. There is an extra sense of the divine presence of the Spirit of God bathing the human situation with something beyond time.

A hymn of J. S. B. Monsell (1811-1875) well sums up the truth of this chapter:

> Worship the Lord in the beauty of holiness;
> Bow down before Him, His glory proclaim;
> Gold of obedience and incense of lowliness
> Bring, and adore Him; the Lord is His Name!

Low at His feet lay thy burden of carefulness;
  High on His heart He will bear it for thee,
Comfort thy sorrows, and answer thy prayerfulness,
  Guiding thy steps as may best for thee be.

Fear not to enter His courts, in the slenderness
  Of the poor wealth thou canst reckon as thine;
Truth in its beauty and love in its tenderness,
  These are the offerings to lay on His shrine.

These, though we bring them in trembling and fearfulness,
  He will accept for the Name that is dear,
Mornings of joy give for evenings of tearfulness,
  Trust for our trembling, and hope for our fear.

Holiness is beautiful. Strength and beauty combine in the servant of God to give him great influence of character. Our Lord in the days of His flesh was full of grace and truth; He is our standard and inspiration for ministry.

7

The Standard of Excellence

"One thing have I desired of the Lord, that will I seek after; that I may dwell in the house of the Lord all the days of my life, to behold the beauty of the Lord, and to enquire in his temple." (PS. 27:4)

"Let thy work appear unto thy servants, and thy glory unto their children. And let the beauty of the Lord our God be upon us: and establish thou the work of our hands upon us; yea, the work of our hands establish thou it." (PS. 90:16, 17)

AMID THE DAILY ROUTINE of the minister, including preparation for the return of the Sunday services, Bible classes, and other meetings at which he must preach or teach, it is possible to lose the vision of the highest ideals and beauty. Beauty may be a word that is infrequent in his vocabulary when the daily and weekly stint of work is pursued. Nevertheless, the passages from the Psalms which head this chapter have something to say to us.

Plotinus, who was not so inspired as the writers of the Bible, in his tractate *Of Beauty*, has cited a similar truth which has reference to philosophy, aesthetics, and theology:

Let us, then, go back to the source, and indicate at once the Principle that bestows beauty on material things. Undoubtedly this Principle exists; it is something that is perceived at the first glance, something which the soul names as from an ancient knowledge and, recognizing, welcomes it, enters into union with it. But let the soul fall in with the Ugly and at once it shrinks within itself, denies the thing, turns away from it, not accordant, resenting it. Our interpretation is that the soul—by the very truth of its nature, by its affiliation to the noblest Existents in the hierarchy of Being—when it sees anything of that kin, or any trace of that kinship, thrills with an immediate delight, takes its own to itself, and thus stirs anew to the sense of its nature and of all its affinity. But is there any such like-

> ness between the loveliness of this world and the splendors in
> the Supreme? Such a likeness in the particulars would make
> the two orders alike: but what is there in common between
> beauty here and beauty there? We hold that all the loveliness
> of this world comes by communion in Ideal-Form.

Thus Plotinus (205-270), philosopher and thinker, engaged in the
quest for mystical union with God through the exercise of pure
intelligence. The Good to him was in essence that which was
beautiful.

The minister in his preparation and in his service is confronted
with the temptation to choose the lesser instead of the higher, the
ugly instead of the beautiful. Sin is ugly and distorted; grace is
beautiful and luminous. The former demeans life and the latter
brings harmony. When Arturo Toscanini (1867-1957), one of the
great virtuoso conductors of the first half of the twentieth century, brought grace to the interpretation of symphony and
opera, lovers of music were caught up in beauty. Suffering from
poor eyesight, he conducted from memory. Yet devotion and
passionate involvement characterized his interpretive con-
ducting.

The maestro was once approached in his latter years by a colleague who asked him for advice in attaining a standard of
excellence as a musician. Normally such a naive question would
have been brushed impatiently aside; but the old man was silent
for a moment, then replied: "I shall tell you a secret. All my life
I have been studying scores. You must not conduct a piece of
music until the notes have marched off the paper and come alive
in your head and heart." To Toscanini this meant the moment
when form and symmetry banished distortion, when beauty banished ugliness. The minister has similar opportunities to plan
and prepare for service. There are years spent in cultural studies
and theology. Eventually he hears the music of the spheres as he,
by saturating himself with the Scriptures, cultivates devotion,
discipline, and an appreciation of the Lord of glory, even Jesus
Christ Himself. If he is to make plain and clear the Christian
message, a minister must not undervalue the hours of preparation at the heart of the mystery.

> My God, how wonderful Thou art,
> Thy majesty how bright!

How beautiful Thy mercy-seat,
In depths of burning light!

How dread are Thine eternal years,
O everlasting Lord,
By prostrate spirits day and night
Incessantly adored!

How *beautiful*, how *beautiful*
The sight of Thee must be,
Thine endless wisdom, boundless power,
An awful purity!

O how I fear Thee, living God,
With deepest, tenderest fears,
And worship Thee with trembling hope
And penitential tears!

Yet I may Love Thee, too, O Lord,
Almighty as Thou art,
For Thou hast stooped to ask of me
The love of my poor heart.

No earthly father loves like Thee;
No mother, e'er so mild,
Bear and forbears as Thou hast done
With me, Thy sinful child.

Father of Jesus, love's reward,
What rapture will it be
Prostrate before Thy throne to lie,
And gaze and gaze on Thee!

(Frederick William Faber, 1814-1863)

In those moments when the mind and heart are transported in the vision of the Eternal lies the secret of the inner vitality which will sustain God's servant in the discharge of his tasks. Some have a special sense of the divine presence which distills a gracious spirit within them. For example, it was reported of Daniel: "An excellent spirit was in him" (Dan. 5:12; 6:3). We might also cite Henry Drummond (1851-1897), who was chosen by Dwight L. Moody as a partner in evangelism, both in Scotland and in America. What was the geniality or charm which radiated from

Drummond as evangelist? How explain the radiance of the sunshine, the perfume of flowers, or the persuasion of music?
Among students in particular he wielded an unusual excellence
of character which filled his messages with light and love. He
believed there was need for transformation, the new birth; but
his contact was not with the outcast, but with men like Nathaniel and Nicodemus. He held up the beauty of Christ and the
supreme glory of the Christian life in fullness and in completeness. Every minister whose aim is to "present every man
perfect [or mature or complete] in Christ" (Col. 1:28) should also
strive to reach this goal.

Think of all the moments of beauty which have enveloped the
minister's life and work! Those joyful hours when a wedding is
celebrated in church or chapel for two young people whose love
is crowned by the love of Christ, whose they are and whom they
serve. I can think of many marriages in which mutual devotion
has continued to increase. Or think of the music of the organ
pealing forth magnificent notes and harmony from some of the
masters of composition. Nothing cheap or tawdry or saccharine
is fitting. Or think of a soprano soloist singing Mozart's "Al-
leluia," with its majestic repetitions. Or a tenor voice ringing
out the Mendelssohn aria from the oratorio *Elijah:* "If with all
your hearts ye truly seek me, ye shall ever surely find me: thus
saith our God." What an hour for the congregation!

The majestic hymns of the universal church throughout the
ages have also offered moments of beauty and grace at the hours
of worship, touching and moving the minds and hearts of the
worshipers, but especially the minister who must lead in worship. Only as he himself is engaged in the act of worship, can he
effectively lead his people. The hours of beauty have been many
throughout the years. Celebration of the Lord's Supper transcends the ordinary. How moved we have been at the climax of
"The Twenty-third Psalm" sung to the tune "Crimond": "And in
God's house forevermore, My dwelling-place shall be!"

The apostle Paul has reminded us that all things are ours.
"Whether Paul, or Apollos, or Cephas, or the world, or life, or
death, or things present, or things to come; all are yours; And ye
are Christ's; and Christ is God's" (I Cor. 3:21-23). This is warrant sufficient to take the whole universe as our possession in

Christ. Then everything in human life as well as in the creative order belongs to the Christian mind. We therefore should think "Christianly" in our view of God and the world. Nothing needs to be common or unclean. We need not be afraid of our cosmos, for certainly we can see it marked by the sign of the cross and upheld by the living, ascended Lord of glory. The astronauts have told us that when they entered space to explore the vastness of the universe they saw the earth with its beauty as they had not seen or known it while on the earth. They saw from new dimensions and lived by transcendent laws unknown before. They bowed in awe and wonder as they began to worship the Creator-Redeemer whose universe it is. Against this background the minister can relate the beauty of the universe in all its branches of knowledge and interest. "We are God's workmanship, created in Christ Jesus unto good works" (Eph. 2:10). The Greek word for "workmanship" is *poiema*, or the poetry of God. Here then is a hint of that beauty which God has given in His acts of creation. Now we as His workmen can utilize similar beauty for our work—not the ugly (cf. Plotinus), but the beauty of the Lord our God.

Sydney Walton contributed to the *British Weekly* a column devoted to "The Poetry Hours" he found in London. In the midst of the bustling metropolis with its commerce, finance, politics, and crime, he spoke of the promise of the psalmist that there shall be green in the midst of the city. After walking the hard pavements, one can find an oasis in a library where a few congenial friends gather once a week. The Poetry Society was founded in 1909 to cultivate "a clearer, deeper sense of the best in poetry and of the strength and joy to be drawn from it." There, among others, would be found Lord Wavell, an army general who, when facing the onslaught of the enemy in 1941, found strength and poise by reading poetry.

Strength and comfort come in the quiet confidence of our souls, and we look instinctively to the seers and poets who write of loveliness and lovingkindness. As Isaiah 61:3 puts it, "The garments of praise [replaces] the spirit of heaviness." The Bible is replete with poetry which reaches heights surpassing knowledge and calling the minister not to neglect that treasury of the best of the ages ready at hand. To live with such beauty is an

opportunity open to all without difficulty or even extra expense.
How rich are we to have rare beauty at home and in the study,
where we can share with family and friend!

Among the many hymns we could cite in which poetry blends
magnificently with music is the following by Oliver Wendell
Holmes (1809-1894):

> Lord of all being, throned afar,
> Thy glory flames from sun and star;
> Center and soul of every sphere,
> Yet to each loving heart how near.
>
> Sun of our life, Thy quickening ray
> Sheds on our path the glow of day;
> Star of our hope, Thy softened light
> Cheers the long watches of the night.
>
> Our midnight is Thy smile withdrawn;
> Our noontide is Thy gracious dawn;
> Our rainbow arch, Thy mercy's sign;
> All, save the clouds of sin, are Thine.
>
> Lord of all life, below, above,
> Whose light is truth, whose warmth is love,
> Before Thy ever blazing throne
> We ask no luster of our own.
>
> Grant us Thy truth to make us free,
> And kindling hearts that burn for Thee,
> Till all Thy living altars claim
> One holy light, one heavenly flame.

Part of the minister's life and work provides open doors
through which we can see the beckoning light which leads to
fuller light. Throughout the Scriptures there is a stress upon that
which is good, very good, and excellent. The ordinary man is
satisfied to choose between the good and bad, or he may find
that the "better" is a hindrance to the "best." It is in this area
that we discover the secret of mental and moral growth, for as
Robert Browning wrote:

> When the fight begins within himself,
>   A man's worth something.
> God stoops o'er his head, Satan looks

Up between his feet—both tug—
He's left, himself i' the middle:
The soul wakes and grows.

The apostle Paul expressed a similar thought when he prayed
for the congregation at Philippi:

I pray that your love may abound yet more and more in
knowledge and in all judgment; That ye may approve things
that are excellent; that ye may be sincere and without offence
till the day of Christ.

(Phil. 1:9, 10)

J. B. Phillips in his *The New Testament in Modern English* has a
refreshing translation in speaking of being "able always to recognize the highest and the best."

All this is to introduce the minister to the growth that is possible in going on to that maturity of life and character which be-
fits a man of God. Jacques Barzun issued an unusual challenge
in *The House of Intellect* (Chicago: University of Chicago Press,
1975 reprint). To the ordinary man among the mediocre in our
culture there is a challenge to face up to his limitations. But the
thrust (and it is a rapier thrust) is rather to those in the ministry,
who are among the privileged and have trained intellects.

If the minister in our contemporary world imagines he can
drift along in casual and careless service without much preparation, a judgment day is inevitable. In I Corinthians 3:9-15 Paul
writes about alternative ways of building our character upon the
enduring foundation in Christ. Whether we use gold, silver, and
precious stones or wood, hay, and stubble "each man's work
will one day be shown for what it is. The day will show it plainly enough, for the day will arise in a blaze of fire, and that fire
will prove the nature of each man's work" (Phillips). The final
and incontrovertible test is that of character, Christian
character, and judgment day will reveal what sort it is!

Barzun's friendly criticism stabs and wounds the conscience
when we think of our opportunities for mental and moral development. Who besides the pastor and minister has been given
five days each week in which he is set apart from the regular
round of earning a living to use the morning hours (at least) in
reading, study, and writing in order to become a man of excellence, able to discriminate with wise sense and judgment the

things which belong to the whole counsel of God? Lay people in the church are engaged in their employments to provide the bread that is temporal; they expect the pastor to come from his rich hinterland of study to share with them the Bread which is eternal.

The true Christian is not antiintellectual. He engages God with his mind as well as with the rest of his total person. The American method of preparation for the ministry involves the study of theology and correlated subjects within a college or seminary set apart from the regular university. In the climate where I was nurtured (Scotland), we studied biblical literature and language, church history, and theology along with philosophy and science as part of the university degree. Thus our student world was not sheltered from confrontation with those who had in mind vocations other than the ministry of the church. Whereas the former method has its special place in ministerial training, the latter offers a distinctive and unique conditioning which prepares proponents of the Christian faith to meet the challenge of their culture.

After trial and testing in the classroom, the newly ordained minister will meet increasingly the thought and belief of those who do not readily accept the Christian view of God and the world. Those who have utilized the quiet of a study (either in the home or in the church building) to prepare to meet this challenge testify to the dividends which accrue to that investment of time and intellect. Christianity does have a solid intellectual base. No age ever needed this base as much as does the present, in view of the blatant anti-Christian attacks and the biblical illiteracy which abound.

When David S. Cairns (1862-1946) became the principal of the United Presbyterian Church Theological College in Aberdeen University, Scotland, he looked back in thanksgiving at his years of preparation when he had struggled to build a solid faith. His early conversion experience was followed by doubt; and when he was dogged by ill health, his studies were interrupted for a number of years. In retrospect he never regarded these years as wasted. One of the discouraging experiences of failure came after he was fully trained to be a minister. He was an unsuccessful candidate for the pastorate of no fewer than sixteen vacant churches. But he used the time to read widely, and to pursue his intellectual and religious goals.

Finally, a door opened and up to the age of forty-five he served as minister of a small country church. This position might be deemed totally inadequate for his intellectual powers, for his name began to be known as he wrote for a wider circle. During those years in the Scottish countryside, Cairns was not in a hurry but continued to lay the foundation in preparation for larger ministries. What might have been lonely years were not unproductive, for he gave to the theological world books like *The Faith That Rebels* and *The Riddle of the World*. From his example we learn that a minister should invest the greater part of his time in his congregation (whom he as pastor knows intimately); then from that storehouse of interchange and reflection he can send forth streams of influence beyond his dreams. Cairns's concern was to unfold the biblical view of life as set forth in both the Old and New Testament. No beginning minister today need be discouraged for he has all the tools of learning which are available to the seasoned pastor.

A certain denomination in an hour of need sought for a man to be the head of their Department of Christian Education and lead their staff in producing something exciting for a new day. After considering the scores of names submitted, the decision was finally made in favor of a younger man who was not known in metropolitan areas or even at the national headquarters of that church. Where was he discovered? After seminary he had accepted the challenge of Montana (which, with its rigorous climate and vast, open spaces, was not so accessible nor comfortable forty years ago). While isolated and lacking a large congregation, the minister invested his money and time in the *Encyclopedia Britannica*. Since the theological library he had acquired from seminary days was limited, he spent the first part of his ministry reading the *Encyclopaedia*—a library in itself. He became one of the best-informed pastors around and his ministry deepened. Though virtually unknown, he was chosen when the church required a leader.

Austin Farrar (1902-1968), professor at Oxford University in philosophical theology, dealt with the theme that "moral perfection is not enough." He pointed out that "it is easier to keep up a round of religious activities than to be a good man, easier to repeat accepted dogmas than to be mentally alert, easier to perform routine pieties than to answer the claims that humanity makes upon us." Every minister has his tests and temptations and obstacles to growth. Hebrews 12:1 enjoins us to "lay aside every weight, and the sin which doth so easily beset us." Not every weight is a sin, but every sin is also a weight. In the light of Hebrews 11 with its honor roll of those who lived "by faith," we understand that the sin the writer has in mind is that of unbelief and disbelief. No Olympic athlete would run wearing a long, clinging robe which might easily cause him to stumble and fall. So in the advance of Christian character, the man of God is cautioned to beware of the weight and sin which might beset (upset) him.

In response to a daily radio program an American minister received thousands of letters requesting answers to life's problems and pains. He reported that in human experience *fear* is enemy number one; *worry* is number two; and *loneliness* is number three. Every minister in his personal life as well as in his public ministry must deal with these threats to moral and spiritual strength of character. A pastor who is committed to his vocation will testify that his own life is not exempted from these obstacles and that they never cease to intimidate and tempt him. Faith overcomes fear; trust cancels worry; and God's presence banishes loneliness.

The fears of life are many and they manifest themselves as the minister faces the unknown quantity of each new day. How shall he act and what shall he say? Will he act in such a manner as to satisfy those seeking help from him? Does he have sufficient background to be able to stand on his own feet to minister? What of those in his congregation who are better equipped by education and culture? Will he feel a lack of polish and poise among those who seem superior? Let the emotion of fear be set aside by his faith in God. Let his mind be ever aware of the promises of God. As the minister of a congregation, he must demonstrate that he is not afraid of the unknown or of the risk of a new venture and certainly not of death, the last enemy.

As for the anxieties of life, we tend to be instinctively concerned and worried about what may happen to us or our family or our people. To cast our care upon God is the avenue of release, for God cares for His own. The enemies of the body are many: ill health, suffering, and facing death. Lack of health and strength can bring a mood of depression or discouragement. Yet George Matheson, who lost his sight and faced a future without a life's companion, could write about the "Love That Wilt Not Let Me Go." We imagine much that never materializes. Why not imagine a better life instead—one not torn apart by tension or the forces of evil?

The loneliness of life can be heart-rending. There is the loneliness of a solitary man in the crowd. The minister will find himself alone in situations when he represents the church and his Lord. He may have little in common with people whose habits and ways of life seem radically different from those within the walls of the church building on a Sunday morning! But he will find himself in strange places and situations and there he can witness by his character (sometimes by his words); he can be a mighty influence for the kingdom of God. He should be in the world, but not of it (cf. the prayer of our Lord in John 17:15). Separation does not require physical or geographical separation; rather, contact with the community will find the pastor lonely, separated in spirit. The divine presence is a shield from evil and a means of gracious, irenic, outgoing concern for others.

When the apostle Paul was near the end of his ministry, he wrote to Timothy, "The cloke that I left at Troas with Carpus, when thou comest, bring with thee, *and the books*, but especially the parchments" (II Tim. 4:13). He who was the writer of much of the New Testament and who had remarkable experiences during his missionary journeys and ministries—he wished to have books. The fears, the anxieties, and the loneliness of life can in large part be overcome through books.

In preparation for the hour of worship certain guidelines are obvious. No one needs to stand at the foot of the pulpit steps and hesitate if he has taken time to meditate, pray, and seek divine guidance concerning what to preach to the people.

What a God-given opportunity and privilege for the pastor to be set free to read and study morning after morning in anticipation of the Lord's Day! Ian Pitt-Watson, professor of practical theology at Christ's College in Aberdeen, has stressed various as-

pects of preparation for preaching in his *A Kind of Folly* (1976).
With pastoral concern and incisive words he reiterates that the
preaching of the church is the heart of Christian theology and
theology is the conscience of that preaching. Each needs the
other. In this context preaching involves the whole person—
intellect, will, and emotions. The end of the sermon exposition
should be the beginning of action. A verdict is expected in the
response of the whole person to the message. This response may
on occasion be given publicly, but generally it lies in an inner
commitment to Christ and a conviction that divine guidance is a
reality in daily life. The outworking of that moment may take a
lifetime.

Every hour of worship contains the essence of the beautiful.
The ideal expressed in Psalm 90:17 ("Let the beauty of the Lord
our God be upon us") may be realized in the vastness of nature's
panorama or in the loveliness of human relations at the highest
level. But certainly it is realized when the glory of the Lord
shines in our hearts in worship.

As leaders in public worship we are not left to decide at the
spur of the moment what to do in praise, prayer, and ministry.
The Bible is full of guidelines to instruct and enrich us in our
ministries. In addition, we are ministered unto by all those who
share in the worship and praise of the congregation.

The Book of Psalms, the hymnbook of the Hebrews, can be of
rich service in public worship. David's introduction of liturgical
singing is recorded in I Chronicles 16. The psalm of David offered here is a fine example of what hymns and spiritual songs
should be like. David led his people in worshiping the Lord "in
the beauty of holiness" (v. 29).

While there are unusual times of Spirit-filled worship and ministry, stress should be laid upon the normal. Order in worship is
important to the enrichment of a congregation. Today as in
David's time, the emotions of people can be stirred, but true
worship must be orderly. Had David neglected this principle, the
religious excitement of the people might eventually have
evaporated. Paul also teaches that all things should be done "de-
cently and in order" (I Cor. 14:40). In modern days there is need
for balance in worship.

Pastors owe much to choir leaders, choirs, soloists, and organists for the uplift they provide to the hour of worship. Hymns, anthems, oratorios can bring a sense of majesty to the service. Who can forget the heritage of church music experienced while he was growing up? I retain in special memory the Scottish version of the Psalter.

When God's people are living their lives in such a manner as to be witnesses (Acts 1:8), they are as salt and light in the society of which they are a part (Matt. 5:13, 14). It is by Christian character in faith and habit that God in His sovereign grace touches and influences non-Christians. More is accomplished in this manner than by special methods and church campaigns to promote evangelism. The Christian character is filled with holiness. The result is a contagion of joy and gladness which touches life in general and individuals in particular.

Every century has witnessed movements of the Spirit of God: the Great Awakening in New England, the Evangelical Revival in England, the Second Great Awakening, the Welsh Revival of 1900. Associated with all these movements has been an outburst of *song* and *music*. During the Reformation Martin Luther composed hymns and encouraged his people to sing chorales in tunes familiar to their time. John Calvin was instrumental in preparing the Psalter; from 1537 on he persuaded others to stir their hearts by singing. Other Reformers of that period contributed poetry and music. Calvin stressed that music should be in four-part harmony, and this became the standard practice. Throughout the Reformation lands of Holland, Switzerland, Germany, England, and Scotland, the Psalter blessed and enriched emerging congregations. The Scots under John Knox were eager converts to singing and over the centuries have claimed the Scottish Psalter as a special part of their national existence!

When revival advanced in eighteenth-century England, the preaching of John Wesley was matched by the more than six thousand hymns of his brother Charles. The nation was saved from the horrors of the French Revolution, and the church in its wider fellowship began to sing its creed and spread its message of salvation and assurance with joy. Oceans were no barrier, and the words and music celebrating God's presence in the midst of His people were carried not only to the New World, but around the globe as sea lanes opened up for commerce and colonization. Merchants and missionaries also wafted the Christian faith in music and in song everywhere. Whether the church term the persuasive ministry of the Holy Spirit "return" or "renewal" or "revival," there is always an outburst of song. "When the burnt offering began, the song of the Lord began also" (II Chron. 29:27).

Like the musician, the artist strives after perfection in his work. Christians throughout the centuries have striven to become saints, separated unto God and placed as members in the church, the body of Christ. The paradox is that though we by virtue of being "in Christ" are now perfect in God's sight, yet we are to go on to perfection. The heights beckon. We have a faith to keep. We have a course to run. We have a struggle to endure (II Tim. 4:7). By following the apostle Paul's advice to young Timothy, the minister has opportunity to demonstrate in his own life and work the grand particularities of which he speaks from Sunday to Sunday. His whole life is wrapped up in the eternal. He preaches of the eternities when all around him men are speaking of the times.

William Blake caught the vision and mood of the eternities:

> See a world in a grain of sand
> And a Heaven in a wild flower.
> Hold infinity in the palm of your hand
> And Eternity in an hour.

God is the eternal artist who shaped the cosmos of beauty and perfection. We are also God's *poiema*, His workmanship (Eph. 2:10). Made in the divine image and likeness, we plan for the ministry as does the artist for his work. We, too, are craftsmen. We, too, aim at a standard—even excellence.

8

The Wisdom of Experience

"It is the man of God, who disobeyed the word of the Lord; therefore the Lord has given him to the lion." (I KINGS 13:26, RSV)

"A great door and effectual is opened unto me, and there are many adversaries." (I COR. 16:9)

"A wide door for effective work has opened to me, and there are many adversaries." (RSV)

"A great opportunity has opened for effective work, and there is much opposition." (NEB)

"There is great opportunity of doing useful work, and there are many people against me." (PHILLIPS)

"Ample opportunity for effective work lies before me here, although there is strong opposition." (BARCLAY)

"A door that offers wide and effective service stands open before me, and there are many opponents." (WEYMOUTH)

"I have wide opportunities here for active service, and there are many to thwart me." (MOFFATT)

"A wide door, full of opportunities for work, has opened there before me, and many are they who are trying to shut it in my face." (A. S. WAY)

THE APOSTLE PAUL in I Corinthians raises crucial questions of character and conduct, especially in chapter 10. There he commands the servants of God not to be ignorant, not to be idolaters, not to yield to immorality, not to be presumptuous and test Christ, and not to murmur. Then in summary he writes:

> Wherefore let him that thinketh he standeth take heed lest he
> fall. There hath no temptation taken you but such as is com-
> mon to man: but God is faithful, who will not suffer you to be
> tempted above that ye are able; but will with the temptation
> also make a way to escape, that ye may be able to bear it. (vv.
> 12, 13)

The man of God is given a high place in the divine revelation
of both the Old and New Testament. Called and chosen by God,
he experiences grace and a growing series of divine unfoldings.
Like Jacob, the individual "learns by experience" (Gen. 30:27).
Spiritual wisdom is acquired and, consequently, service is accepted wherever God places His servant.

A Minister's Obstacles brought out the many perils and pitfalls
as well as tests and temptations common to all Christians, but
especially dangerous for the man of God who is placed in a
special ministry. Chapter 8 dealt with the "Fear of the Cast-
away" and chapter 18 with the "Waste at Noonday." There is
abundant warning that the ministerial position does not give
immunity from peril, that profession is no substitute for reality,
and that whoever is strong or faithful in the Christian life is the
target of evil and subject to attack. The faithful may become a
failure and the servant of God may become a servile slave of
evil. Position and prestige do not guarantee power for survival
in the battle of life. Inner resources are necessary, even the Holy
Spirit of God.

How often the same tragedy is repeated in the Old Testament:
the man of God (the highest endorsement for service and ministry) is disobedient (the heinousness of inner anarchy of spirit)
unto the word of the Lord (the holy standard to be followed
without question). It is no sin to be tempted, but yielding to
temptation becomes sin. The tested life is a means of demon-
strating our worth and value in the sight of God and in the service of the church.

When the servant of God stands in the holy place, he represents all God's people. Those set apart for special ministry know
that in their office there are both privilege and peril. Leviticus
21:8 deals with the priestly office in Israel: "He shall be holy unto thee: for I the Lord, which sanctify you, am holy." This
separation or devotion to God sets the standard for ministry.

Obedience is the law of that office. In *A Minister's Obstacles*, chapter 5, it was pointed out that King Uzziah was judged by God when he presumed to act in the office of the priest. Pride was his undoing. Self-will and self-love bring inevitable judgment. Numbers 16 records how Levites led by Korah, Dathan, and Abiram were guilty of intruding into the high and holy office of Aaron when God had not appointed them to it. They were presumptuous and judgment followed. Likewise, Judges 17-18 tells the story of the counterfeit priest and his graven images. Acts 8 condemns Simon the magician, who imagined he could buy the power of the Holy Spirit.

These samples of irresponsible self-love are from the biblical period, but let us not be blind to the contemporary world wherein religious leaders and groups and cults pander to the sensational. Driven by self-interest, multitudes are swayed by the appeals of personalities who, without ethical norms, claim to be able to work the unusual and the miraculous.

In I Kings 12-13 there is a tragic story of presumption, rebellion, and disregard of divine revelation. Jeroboam was guilty of setting up duplicate, rival centers of worship, providing the people with symbols, feasts, and sacrifices. To save the time and trouble of traveling to Jerusalem to sacrifice, Jeroboam set up more accessible high places at Dan and at Bethel. Convenience and not consecration won out. God's verdict is the repeated pronouncement, "This thing became a sin" (12:30; 13:34).

In more recent times Adolf Hitler was the religious-political embodiment of presumption. In effect, he claimed messiahship as commander and leader, Fuhrer and savior, and engulfed millions in hatred and holocaust. But his symbol was a crooked cross; only the cross of the Lord of lords and King of kings will usher in the kingdom of God. Hitler's presumption inevitably issued in judgment and disaster.

In all cases of human presumption, including Jeroboam and Hitler, in the end the true wins over the false; the genuine outlives the counterfeit. Those who have been set apart for special ministry continue to lead their people. "We have priests ministering to the Lord who are sons of Aaron, and Levites for their service. They offer to the Lord every morning and every evening. . . . For we keep the charge of the Lord our God, but you have forsaken him. Behold, God is with us at our head, and his priests with their battle trumpets to sound the call to battle against you. O sons of Israel, do not fight against the Lord, the God of your fathers; for you cannot succeed" (II Chron. 13:10-13, RSV).

The deterioration in ancient Israel warns us who minister in sacred worship and service. The charlatan is always present in contemporary life, seeking to establish substitute religions. Power and the lust for power are not confined to the political scene. Religious life is shot through with similar personalities seeking power. But who are we to judge? In the most orthodox churches will be found individuals who seek and often receive adulation which feeds their desire for power. We may be free from the snare of sloth, but who among us has not known a moment when dreams and visions of power blinded us? To be presumptuous in the church could be our undoing. When we accept in humility our limitations, we are liberated afresh to serve. The secular mind of our generation is subtle in seducing the man of God. We are always in need of that insight which discriminates wisely between the genuine and the counterfeit.

We stress "the Christian mind" over against all other claims and ways of thought and life. There is also what we call "the Christian view of God and the world." In speaking of "the modern mind" we must be cautious, lest we be out of date. Harry Blamires speaks of *The Christian Mind* (New York: Seabury Press, 1963) as something lost and forgotten in a day when a Christian ethic, a Christian practice, and a Christian spirituality are still discerned in our society. These, however, are the dividends of an earlier investment of the Christian mind. Contemporary man at his best is rapidly spending those dividends and then what? Blamires pleads for a recovery of the Christian mind. We should think "Christianly" upon the total life of our time. Man claims to be and acts as if he were self-sufficient. When he senses his lostness and alienation, the preacher can bring the Christian mind and spirit to confront him with the divine good news which offers fulfillment and satisfaction. In our secular age when a majority of voices deal with time and the temporary, Hamish C. MacKenzie would plead for *Preaching the Eternities* (Warrack Lectures, 1961).

This opens the door of opportunity for the preacher to deal with values and absolutes under God. Cultivation of the spirit does not neglect the mind. Discipline of the will does not by-pass the intellect. When the goal of man is reviewed, death is not the worst that can come to us. Kenneth E. Kirk in *The Vision of God* (Greenwood, SC: Attic Press, 1978 edition) deals with the *summum bonum*, the ultimate, the goal, the end of our living, loving, and aspiring. Out of the belief that the pure in heart shall see God (Matt. 5:8) new dimensions of faith and confidence are born. A Christian mind and point of view will then illumine all aspects of life and transform character and conduct.

In *The House of Intellect* (Chicago: University of Chicago Press, 1975 reprint) Jacques Barzun issues a plea that we stop to think about our heritage in an age which has prostituted the things of the mind. Education without real instruction and instruction without authority have led a generation into a darkness where people grope to express themselves but lack the discipline to read, write, and express themselves adequately when thrust into the matrix of secular society.

Barzun speaks of the enemies of intellect and pleads for those qualities which will safeguard the master virtues of intellect. Those qualities are *concentration, continuity, articulate precision,* and *self-awareness.*

> Intellect needs the congregation of talents spurring one another to higher achievements by the right degree of proximity and intercourse; it needs the language and the conversation that maintain its unity like a beneficent air; it needs precision to dispel the blinding fogs of folly or stupidity; it needs self-awareness to enjoy its own sport and keep itself from vainglory.

Concentration is a key to growth and progress in our studies and service. What is spoken of as "consecration" to God's will and service is better spoken of as "concentration." This dedication reverses the maceration of the ministry. The demands made upon the pastor are legion and many are caught in the whirlwind of bits and pieces, blown here and there in attempts to be busy. Such busyness is not the business of the kingdom, but wasted time and energy. Concentration is the basis of all study and development. W. B. J. Martin in his *Little Foxes That Spoil the Vines* (New York: Abingdon, 1968) deals with the "sneaking, wee sins that undermine life." The obvious and glaring sins which beset the minister lie in the realm of pride, jealousy, greed, laziness, and many other obstacles easily recognized. But Martin has put his finger on the not so obvious. He deals with boredom, discourtesy, flippancy, restlessness, ingratitude, careless listening and careless talk, and much besides. This is a sharp thrust penned by someone who has the imagination and the skill of a wise diagnostician and also experience in the healing of so-called little sins. Engaging as he does in the cure of souls, certainly the pastor needs someone to minister to him in that most needy area of his own life.

Continuity is another prime demand upon the minister. There is abundant temptation to yield to interruptions and to lay aside what requires our utmost attention each day or week. The main priority is to spend our morning hours in the study, adhering to a plan of reading, writing, and devotion. Sometimes we give the impression that we are "Mr. Fritterday" in that we jump from one thing (unfinished) to another as our interest comes and goes. We must have a plan before us with each hour set out for its particular aspect of work.

There is in adhering to a specific plan a cumulative aspect which should not be minimized or disparaged. Reading a book of the Bible for mastery of the whole takes time. For example, to read the Book of Genesis will require an uninterrupted period of three hours. The Gospel of Mark will take two hours. To read lengthy passages of the Bible at one sitting and to repeat the process is a simple and enriching method of Bible study. G. Campbell Morgan testified that he did not begin to master (and teach) a book of the Bible until he had first read that book some fifty times by way of preparation and foundation. After synthesis come analysis of the parts and then the exegesis and exposition of the details. In preparation for the Advent season or the Lenten-Easter season, a man does well to spend three months in advance in reading continuously the relevant biblical material as well as appropriate theological studies which stimulate his mind. Such continuous investment several days each week will bring its dividends in teaching and preaching.

There is a great danger in spasmodic work. In II Chronicles

30 we read that celebration of the Passover was delayed. Apart from the suggestion that there was an insufficient number of priests available (RSV), the King James attributes the delay to the fact that "the priests were not sanctified sufficiently" (v. 3). Perhaps the spasmodic nature of our work is due to a casual or careless disposition on the part of us ministers. Has the clarion call of Romans 12:1 to "present your bodies a living sacrifice" lost its meaning in the plethora of competing demands upon our time and devotion? Steady, day-to-day, and continuous giving of ourselves may well be the key to a fruitful ministry.

Articulate *precision* is another quality demanded of those who live in the house of intellect. Recall John Bunyan's description of the Interpreter's house in *Pilgrim's Progress*. What discoveries awaited the pilgrim as he was led from room to room. How marvelous God's provision for the pilgrimage ahead! The armor of defense to ward off attack, the sword which is the Word of God, the instructions mediated by the Holy Spirit from that scroll of the Scriptures—all these items brought enthusiasm to Bunyan's pilgrim. From this time on he would venture into the unknown and face many tests, trials, and pressures. But he would always win his victories, even in times of rebuttal and discouragement.

There is steady progress in growth in character when the minister knows his way to be clear and precise. No sentimental emotional states will divert him from the precise insights he has gained from divine revelation concerning the Christian experience which is "in Christ." By bringing his personal experience to the court of the Word of God and allowing the light of divine revelation to attest or interpret anew what his personal life has achieved, he acquires a balance and a quickened sense of the presence of God.

Self-awareness is the joy and strength that accrue to the minister whose faith and knowledge dispel any vainglory or any foolish notion that as a pastor he has accomplished what the secular society would term "success." This term is foreign to the spirit of the New Testament. Any ministry which is allowed to last is appraised only by the divine Taskmaster under whose eye we have done what we could and still think of ourselves only as "unprofitable servants." Appraisal will be made not in terms of the "successful" ministry but the "fruitful" ministry. At the last there is the promise that some will receive God's endorsement: "Well done, good and faithful servant."

Self-awareness will enable the minister to obey the dictum of Romans 12:3—"not to think of himself more highly than he ought to think, but to think soberly. . . ." Humility will be the best companion of the minister as servant of God when he reaches the end of his life. The Covenanter Hymn of Samuel Rutherford's day ascribes the credit where it belongs:

> With mercy and with judgment
> My web of time He wove;
> And, aye, the dews of sorrow
> Were lustered on His brow.
> I'll bless the hand that guided,
> I'll bless the heart that planned,
> When glory, glory dwelleth
> In Emmanuel's land.

To advocate self-discipline is easy, but each person must find his own ways and means of achieving this end. What is a working ideal for one cannot be made a rigid practice for others. In the matter of devotion there are many variations. John Henry Jowett (1864-1923), on arriving at his first pastorate in Huddersfield, a Yorkshire mill town, was awakened the first morning by the sound of hundreds of feet (in clogs) hurrying past to begin the day's toil in the mill. It was only six o'clock. Jowett there and then decided that if the people within that society had to arise early to work for the bread that perished, then he should likewise arise early to engage in his pursuit of the Bread of Life. In consequence, he found his mind and spirit had a bent toward prayer at seven o'clock in the morning.

There are helps to discipline for anyone seeking with open mind and heart. Ignatius Loyola (1491-1556), a soldier converted to Christ to become the head of the society we know as the Jesuits, brought his military training to bear in the spiritual discipline of devotion and prayer. In *The Spiritual Exercises of Ignatius Loyola* the day's military periods and exercises are transmuted into a similar structure of spiritual exercises. Thus Loyola continued the habits he had learned earlier and made them a means of growth and strength for godliness. If this seems too mechanical a means for our evangelical position, we should beware, on the other hand, of becoming so casual and careless that we wind up with whims and fancies, without structure and development.

The self-disciplined mind will steep itself in dogma. John Henry Newman (1801-1890) informs us in *History of My Religious Opinions* that from the time he was fifteen, dogma had been the fundamental principle of his religion. He said, "I know no other religion; I cannot enter into the idea of any other sort of religion; religion, as a mere sentiment, is to me a dream and a mockery." How true it is that modern man is suspicious of dogma while wistful for faith. Our task is to bring to this generation the message that the eternal God has revealed Himself as Creator of the universe and sovereign director of history, and that at the center of man's life is the cosmic significance of the cross. The dogma is that God in Christ has redeemed the creation which He brought into order and design for man's dominion.

John Hunt's *The Ascent of Everest* (1953) recounts the amazing story of how for the first time in man's recorded history the pinnacle of Mount Everest, 29,028 feet high, had been scaled by two intrepid mountaineers, Edmund Hillary and Tenzing Norgay. Their reactions in that hour were awe, wonder, humility, pride, exaltation. These surely ought to have been the confused emotions of the first men to stand on the highest peak on earth, after so many others had failed. But the dominant reactions were relief and surprise. Relief because the long climb was over and the unattainable had been attained. And surprise that it had happened to them in particular. In Hillary's words: "It had happened to *me*, Old Ed Hillary, the beekeeper, once the star pupil of Taukau District School, but no great shakes at Auckland Grammar and a no-hoper at University, first to the top of Everest! I just didn't believe it." But Hillary did not keep all the glory to himself. He paid fitting tribute to all those anonymous people and circumstances that had contributed to the assault:

> To all who had climbed on Everest before; to our planning and other preparations; to the excellence of our equipment; to our Sherpas and ourselves; to the favour of the elements. And I would *add one more asset*, intangible, less easy to assess; the

thoughts and prayers of all those many who watched and
waited and hoped for our success. We were aware of this hidden force and we were fortified by it.

The same can be stated concerning the minister and his work
and service. He is the inheritor of the experiences of those who
have gone before. He is the heir to a rich tradition and legacy.
He has the benefit of excellent equipment in the history of the
church. The unnamed and unknown Christians who have been
faithful over the centuries bring to him today their support and
spiritual encouragement. The intangible asset of prayer and
more prayer as congregations surround their pastors with that
unseen force of the Spirit brings strength and courage in the day
of ordeal. We have the opportunity to know the power of the unseen.

One modern man of letters whose writings have prodded and
probed the minds of our generation is C. S. Lewis. In *God in the
Dock* (Grand Rapids: William B. Eerdmans, 1970) he states:

> To conclude—you must translate every bit of your Theology
> into the vernacular. This is very troublesome and it means you
> can say very little in half-an-hour, but it is essential. It is also
> of the greatest service to your own thought. I have come to the
> conviction that if you cannot translate your thoughts into an
> educated language, then your thoughts were confused. Power
> to translate is the test of having really understood one's own
> meaning.

Here is wise counsel for any minister of the gospel. To spend
the morning hours in reading and in study provides an opportunity not given to many. The wealth of literature, the lure of
theology, the preparation of the sermon, and the gathering of resources in teaching a congregation provide a continuing education and that without travel to some college or center of learning. The learning center is in the home study or church study, a
considerable saving in the time invested for these glorious goals.

When we reflect upon our days and weeks of such study, we
owe a debt of gratitude to a generous congregation which has set
us free to utilize those precious hours. We are not like some who
have to engage in the business world or as teachers in a school
or college in order to earn sufficient salary to cover our ex-
penses.

Whenever the subject of dogma is mentioned among students or in a congregation, there is the feeling that it is something unreal. There is a difference between what we call "dogmatic" speech or manner and what is divine "dogma." The question of dogmatic finality has been raised by Alfred North Whitehead (1861-1947), professor of philosophy at Cambridge and Harvard. In his *Dialogues* (Westport, CT: Greenwood Press, 1977 reprint) he tells how he accumulated a sizable theological library. After eight years of reading theology in addition to his other work, he suddenly sold the library and from then on dropped the subject. Was that because he could not accept the current dogmatism and what he regarded as the unwarranted claims made by religionists? Whatever it was, the realm of theology lost a great mind. What if Whitehead had come to a reasonable faith and declared himself a committed Christian?

There is *a place to stand*, as Elton Trueblood has so richly affirmed as a philosopher and Christian. We find that in the vastness of the universe truth has depths which no one can exhaust. Whitehead in this context said:

> The Universe is vast. Nothing is more curious than the self-satisfied dogmatism with which mankind at each period of its history cherishes the delusion of the finality and of its existing modes of knowledge. Sceptics and believers are all alike. At this moment scientists and sceptics are the leading dogmatists. Advance in detail is admitted; fundamental novelty is barred. This dogmatic sense is the death of philosophic adventure. The Universe is vast.

If he had lived to enter the Space Age, what would he have said?

We have the opportunity to learn from Whitehead and other philosophers whose wrestling with truth should not leave us behind in that exercise. We, too, confront the vast unknown hinterland of knowledge awaiting investigation, especially as we deal with divine revelation and the mysterious universe of which we are a part. God set man at the center and crown of creation to be His instrument. What others miss is that divine-human encounter wherein we have been found of God in Christ. We find the old has gone and the new has come.

The philosopher, scientist, mathematician, and theologian learn *humility* and bow before the unlocked secrets of the universe in an attitude of expectancy awaiting response. So, too, the preacher-teacher, the minister of God, bows down with similar spirit, knowing that God will be pleased to unveil His mind and will. When Joseph Parker of the City Temple in London ended his ministry, he confessed he had spent fifty years in study, but now felt like a boy on the seashore who had picked up only a few pebbles on the beach. So vast was the untapped territory of the Scriptures still to be worked.

There is a danger in dogmatic speech when it is devoid of humility or when the truth is not spoken with irenic emotion. One of the perils in the ministry is our glib and easy way of expressing our ideas, ideals, and sometimes our judgments in public worship as we lead a congregation in acts of devotion. Our facility in speech is often nothing more than the art of saying something learned the night before with the air of having known it from all eternity.

Yet there is a place for dogma—if not for the unlovely speech of dogmatism! Dorothy L. Sayers, noted writer of mystery stories, was also a devout member of the Episcopal Church in England. When asked to address a conference of Anglican clergy, she grasped the opportunity to state her criticism of that august body. It was a time when the churches were under attack and the preacher censured because of what the public called "dull dogma." She startled her hearers and the press by insisting that *it was the neglect of dogma that made for dullness.* "The Christian faith is the most exciting drama that ever staggered the imagination of man—and the dogma *is* the drama." At the heart of dogma is the question, "What think ye of Christ?" The answer involves both that strange and mysterious death on the cross and the resurrection. Without a creed to possess the mind there is only chaos. Dorothy Sayers's essays on theology are as relevant now as when first issued. If we cannot get excited and be moved by passion when we are proclaiming the eternal redeeming acts, we may be undone.

The Bible, our supreme Book of books and our one guidebook in the spiritual life, is full of divine disclosures of the nature and being of God. We affirm in the Apostles' Creed: "I believe in God the Father Almighty, Maker of heaven and earth, and in Jesus Christ, His only begotten Son, our Lord. . . ." From that

confession of faith come the conduct and behavior for moral and
ethical living. Thus dogma is inescapable.

Our individual experience of God's grace and call to service
builds an intellectual basis for faith. Our minds wrestle with
profound truths. By "intellectual" I do not mean jargon mixed
with abstract statements of theology. Rather I mean simply the
common-sense wisdom and understanding of those ordinary people who have Christian belief and committal and who live their
lives for God day by day. Paul prayed that his friends at Ephe-
sus might have "the spirit of wisdom and revelation in the
knowledge of him [Jesus Christ]: the eyes of your understanding
being enlightened; that ye may know . . ." (Eph. 1:17, 18).

There is a tendency for people to accept the emotional appeal
or topical or practical exhortation while downgrading what they
term intellectual preaching. As if people who listen to systematic
preaching of biblical principles do not have the capacity to appreciate the deep truths of Christianity. As if all they need to
hear is good advice. Such a distinction cuts the nerve of the basic idea of the Christian faith. The worth of an emotion and of
any action that might be taken in response to it depends upon
the truth which inspires and directs commitment of the will.
Hence the need of theological preaching which is rooted and
grounded in biblical revelation. The truth of *God in Christ* is of
direct and vital importance to every Christian; Christian life to
be real and valid must be based on that truth.

The vague, indefinite, inarticulate, and hazy ideas which pass
for Christianity today are the result of lack of clear and definite
intellectual proclamation of biblical theology. History testifies to
the vitality of renewal and revival when men's minds have been
moved by the dogmas of Christian faith and life. Witness the
Evangelical Revival in the eighteenth century and the results. In
like manner, during the Great Awakening in New England at
the same period of history such presentation of theology captured the minds of a generation and motivated them to action.
While the emphasis differed theologically in Old England from
that in New England, the results indicated the re-creative power
of the Holy Spirit's applying truth as absolute and final to conscience and life. Vital Christianity does not yield to the popular
demand that strenuous mental activity be avoided. Our Lord's

words were "to love God with all our heart, soul, *mind*, and strength."

We learn in the ministry that the basic questions of mankind are theological. Creation, History, Providence, Life, Suffering, Death, Time, Eternity, Destiny—these words demand reading and study so that we may be able to give an answer (in part at least!) to questing people who are disturbed by life and seek guidance on the journey of experience. Ministers who are honest and diligent must pursue truth in the light that God gives through Scripture and nature. Divine revelation and divine grace are the ultimate grounds of all human hope; they are concepts which are destined to rise to new power in our thought and experience. We accept "dogma" in the word of the lawyer, the doctor, the scientist, the architect, the astronaut—yes, even the carpenter with his tools—so why not divine dogma, the canon, which, with its principles of theology and revelation, is as straight as a plumbline?

The relationship of science and Space-Age Christianity may not be seen as an area of concern to most ministers of the gospel, but to some it is crucial. There is a growing conviction that, while the work of the Holy Spirit in creation, incarnation, and inspiration reveals the same eternal values, this new age requires a Christ-centered view of the universe in His cosmic significance. Charles E. Raven in 1927 as a theologian-scientist was exploring that concept. Here was not an accommodation to natural theology, but a new method of Christian apologetic. Our Lord Jesus Christ is central and final in divine revelation as Scripture testifies, but He is also the Lord and Creator of the universe wherein the glory of the Godhead is manifested. We learn by experience, and the fear of the Lord is the beginning of wisdom.

9

The Power of Ambition

"Whosoever will be chief among you, let him be your servant." (MATT. 20:27)

"He must increase, but I must decrease." (JOHN 3:30)

"If anyone aspires to the office of bishop, he desires a noble work." (I TIM. 3:1, RSV)

"Seekest thou great things for thyself? seek them not." (JER. 45:5)

"Seek ye first the kingdom of God." (MATT. 6:33)

THE TENSION CREATED by these statements is a constant concern of the devoted minister in his life and work. How to resolve it is a difficult task. On the one hand is the call to self-sacrifice and to lowly service in the ministry. The nature of that call invites a man to a vocation which cannot be measured in terms of modern ideas of success and monetary rewards. The pastor or would-be pastor must not allow himself dreams of grandeur and aggrandizement. Nevertheless, there is a stage in experience where even the most selfless person finds he must allow for a measure of ambition or fail and be nothing.

The peril lies in the pursuit of an *unworthy* ambition. Selfish desires may tempt us to take the easy way or to become ruthless and evil in pursuing our career. There is no simplistic way of resolving the dilemma. All other vocations demand and invite the best minds and people for the tasks and openings available. It is assumed that there will be those who will seek to advance in skill and experience, who will be interested in greater responsibility and larger monetary rewards. That is not frowned upon in our congregations. However, the minister is thought of as one who has more altruistic motives and aspirations. Thus there are constant tensions upon the man of God lest he be caught in something deemed unworthy of him.

George E. Sweazey, professor of homiletics at Princeton Theological Seminary, discussed this in an address given in Miller Chapel at the seminary. His insights into the problem are among the most significant in print. Coming from a rich and long ministry in the pastorate, he was qualified to speak out of experience. He distinguishes true ambition from counterfeit. Paul was ambitious—he made it his aim—to do three things: (1) not to build upon another man's foundation; (2) to be well-pleasing in the sight of the Lord; and (3) to preach the gospel in the regions beyond (where others had not yet gone).

A disciplined and dedicated servant of God will have similar motivations. The idea of being "nothing" or of failing in his task will not arise. The aim of such a person is simply to do his best and to serve without reservation. If the favor of God should rest upon his work, then he will be thankful. If he sees little or no return from his labors, he will still be faithful in the field of service where he has gone. The measure of what is accomplished is not by the standards of our secular age. An apparent failure in the eyes of the world may be a singular success in the judgment of God. Faithfulness brings its crowning of life and ministry. Canon Peter Green could have occupied one of the higher posts of leadership in the Anglican Church, but he remained in the slums of Manchester in his belief that he must identify with the people there in their social, economic, moral, and spiritual need. Such an ambition takes time and a long pastorate. Green did not lack open doors of evangelism on the street, in the tavern, at the labor exchange; he "sat where they sat" (cf. Ezek. 3:15). From that vantage point he also wrote for the *Manchester Guardian*, and published books on ethics and theology as well as the devout life. Ambitious? Yes, in that he sought first the kingdom of God and then accepted whatever came in the bundle of life.

As George Sweazey has pointed out, just to be allowed to be a minister might well be the heart of ambition for many of us. In the work of reconciliation and the declaration of the good news in Christ, the minister is there at the center of the struggle in our world. "Farmers and doctors work to keep people alive; the minister works to make their lives worth living." The glory of our vocation is that we are privileged to be undershepherds for the Great and Good Shepherd.

Who like the minister has the open door to families when tragedy strikes? Let an accident befall someone. Witness the rush to the hospital in an emergency. The minister can stand alongside the doctor in ministering to human need. The congregation and the community (or parish) will respond to any pastor who cares when a child is born, when a funeral or memorial service is planned, and when a wedding ceremony is performed. In the crisis hours of life and in those moments when guidance is sought at the forks of the road, how often the minister is invited to share in life's secret aspirations and in the decisions of those who trust him!

When the nation is faced with a crisis or choice of leadership, a minister has a supreme opportunity to speak words of counsel and strength to hundreds of people. When moral issues are to be faced in a community or when a nation must be like the "multitudes in the valley of decision" (Joel 3:14), then the minister brings from the eternal Word of God that word which sifts, enlightens, warns, and appeals for the highest and the best. No other person in the community compares to him in this respect. No politician is so favored by a loyal and faithful people who as a constituency rally week after week, month after month, to hear what that one man has to say. Politicians do not have many to listen to them after this fashion, but the minister? Yes! Thus we shape the destiny of people and communities, and by our words and interpretation of truth we fill the minds of countless numbers throughout our ministry.

Any discussion of a goal for the minister raises the question of ambition and what is termed success in life. A healthy ambition is a must for most people if they are to succeed. Hence the exhortations and inducements to seek after the glittering prizes of life. Jack Anderson wrote about Jimmy Carter *(Sunday Parade Magazine,* Nov. 13, 1977):

> He could have remained in the Navy and sought to be its leader. Instead he went into business. He was motivated by a desire to expand his life and experiences and his ability to learn and to encompass a new circle of friends or to make the most of his own influence.

This led him into politics, and in 1972 *he set his sights upon the White House*. "I always felt," he explained, "that whatever talent or ability we have, it ought to be used to an optimum degree in the service of fellow human beings and in the service of God."

Yet he acknowledged that *he was also propelled to the top* "a great deal, maybe *mostly, [by] personal ambition* and gratification, a sense of having done well, of having achieved. . . . It has been a gratifying thing to do it and to achieve in a contest, like winning a game, that has also been with at least the rationalization . . . that I was making the most of the life that God has given me."

Those who influenced Carter most included his father, James Earl Carter, Sr. ("he demanded and got my respect"); Admiral Hyman Rickover, who instilled in Carter the commitment to excel; and President Harry Truman ("he had a lot of courage, was basically honest"). After his Christian experience of "new birth" Carter developed a rigid self-discipline which prepared him for the exacting life and work of the White House.

No one can find fault with the healthy ambition of a president or of others in walks of life different from the ministry. Who can say whether ministers in early years had similar ideas? As far as information is shared, few, if any, set out with their sights upon a prominent church in a metropolitan area. The majority of would-be ministers do not share the same motivations as other young people, for they know that God has called them to special preparation and opportunity to serve in some phase of the church's ministry. The compelling idea is not to get to the top by personal ambition. The call finds a young person humbly and modestly committing life to the will of God, which must unfold gradually. The element of sacrifice and the language of "taking up the cross" are pertinent and a powerful motive at that stage. Who has not been touched and moved in a service in church when volunteers have offered themselves for missionary tasks? Who has not witnessed the dedication and commitment of youth at a student or missionary convention to present their bodies a living sacrifice to God? And then to go actively to the needy places of the earth? When that spirit is lost amid the professionalism of contemporary life, when a cushion is sought instead of the cross, then the heart of the ministry is lost.

"Seekest thou great things for thyself?" asked the prophet Jeremiah (45:5). "Seek them not." *"Seek ye first the kingdom of God,"* answered our Lord (Matt. 6:33). The success syndrome and self-centeredness with our sights set on some goal and working to reach the top by personal ambition are not what we have understood by our call to the ministry of the gospel. Rather we hear the word: "Thine ears shall hear a word behind thee, saying, This is the way, walk ye in it, when ye turn to the right hand, and when ye turn to the left" (Isa. 30:21). If this is foolish in the eyes of the world, so let it be. The history of Christianity is a record of a noble band of witnesses who advanced through storm and trial to build the church.

Many indeed are the opportunities showered upon the pastor-preacher by the open doors of the ministry. He meets others who can exercise their natural gifts and disciplined abilities to produce lasting joy. The building called the church may be plain, soot-stained, and lack much of human adornment—but in it there is the God-given opportunity to sense the divine presence and to join with the whole church of all the ages in the highest act before God—worship. More than any other person the servant of God is granted these privileges because of his calling and vocation.

Even the apostle Paul speaks of the proper place of ambition:

> My constant *ambition* has been to preach the Gospel where the name of Christ was previously unknown, and to avoid as far as possible building on another man's foundation. (Rom. 15:20, Phillips)

> We therefore make it our *ambition* . . . to be acceptable to him. (II Cor. 5:9, NEB)

> Make it your *ambition* to have no ambition. (I Thess. 4:11, Phillips)

Paul's use of the word *ambition* may be startling to some. Ambition is a healthy spirit for the full-blooded person who is active in good deeds and seeks to do something with life and to insure that at the end he will be remembered as a person who realized that dream. This becomes in some instances the motive and wellspring of action and deed. When Paul speaks of ambition, the word always carries the suggestion of wise and discreet choices.

Among many obstacles that would hinder and discourage the minister there is often a temptation to lack of depth. Conditions of our day are prone to offer any easy way out by being superficial. Another age talked much of being in earnest; this meant the minister should be serious in his work. It did not mean a soberness of disposition and facial expression as if the minister had lost his sense of humor and his enjoyment in life. John Bunyan's Interpreter in *Pilgrim's Progress* was characterized as "a very grave person" *(gravitas)*, which spoke of a sense of what is appropriate. Who like the minister faces the sorrows and sufferings of life? Who knows the heartaches and tensions of people torn by temptation and trial? Who shares the burdens of loss and tragedy common to man? The minister knows that a frivolous spirit is no substitute for the undershepherd who carries the griefs of others and who "sits where others sit" in the day of ordeal.

It is good not to live on the surface of life, but to have a deep awareness of the tragedies which can beset mind and heart. It is good to have encountered the challenge of rocky ground and soil choked with weeds and thistles needing to be plucked. It is good to have helped to clean the soil of the human heart and ready it for the divine Sower. We have the opportunity to cultivate our own lives in this respect. To be a man without depth in the ministry is tragic. Only as a minister cultivates the inner life of devotion in the hours of worship and study can he bring forth a harvest in his character surpassing the ordinary and can he rise above the commonplace. Too many of us in the sacred calling are content with the externals. In our routine duties we are burdened by monotony and lack of enthusiasm. We become stale in our utterance, flat in our moods, and the zest goes out of our ministry. One remedy is to get outside of the city and contemplate the infinite variety of nature. There is an ever changing vision of sky and land, if we but look for it. God is the eternal Artist of infinite beauty and design.

The minister learns from the variety of creation that his own life and work need not be humdrum or tedious or dull. The excitement of each day's new beginning brings venture and vision of something not known before. New events and people will confront him. Each demand upon his time and counsel will open new vistas of human dilemmas to be resolved and of God's grace to be given so that he can minister once again. A minister is a realist in a world torn between pessimism and optimism; he has untold opportunities to show that Christianity does provide a way of life to deal with good and evil. And all of this is to the glory of God.

As we saw at the opening of this chapter, the man with a worthy ambition will forgo the self-centered life and redirect himself in the service of the Christian virtues. Without this proper sort of ambition, a man daily engages in tedious routine devoid of inspiration and dynamic thrust. Paul confessed: "I count not myself to have apprehended [attained]" (Phil. 3:13), because he knew by experience the goal of the Christian life. Nevertheless, he "pressed toward the mark" (Phil. 3:14). The context suggests Paul was thinking of a fullness of life which could be spoken of only as a state of perfection.

In reference to a choir which practiced daily and thus increased in quality, a wise inspector of educational facilities said: "The attempt to do one thing perfectly every day is the best medium of education." There is truth in this. The Huddersfield Choir of England spends months practicing Handel's *Messiah* for one rendition annually. A critic might say that this is not necessary for the famous choir already knows the score. It is probably by now a monotonous task and drudgery to do it once more. Nevertheless, when the three-hour oratorio is actually presented, what happens? Because the score is familiar after years of rehearsal, there is striving after perfection. Each occasion is a new opportunity to rise to higher heights of expression and to pursue ultimate and final harmony and balance. Having acquired a sense of the perfect, the choir strives to achieve it. The minister, likewise, with his knowledge of the Christian faith and the Bible, continues to learn by experience as he pursues the goal that is in Christ.

"Success" is a catchword of our secular age. The minister is rated by the measurements of the spirit of our age either as successful or as a failure. The workaholic drives himself and pursues a goal of reaching great heights. In business, athletics, politics, law, medicine, television, radio, and other realms of the entertainment world, success is equated with publicity and prestige. Inevitably this all links up with financial gains. Tycoons of industry turn millions of dollars into billions and wield unparalleled influence and power over others. "If power corrupts, then absolute power corrupts absolutely," according to Lord Acton, Roman churchman and professor of modern history at Oxford University.

In our material order the holding of astronomical assets signifies power over others. Our society has been so cheapened that the dollar sign spells success in this mortal life. Only stewardship of life and means can bring a balance and equilibrium. The idea of success has so permeated our social and economic order that it has invaded the church of God. Too many refer to churches in terms of success. They mean a rise in membership statistics and attendance at services. Or they may refer to the giving of a congregation as above average. All this may be laudable from the point of view of those who think in terms of numbers and growth possibilities. Certainly in the Book of Acts, which was written by Luke, travel companion of the apostle Paul and a reputable historian, there are recorded no fewer than *seven summaries* (2:47; 5:14-16; 6:7; 9:31; 12:24; 16:5; 19:20) of multiplications in the fellowship of the church. Across the centuries church history provides similar accounts of progress. By renewal and revival and awakenings each century has recorded growth and development numerically by the tens of thousands.

None of this need blind us to the fact that while we are prone to rejoice in progress and so-called success among congregations and in achievements by individuals within the church, there is a peril. In keeping with the spirit of the age, the minister can be lulled into regarding numbers as a status symbol. We need to guard well our aims and goals, our earthy ambitions and personal desires as ministers. We must be wary of the lure of a larger congregation, a more adequate salary, and the pursuit of hidden expectations which we think are in accord with our talents. Where we serve needs careful scrutiny as we seek the divine will for our lives.

To the minister, academic success is something which appeals insistently. If we are to love God with our mind as well as with all our might, soul, and heart, then the pursuit of knowledge is not an unworthy goal. Truly this is enjoined upon the minister as he continues his biblical and theological education over the years. He may not receive publicity because of church statistics, building programs, financial goals, or community prestige. However, he should be known for his growth in knowledge and spiritual power as a man of God. Failure is to be avoided in this realm. Here is where he should excel. He has the morning hours free for study and meditation. He should use them well for preparation and spiritual growth.

The paradox is that what the world deems "failure" is allowable in other areas of our common life, for in these areas the minister has laid aside his full-time involvement. Probably he has given up the life of business for the business of his life in the ministry. He has been called out of teaching, sales, engineering, construction work, farming, military service, medicine, or law. He may have heard a clear call to leave what was legitimate and good for something more excellent in the plan and purpose of God for his life.

As a student at Aberdeen University I had the privilege of sharing in a conference where I met Alexander Frazier (1870-1964), who had left Edinburgh for Aberdeen. He had had a large and responsive congregation in Edinburgh, but now in the new field the situation was otherwise. I inquired about his work. With humor and gentleness of speech, he said he was going in for subtractions that year! He went on to explain that the Aberdeen congregation was losing members. Statistically there was a heavy loss at the end of the year. However, his face lit up as he remarked that after those who did not like his emphasis had left, he expected to add others whom he had evangelized and who responded to his teaching and preaching ministry. After the sifting would come the seeding for a new harvest.

At that same period the university had as its rectorial speaker the well-known orator and politician, Lord Birkenhead. I recall his scintillating address entitled "Loose Thinking and Other Matters." His thesis was that the graduates should go out into all walks of life and make success their goal. That memorable oration was a stirring call to effort, a summons to be the master of personal destiny, and to seek "the glittering prizes of life"! A rereading after the lapse of time is revealing. More so when we recall that the eminent speaker was the incarnation of his theme. In his own life he rose to the highest legal position in Great Britain and was a national leader in government. Financially he prospered. However, the publication of his biography by a son unveiled the emptiness of ambition and success. Birkenhead had "gambled" with life and material things. He was so clever that he was able to avoid certain taxation, but when he died he left behind a train of debts and legacy of sorrow. His son published the life story of his father in order to acquire income out of which to pay debts of the past. The "glittering prizes" were tarnished for many of those who as young students had heard a false philosophy of life stressed by one who seemed to be the epitome of what he advocated. In contrast, our Lord in His call to young people to follow Him gave as His symbol a cross and not a cushion for life. "Whosoever doth not bear his cross, and come after me, cannot be my disciple" (Luke 14:27).

Why is success so important in the ministry, and why do we refer to ministers in terms of success or failure? Is it that we are brainwashed by secular standards and believe a lie? Everyday life is filled with examples of people who are lauded for their success, and it is assumed that the pastor (whatever his ministry) should be given similar praise. This is not to decry ambition (of the right sort—recall Paul's wholesome admonition). When the yoke is accepted, the cross is implied.

Paul's life concluded not with apparent success but failure. Instead of arriving at Rome to proclaim the gospel to thousands, he was given welcome by a few disciples, then placed in protective custody under Caesar's edict. This was his reward after trials before Felix, Festus, and Agrippa (Acts 24-26), and after a perilous voyage and shipwreck. Paul was apparently expendable. When shut off from public ministry, he received those who came to visit him in his quarters. There, under Roman guard, he continued teaching and preaching (Acts 28:23-31). He used the time to write letters to churches and individuals. Paul left no fortune in money or material possessions, but his failure in the eyes of the world was transmuted into influence beyond his lifetime and throughout the centuries which followed. His letters preserve his legacy of faith and devotion and are beyond price. Whereas the name of Nero, the emperor under whom he was held in custody and eventually died, is much maligned today, Paul's name is forever enshrined in history and in the annals of the church.

Others who have not been rated as successful would include John Milton, who in blindness wrote his epics *Paradise Lost* and *Paradise Regained*. All that he received for this work was about fifty dollars. John Bunyan, imprisoned periodically for preaching, used his incarceration to write his immortal allegory *Pilgrim's Progress*.

Over against the lure of success lies the story of countless people in the ministry who have weathered long days of service without much encouragement and worldly attainment. Churches, schools, colleges, seminaries, mission boards and societies, hospitals, retirement homes, orphanages—these have been the arena of devoted people who have carried heavy burdens. Many stories of sacrifice and service have not made headlines in the press or in magazine articles or in books. The unsung heroes and heroines of the faith seem not to have succeeded after their long pilgrimage. Yet their seeming failure to receive awards and rewards entitles them to another kind of accolade by the Master Himself.

In material possessions, John Wesley at his death left but two silver spoons, his spectacles, preaching bands, cloak, prayer book, and the usual odds and ends common to an aged person. But his writings fortunately had also been preserved so that his journals, letters, essays, sermons, and tracts were given safekeeping for all subsequent generations. What a priceless legacy!

In the recent Olympic Games at Montreal (1976) some who gained either a silver or a bronze medal spoke of their lack of success in missing the gold medal. This to them was failure. What they failed to recognize was the achievement of *having taken part in the events!* They forgot that they had been chosen to be members of the team. Though they did not win gold medals, they had been crowned already. That was sufficient!

Ronald Ross of England devoted his life to tracking down the mosquito which causes malaria. After a lifetime of research and publication, into which he had poured all his assets and resources, his widow was left with a pittance (and a small pension from the government). She had to sell his papers in order to survive, yet, paradoxically, such failure greatly benefited mankind.

The measure of success in our world would exalt financial returns, personal prestige, and publicity. Television and radio have given to the minister opportunity for proclamation, but also an open door to adulation. The leaders in this type of public ministry seem to attract large audiences and a wide hearing. In addition come offerings and financial returns. In recent years contributors have asked for an annual audited statement of income and expenditures (in the millions of dollars). With the disclosures over recent years of irregularities and even unethical standards, the question of accountability keeps cropping up. In most local churches there is a board of elected officers to serve as a check on pastor and congregation. Likewise denominations have presbyteries, synods, or conferences, while transdenominational enterprises have specially appointed boards. It is high time to establish an effective means of check and restraint on religious leaders in the media.

Our modern society worships at the shrine of success. Every realm of life is estimated according to man's achievement or his loss. Success and failure are the marks of judgment. Do we not see this in our sports when the winning team or the Olympic athlete is applauded for his prowess in being first? Others are reckoned to be failures. Even second place or a silver medal is dismissed as failure. The big corporation whose executives amass large salaries is spoken of in terms of adulation, whereas the independent individual who struggles in a small business is not given much attention. How easily the latter is written off as second-rate or lacking in ambition!

The danger here is that with regard to the special calling of the ministry, we are easily seduced into adopting the same standards of our society when we measure service for God through the church. Donald A. Miller, former president of Pittsburgh Theological Seminary, has said, "The value of a man is measured both by the way he carries his successes and by the way he deals with his failures."

Two biblical characters come to mind: Jonathan and the apostle Andrew. Each was closely related to a stronger, more prominent character. In I Samuel 14 and 18 Jonathan is depicted as a man of principle and achievement, yet one who was willing to take a secondary place when it came to awards for service.

Jonathan was King Saul's heir; a soldier and leader in the nation, Jonathan had great strength of character. He displayed discipline and dedication in times of national crisis. A man of faith, he also manifested judgment in leadership which resulted in the defeat of his enemies in battle. His victory surely should have received the acclaim of the nation. Strange as it seems, Jonathan did not seek public recognition, but modestly and humbly accorded the victory to his father and king. "Jonathan smote the garrison of the Philistines. . . . And all Israel heard say that *Saul* had smitten a garrison" (I Sam. 13:3, 4). Here was a man ready and willing to go unrecognized and to take the second place. Later, when he understood that David would be king after Saul, he expressed joy and supported his friend David, even entering into a covenant with him. Moreover, Jonathan gave David the royal armor, robe, sword, bow, and girdle.

In the New Testament we encounter Andrew the apostle. The Gospels speak of him as second to his highly active and prominent brother Peter. Three events indicate traits in Andrew which mark him out as a man of modest bearing and sensitivity to the needs of others. He did not seek the public eye; in lowliness of spirit and in humility he sought no reward or recognition.

Andrew is mentioned in three special events of the Gospels:

> He brings his brother Peter to Jesus (John 1:35-42).
> He brings the boy with fish and loaves to Jesus (John 6:8, 9).
> He brings the Greeks to Jesus (John 12:20-22).

Somewhere it has been pointed out that here we have the insight and humble service of a man who takes second place to his brother.

> He is the first soul-winner.
> He is the first youth-worker.
> He is the first missionary.

The ministry provides opportunities for individuals to serve in the Order of Saint Andrew!

It is fitting to close this chapter with the words of Joseph Parker (1830-1902) of the City Temple of London, who, in giving advice to a young preacher in a volume entitled *Ad Clerum*, wrote of the signs of a successful ministry:

> Success in ministerial service is not to be confounded with success in any other engagement of life. Naturally you think of

success in connection with crowded chapels, ample financial resources, and a sounding reputation: far be it from me to say that these things are not to be desired in a proper measure; at the same time I hold distinctly that *it is perfectly possible* to fall short of them, and yet to be realizing a very high degree of success in the Christian ministry.

10

The Sense of What Is Vital

"For he [Judas] *was numbered among us, and was allotted his share in this ministry. (Now this man bought a field with the reward of his wickedness.) . . . 'His office let another take.' "* (ACTS 1:17-20, RSV)

"Inquire in the house of Judas *for a man of Tarsus named Saul."* (ACTS 9:11, RSV)

"Ananias, why has Satan filled your heart to lie to the Holy Spirit? . . . You have not lied to men but to God." (ACTS 5:3, 4, RSV)

"A disciple at Damascus named Ananias . . . *said, 'Here I am, Lord.' "* (ACTS 9:10, RSV)

"Simon . . . offered them money, saying, 'Give me also this power. . . .' Peter said to him, 'Your silver perish with you. . . . Your heart is not right with God.' " (ACTS 8:18-21, RSV)

"Simon called Peter . . . will declare to you a message by which you will be saved, you and all your household." (ACTS 11:13, 14, RSV)

THE CONTRAST in the above extracts from the Acts of the Apostles deals with discipleship and deeds. There is realistic judgment as to what is genuine and what is counterfeit. One disciple acts as a traitor and eventually commits suicide, while another with the same name is characterized by his outgoing hospitality and gracious actions. The name Ananias is associated with lying and hypocrisy until another disciple of the same name renders obedience in service. The name Simon is tarnished by the magician's "simony" and lust for power, but another weakling named Simon is granted rocklike strength to bring salvation to others.

We see here the unmasking of the betrayer of our Lord and Master. There is the unveiling of the hypocrite who lies within

the community of the church. There is the unwarrantable attempt to claim spiritual power by mercenary means.

Both English and American literature present a wide variety
of depictions of the minister. Geoffrey Chaucer obviously had a
high regard for the parson of his *Canterbury Tales:*

> A good man there was of religion,
> That was a poor parson of a town.
> But rich he was of holy thought and work:
> He was also a learnèd man, a clerk,
> That Christes Gospel truly would he preach.
> His parishen devoutly would he teach.
> Benign he was and wonder diligent
> And in adversity full patient.

But other authors felt a disquiet concerning the status of the
minister. Witness Sinclair Lewis's portrayal of *Elmer Gantry*
and other modern novels treating men who defected from their
holy vows. The hypocrisy of charlatans needs no elaboration.
The church shamefacedly confesses the failures of pastors who
have fallen in the fight without honor.

Then there are many novels which caricature ministers. The
novels of Anthony Trollope literally bristle with parsons. The
prime example is *Barchester Towers*, with its hen-pecked bishop,
the unforgettable Mr. Cromlin, the learned Mr. Arabin, Dr.
Grantley, the dean, and the canon who, instead of performing
his duties, lounges in pleasure and idleness. The clever psychological novels of George Eliot also depict a wide variety of
clerics. Take Mr. Gilfil, a plain, goodhearted man who did not
shine in the more spiritual functions of his office. Or Amos Bar-
ton, the patient, long-suffering curate. The central character in
Oliver Goldsmith's "The Deserted Village" and *The Vicar of
Wakefield* is a parish minister.

The minister has stood in society as a man set apart by his vocation. The call of the Spirit of God has led him to give up the
regular pursuits of life to devote himself to the supreme task as a
man "under orders." Nevertheless, by obeying that call, which is
ever insistent in his spirit, the minister, in addition to com-
manding the respect of his congregation, has also become the
subject of caricature and distortion. Clever cartoonists and brilliant novelists have displayed the lives of preachers who have

not only had their eccentricities, but their hours of backsliding and sin as well.

In *The Silence of Dean Maitland*, Maxwell Grey presents a character whose outward profession is above reproach. Yet throughout his ministry he lives a monstrous lie until he is unmasked as a tortured soul caught in the trap and the mesh of hypocrisy and deceit. Dr. Clarence Macartney of Pittsburgh called my attention to this almost forgotten (and, unfortunately, out-of-print) novel. It is a vivid presentation of the searing of conscience, the awakening of remorse, and inevitable judgment.

Modern novels are more familiar. We are indebted to Horton Davies, professor of religion at Princeton University, for his *A Mirror of the Ministry in Modern Novels* (New York: Arno Press, 1959). Here we have both literary criticism and religious analysis of the modern depiction of the minister. Among novelists discussed are Nathaniel Hawthorne, Sinclair Lewis, James Street, William Hale White, Mrs. Humphry Ward, Harold Frederic, Georges Bernanos, François Mauriac, Graham Greene, W. Somerset Maugham, A. J. Cronlin, Alan Paton, Hartzell Spence, James Gould Cozzens, and Peter De Vries.

Modern novels have presented the minister in all of his functions: priest, preacher, evangelist, missionary, and community leader. The foibles and failures in each capacity do not escape attention. While there is a measure of respect, there are also satire and condemnation and a call for judgment. Protestants and Roman Catholics, men with doubts and questions, all receive critical analysis.

The necessity to avoid hypocrisy is ever with us in the ministry. The world around is quick to detect the insincere and the charlatan. In the days of Jesus and the early church, occasion was taken to unmask those religious leaders who were caught in the trap of trivia and unreality. They were the Pharisees. Jesus warned His followers against "the leaven of the Pharisees" (Matt. 16:6). What was this leaven? It was their insincere talking of doctrine and their duty and their devotion. Examples are numerous. We are warned. A pastor is faced with the temptation of hypocrisy. No one faces such peril as he who is in the holy office of the ministry.

The appeal of C. S. Lewis, according to one of his close

friends, lies in his tearing away of pretense and his piercing the
veneer of camouflage and complacency in Christian profession.
If Soren Kierkegaard stabbed at the institutional church of his
generation as moribund and barren, so Lewis in more recent
times became God's ambassador to clear away the rubbish of
the unnecessary and the accretions which tend to obscure the inner core of the genuine faith of the Christian.

Vulnerability to the tests and trials of hypocrisy is a major
handicap of the minister and also of the church. The congregation rises or falls by the stature of the pastoral leadership.
Among the evil attendants of hypocrisy may be ambiguity in
speech, fuzziness in thought, compromise in act, refusal to listen
to others, and dilution of truth which is uncomfortable for us
and for others. In a word, the ministry is clouded over; we become time-servers and take the easy way out. This behavior can
work only to our harm.

Among the idols of our church life is the institution itself.
Even as Israel of the Old Testament was warned by her prophets
against this form of idolatry, so we likewise are in similar peril.
Because we are the church, we imagine that as God's chosen
people we are immune from certain risks and dangers. As God's
channel and agent we offer the gift of reconciliation to the people without, but rarely do we sense that we on the inside are
first to need that reconciling grace of God. What congregation
has not known a Diotrephes who loved the preeminence (III John
9)? Leadership is exciting, and as a result there are those who
seek only the first place and brook no rivals. The secular spirit
can pervade the church and a dominant personality assume his
right to rule over his brethren. Then the pastor is faced with a
crisis—should he personally take the situation in hand or compromise or in silence allow a braggart and tyrant to take over
the church session or board to the hurt of all? The lust for power
is not the prerogative of political aspirants or big business executives—it raises its ugly head in the church. Even a pastor may be
guilty of pushing others out of his way in his selfish pursuit of
status and power.

It is to be confessed that the most difficult experience in the
ministry is making our preaching and teaching measure up to
what they ought to be. James 3:1 warns us that to seek the office

of a teacher is to place oneself in a perilous position. Because we traffic in words and counsel others, we are in danger of a greater judgment and a stronger searchlight upon our actions. What we say is to be complemented by what we do. Our Lord in His day warned against the hypocrisy and the leaven of the religious leaders (Matt. 16:6). If the seven Woes of warning and of judgment on the Pharisees (Matt. 23) are preached at all, they are not preached as much as the Beatitudes of the Sermon on the Mount (Matt. 5). A comparison of the Woes with the Beatitudes is startling and revealing.

The original meaning of the word *hypocrite* was "actor." The actor played many parts and so wore several masks to portray different characters. Later the word took on the evil connotation of the religious man acting out religious life with ambiguity and deceit. The minister is tempted in his public life to act many parts. But the real person is disclosed when he stands alone and unmasked before God. Character is what we are in ourselves before God. To pretend in public that we are otherwise is to play the part of an actor.

Idolatry in ancient times was seen as making and setting up idols as objects of worship to replace the one true and living God. Isaiah 44 issues a flaming indictment against idolatry. Those who make idols eventually become like them. Let any institution or program become an end in itself and idolatry has begun.

The call to follow Christ is an initial experience. Discipleship implies discipline. Discipline brings to mind a life beset by rules and regulations of duty. This sometimes stabs the conscience in such a way that we shrug off the idea as too much bother or beyond the potential of human life. After all, why not be free and casual in Christian living? The mood of the moment and the spirit of the hour do not call for a curtailment of what we like best. Whenever we are assailed by such thoughts, it is wise to heed the warning of Romans 12:2: "Don't let the world around you squeeze you into its own mold" (Phillips). Other renderings of this well-known text are, "Do not be conformed to this world" (RSV), and "Adapt yourselves no longer to the pattern of this present world" (NEB).

The demands made upon the preacher are many. There is a

call to self-discipline so that each day may be invested to the full. Only the best is good enough for the life and work of the ministry. Our response to the Master's call implies a total commitment and a dedication to the highest.

The year 1976 was anticipated by thousands of athletes from scores of countries around the world. One thing filled their minds—to participate in the Olympic Games at Montreal. From all nationalities and backgrounds they came. From various cultures, faiths, and social strata, these athletes lived together in the Olympic Village, shared their meals, and practiced beforehand—until the call came to act! When their event was announced, they were ready and eager to engage in the test for excellence. One thing was held in common—not their cultures, faiths, colors, social or intellectual standards, and certainly not their national backgrounds and flags. What was significant was their oneness in *discipline*. Bruce Jenner's idea and ideal expressed the convictions of all. He had lost at Munich in 1972. At that time he said he was determined to win the decathlon in 1976. He aimed to spend the next four years in training and preparation for one goal—to win that arduous and exacting test of the body and mind of the athlete. He spoke of giving himself in committal and *dedication* to this pursuit. Like the athlete, we who are in the Christian ministry should not be negligent in that grand and glorious pursuit of fitness for our tasks and the demands made upon us.

The language and teaching of the New Testament tie in with athletic ideas. Our Lord called His followers to a life of discipline. We are learners who begin and continue in the school of Christ. This was the meaning of His call to the Twelve to follow Him and to be with Him before He sent them out in ministry and service (Mark 3:13-19). To abide with Christ is to abound in Christ. The abiding and the abounding life of the Christian is planned for us. Paul in his letters makes this clear. The first half of each letter deals with the doctrine or what the church believes; the second half is a complement offering instruction about our duty or how the Christian behaves. A rereading of Paul's letters in that light will suggest how moral standards and Christian ethics are interrelated with theology.

Discipline in discipleship does not constrict or narrow the in-

dividual life. To contract in this case actually brings enlarge-
ment. The Olympic athlete is there because he has deliberately
and intelligently constricted his time and strength for one end.
The athlete does his duty each day and disciplines his life in specific ways: strict regimen in drinking and eating; regulation of
sleep and relaxation; daily workouts in his sport. Then, and only
then, does there emerge gradually the necessary fitness for the
day of testing. Just as the athlete is tested by his sporting event,
the soldier by the conflict, and the student by the examination,
so the man of God is tested by the ministry. Paul wrote of this in
II Corinthians 11:23-28 (to be pondered during the quiet hour).
Reflect especially upon his final word: "Beside those things that
are without, that which cometh upon me daily, the care of all
the churches."

We who have but one church or congregation find out our in-
sufficiency and inadequacy when we are confronted by excessive
demands upon our strength and time as well as upon our judgment and wisdom in crucial areas of human need or moral and
spiritual crises. To lead a congregation in the spirit of an undershepherd trained by the Good Shepherd is a test of our inner life
and resources.

The ministry has been construed as a "safe" profession. The
minister is given a high place in the public estimation. For generations he was rated above others in the community because of
the nature of his religious life and work. If temptation came to
the pastor-preacher, he was always regarded as a special person
and almost immune from that blast of evil. However, as I
pointed out in A Minister's Obstacles, the status and nature of
the minister's life and work bring to him the same temptations
common to all men, but often they are thrice-heated in their
fiery nature. The minister has opportunity to demonstrate that
when he is tempted he is able to withstand evil and the seduc-
tions of the world.

The sixties and seventies of our era are decades in which we
have witnessed not only a revolt against traditional standards of
morals, but also an acceleration of unethical permissiveness. Instead of adherence to the absolutes of the Ten Commandments
and the ethical standards handed down within the church of
God, more recent epochs have seen the breakdown of accepted

morality. Situational ethics and existential morals have gradually eroded the ancient norms and removed guidelines for youth.
Whatever is pleasing to the individual is to be the morality of
the moment. Hedonism is rampant.

In more recent days the general public and the Christian
church have been shocked at the unveiling of bribery and corruption in high places. This began before the disclosures of Watergate, which more and more seems to be the watershed or
great divide of our time. Though Watergate applies specifically
to the American political scene, there are similar happenings
taking place in other nations.

Statesmen and politicians, civic and national leaders, have engaged in questionable actions which demean their high office
and their campaign pledges of commitment for the public good.
Newspapers and magazines of several countries have done
thorough jobs of investigative reporting; trials and imprison-
ments have followed. In some instances punishment has been
avoided through pardons or resignation.

In business, corporations have been accused of using agents
who have given bribes and used unethical methods to increase
profits. The humiliation of Prince Bernhard of the Netherlands,
the resignation of President Nixon, the arrest of former Prime
Minister Tanaka of Japan, the cynicism in Italy and the incapac-
ity to react to corruption, the sex scandals in Washington, and
the suggestion that we have seen only the tip of the iceberg have
produced cultural shock!

Business and politics are not the only areas of concern. Social
life is shot through with immorality. Crimes increasingly plague
our neighborhoods. When in 1976 the city of New York experienced a lengthy blackout, so-called decent citizens and ordinary people with acceptable moral standards were suddenly
exposed to the temptation of stealing. During that darkness on
the streets the darkness in people's minds sought to put out any
moral light as a standard of actions. This demonstrates that
when restraints are removed, even for a little while, the natural
man erupts in sinful acts because he is a sinner by nature. We
are what we are and we live in the dark!

What we desire as a free and democratic order is threatened
by permissiveness and situational ethics which have abandoned

the absolutes of the Ten Commandments and the final standard
of enlightened conscience. Without a moral base our modern life
is in jeopardy. Walter Lippmann (1889-1974) said of an earlier
period of moral breakdown:

> Morality has become so stereotyped, so thin and verbal, so en-
> crusted with pious fraud, it has been so much monopolized by
> the tender-minded and the sentimental, and made so odious by
> the outcries of foolish men and sour old women, that our gen-
> eration has almost forgotten that virtue was not invented in
> Sunday schools but derives originally from a profound realiza-
> tion of the character of human life. . . . Virtue is a product of
> human experience. Men acquired their knowledge of the value
> of courage, honor, temperance, veracity, faithfulness, and love,
> because these qualities were necessary to their survival and to
> the attainment of happiness.

In *A Preface to Morals* (Boston: Beacon Press, 1960) he warned
us about "the acids of modernity" and the erosion of moral standards:

> This is the age when the circumstances of life have conspired
> with intellectual habits to render any fixed and authoritative
> belief incredible. The irreligion of the modern world is radical
> to a degree for which there is no counterpart. The passion to
> disbelieve is so strong.

Medical and law students have been known to steal books
from libraries, cheat on exams, and sabotage the work of their
classmates. If aspirants demean the standards of these two lofty
professions even before starting their careers, then what guarantee is there of the quality of medicine and law in the future? We
are shocked at the recent disclosures of the abuse of funds intended to aid the needy and the poor, when under the Medicaid
program there is a high incidence of individual physicians collecting excessive payments in the hundreds of thousands of dollars. Medicaid mills flourish in poverty areas, designed to de-
fraud rather than serve the patient. Unnecessary diagnostic tests
and X-rays are routinely administered for only one purpose—to
enrich cooperating pharmacists and laboratories. Evidence is
coming from all parts of the nation. Profits without honor and
greed without true service are a denial of the highest and the
best.

At this point the Christian church should pause a moment to

ask, "Could this evil penetrate into the fellowship of the unique group known as the body of Christ?" We would like to answer, "Surely not!" Yet with shame and shock we have to confess that we are not immune from the same temptations and we have not taken the opportunity to say no when we should have taken our stand against evil.

Television puts on display to the public certain religious (claiming to be Christian) leaders who teach and preach and make astounding claims of miracles wrought. The format copies the sophisticated ways of show business. Charismatic personalities use chatty speech to lull the unthinking into acceptance of extravagant claims of healing and cures. The gullible welcome relief from the litany of ills plaguing mankind. The millions of dollars which are associated with some of these television programs are a far cry from the notion of the community church and congregation where the faithful serve and give what by comparison seem to be meager amounts. One television leader in defense of the large amounts received said that he believed in the "abundant-life" ministry. A Christian should live as well as a Rockefeller. "Of course," he added, "we try to be good stewards." In connection with this, we mention again the widespread stress upon what the world considers to be success. The question arises: What is the relationship between moral standards and the use of modern high-pressure business methods in religious circles?

John Wesley (1703-1791) lived a long and full life. His work was done in the context of the Evangelical Revival of the eighteenth century in England. His journals and letters as well as his sermons and tracts elucidate his mind and spirit. Behind that public ministry lay an unhappy private life. He had found it difficult to decide whom to marry. That he passed over several opportunities gives hint of an indecisive judgment. When he did finally wed, he experienced marital tension. The home life of Wesley was not what it might have been. His life as an itinerant evangelist, always on the move, traveling from day to day across England, may reflect an unstable home environment.

F. B. Meyer (1847-1929), noted Baptist preacher and exponent of the devout life at the Keswick Convention, was another who found home life difficult. His wife came out of a background of affluence and social standing in Victorian England. Because she was not always with her prominent husband, the term *worldly* was often used concerning her. There must have been great loneliness in the preacher's life, for his wife did not enter into his commitment to the gospel. However, his own words, "I have had a cross to bear in my life, and it has made me the man I am," give evidence of inner discipline and sensitivity. The opportunity to demonstrate the ideal Christian home is open to the pastor who is blessed with an understanding wife and family.

Religious leaders always face the possibility of moral breakdowns (alleged or actual) within their lives. We have the opportunity to be sensitive to conscience and its demands. Henry Ward Beecher (1813-1887) at the height of his ministry in Brooklyn was charged with indiscretions which led to criminal charges. But he weathered the storm and continued his public work. For many years there was a question concerning his innocence; there was a shadow cast over his character because of his alleged unethical behavior. In this realm the minister has the opportunity to live a clean life, free from all appearance of contamination. Mark the perfect man. Because of the special vocation to which he is called, the servant of God does well to withstand in the evil hour.

> In the hour of trial, Jesus, plead for me,
> Lest by base denial I depart from Thee;
> When Thou seest me waver, with a look recall,
> Not for fear or favor suffer me to fall.
>
> With its witching pleasures would this vain world charm,
> Or its sordid treasures spread to work me harm,
> Bring to my remembrance sad Gethsemane,
> Or, in darker semblance, cross-crowned Calvary.
>
> If with sore affliction Thou in love chastise,
> Pour Thy benediction on the sacrifice;
> Then, upon Thine altar, freely offered up,
> Though the flesh may falter, faith shall drink the cup.
>
> (James Montgomery, 1771-1854)

The ministry is not exempt from the lure of and lust for power. Power politics creeps into the church and Christian circles. Bruised and broken lives result from the acts of those who ride roughshod to have their will at the expense of others. Doors of service have been closed and sensitive persons and families wounded. In some instances a life and a ministry have been cut off.

Among the minister's greatest opportunities is the practice of what he preaches. Note the example of which Chaucer wrote:

For Christes lore and his apostles twelve
He taught, but first he followed it himself.

This touches a tender spot in the life of any minister. We who speak and preach to others—what about our own life with the application of the same truth? Two brothers—one a doctor, the other a minister—lived in Glasgow. Being unmarried they had a housekeeper who answered the telephone. On receiving a call for Dr. _____, she had to inquire, "Do you mean the one who practices or the one who preaches?" The point is self-evident!

One thing is clear—no man in the sacred calling should engage in that vocation casually or lightly. We know that the searchlight of truth beats upon our conduct and reveals our character each time we stand to minister. Part of our modern world's criticism of the ministry lies here. The questions are asked: Is the man in that office a hypocrite? Is he in it for what he can get out of it? Or is he a man engaged in his task solely because he believes he has received a sacred call which he cannot decline? Our Lord spoke the final word on this matter when He said: "I am the good shepherd: the good shepherd giveth his life for the sheep. But he that is an hireling, and not the shepherd, whose own the sheep are not, seeth the wolf coming, and leaveth the sheep, and fleeth: and the wolf catcheth them, and scattereth the sheep. The hireling fleeth because he is an hireling and careth not for the sheep . . ." (John 10:11-13). How compelling are these words! The undershepherd must be concerned to pattern himself after the Good Shepherd and to avoid the dread alternative of becoming as the hireling.

The man who enters the ministry must see himself in the light of the Good Shepherd. Why do we engage in the ministry? Is it simply to meet human needs and help people as best we with our humanitarian ideals can? Were we given tests and examinations to find out if we measure up psychologically and emotionally to deal with the major problems of human society? Recent years have witnessed changing ideas concerning the ministry and its servants. The peril of professional status has permeated the life and work of the church. If professionalism in the ministry denoted simply a training of God-given abilities for the task at hand, it might have some place. But if professionalism has come to denote a select group who have been endorsed and granted credentials by a religious body so that others who might not have passed through a particular preparation are then debarred from engaging in a ministry which they may claim to be valid "under God," then we must deal with the question of the *call* to the ministry. After all, there is a call.

That that call comes in various ways becomes evident as we reflect upon the experience and the history of the people of God. The Bible is replete with "case histories" wherein we discern the nature of the call of God and the surrounding circumstances. God called Noah to action to demonstrate faith by obedience. Samuel was called when a child in the midst of training for religious service. Elisha was called from the plow as David was called from the life of the shepherd. Hosea was called amid the trials of a broken marriage; by suffering in matters of love he learned something of the love of God which never lets the sinner go. Amos was called from the rigors of being a herdsman to proclaim divine righteousness to a decadent society. Jeremiah was called with the knowledge that God had already planned for his prophetic ministry while he was still in his mother's womb. Isaiah, probably a temple priest, was called to prophetic ministry in a day of national disaster; the call came while he was engaged in public worship. It is written that our Lord after a night of prayer chose and called twelve disciples to be with Him; later He sent them forth as apostles. During their three years with Him He taught them, and they heard His words and witnessed His deeds. This group included Matthew, who was called from his position as tax-collector for the state in order that he might engage in a systematic proclamation of our Lord's deeds and words. Luke was called from his rich background in medicine to record what Jesus both began and continued to do and to teach. Apollos was presumably called from the University of Alexandria to become an expositor of truth who spoke with passion and accuracy. Paul, the one-time enemy of the Christian and the

Christ, was called to be the missionary-evangelist to the Roman
world and the author of books whose heights beckon us.

Paul has elucidated the reasons why men of God obey their
call and in their ministries emulate the Good Shepherd instead
of the hireling: "Just as we have been approved by God to be entrusted with the gospel, so we speak, not to please men, but to
please God who tests our hearts. For we never used either words
of flattery, as you know, or a cloak for greed, as God is witness;
nor did we seek glory from men, whether from you or from others, though we might have made demands as apostles of Christ"
(I Thess. 2:4-6, RSV).

One of the leading figures in the German Evangelical Church,
Heinrich Vogel, has served both as pastor and as professor in
Berlin. Seeking to help younger men find a solution to their per-
plexities about the call of God and their vocation amid the ruins
of their national structure, he shared in 1962 his firsthand experience of trials and testings. The words *reconstruction* and
reinterpretation occur frequently in his advice, taking us back to
the Scriptures for the answer. Vocation is determined by God's
plan for each individual. This is an intensely personal and private matter. It is up to the individual to face up to the call in all
its seriousness. God's call to His service is so hidden within each
man's personal relationship to Him that it would be presumptuous to intrude upon it and especially to try to define it in
specific psychological terms. In short, by overcoming man by
grace, God makes him willing to serve.

11

The Discipline of Writing

"My tongue is the pen of a ready writer." (PS. 45:1)

"Take a large tablet and write upon it in common characters." (ISA. 8:1, RSV)

"What I have written I have written." (JOHN 19:22)

"These are written, that ye might believe." (JOHN 20:31)

"For whatsoever things were written aforetime were written for our learning, that we through patience and comfort of the scriptures might have hope." (ROM. 15:4)

"I write unto you, little children. . . .
I write unto you, fathers. . . .
I have written unto you, young men. . . ." (I JOHN 2:12-14)

"When you come, bring the cloak . . . also the books, and above all the parchments." (II Tim. 4:13)

THE SCRIPTURES, the treasury of truth, did not come to us by accident. In God's providence selected persons became the transmitters of words through the medium of scrolls and parchments. Scribes assisted in preserving the divine revelation. Across the centuries certain messages were given oral transmission and later written down in the Book of the Law. The Writings and the Prophets, the Gospels, the Acts of the Apostles, the Letters to the Churches, and the Book of Revelation were added to complete the drama of redemption. Divine revelation was transmitted through selected individuals who were inspired by the Holy Spirit to record in writing the sacred message of grace. Thus God's revelation became fixed in literature. The same Spirit gives illumination of that revelation to the Christian and the church. Writing, then, is a crucial element in the annals of faith.

Some members of the Christian church see the ministry as confined to the pastoral office and forget its many-sided nature. The pastoral function is only one aspect within the total work of the body of Christ. All the members of the universal church are directed by the Head. Under His guidance the various ministries (which are His gifts) are exercised. By worship and witness the spiritual, social, political, and physical needs of people are touched. As undershepherd of the flock the pastor-teacher has his special call and work. One of the needs of this generation is Christians who will write and publish the fruits of their reflection and study. Included among this new corps of writers should be members of the pastoral calling.

Theological writing requires a knowledge of the history of doctrine as well as an awareness of the church's interpretation of the biblical truths preserved for our learning and instruction. Spiritual insight and scriptural knowledge are required in order to express in prose and poetry that which might prove of worth for others to grow in grace. Our generation lacks biblical literacy. There is a void awaiting penetration by Christian writers who are prepared to spend the time and exercise the discipline necessary. The legacy of the past and the heritage of the church are with us, but still we require complementary writings of the present if our destiny is to be assured. As I reflect upon the writing I have done as a pastor, certain principles I have learned by experience stand out, principles which may be of value to someone who intends to express his convictions in writing.

The pastor who writes as an adjunct to his preaching ministry engages in an arduous task. Much of his writing must be done as a labor of love. After spending hours in preparation for preaching and teaching, the mind is often too exhausted to pursue writing.

Among the requisites of writing is a moment of inspiration, but even more there is need for concentration of purpose. Persistence at the desk is most vital. Whenever the subject is involved, there may be the requirement of outside reading and research. He is blessed who has hundreds of books to which he may readily turn for reference. A writer must accept the fact that he may sit at his desk for many hours at one stretch and produce very little.

D. Elton Trueblood, now of Earlham College (Richmond, Indiana), knows the discipline of writing. A Quaker in the spirit of William Penn, Robert Barclay, and Rufus Jones, he has produced over thirty books through day-by-day persistence in writing. In his autobiography, *While It Is Day* (New York: Harper and Row, 1974), he shares his method:

> In my case all is done in longhand with a fountain pen, with ink that flows effortlessly. By this method I avoid the mechanics of the typewriter, and the speed of the pen seems to match the speed of my mind. Writing all morning in this fashion, I can without strain produce two thousand five hundred words. Because unbroken speed helps to create smoothness of style, I make only a minimum of corrections as I produce the first draft. Later, of course, especially after the chapters are typed, I substitute, delete, and add to my heart's content. But it is the original writing which is both exhilarating and energy- consuming.

Albert Barnes (1798-1870), pastor of the First Presbyterian Church in Philadelphia, for thirty-five years was able to work at an incredible pace. In addition to fulfilling the demands of a long pastorate, he published essays, sermons, notes for Bible study, and then a Bible commentary of twenty-seven volumes. His expositions served to clarify difficult doctrines. How was this work accomplished? Barnes said all his writing was done before nine o'clock in the morning. Rising regularly between four and five o'clock he would spend several hours in writing. In this way he did not neglect his large congregation and pastoral responsibilities.

Winston Churchill led a full and arduous life. He was the leading statesman of Britain during an intense period of history. His influence is known through his leadership during two world wars. Yet he found time to write. It took great perseverance to produce a two-volume biography of his father, Lord Randolph Churchill; a four-volume biography of an ancestor, the Duke of Marlborough; a four-volume *History of the English-Speaking Peoples*; and the monumental six-volume history of *The Second World War*. How was this accomplished? He would sit down at his desk and begin to "doodle" on a piece of paper. Eventually words would begin to flow. What he wrote he polished later. He himself said that inspiration is nine-tenth's perspiration.

John A. Hutton said that he, too, would sit at his desk and write just anything until he felt the urge and impetus of ideas surging through his mind and emerging as words and sentences. When I asked him concerning the long, involved sentences (often running to one hundred words) in his editorials for the *British Weekly*, he smiled and said that if I found them difficult, I should be thankful he was able to interrupt himself and insert the periods where he did! Exuberant phrases were typical of his style, whether he was writing an editorial or a sermon. Hutton set a fine example of making full use of the limited "spare" time available.

François Fenelon (1651-1715), French mystic and teacher, in his *Christian Perfection* (Minneapolis: Bethany Fellowship, 1976) touches upon the theme that the devout life which aims at the heights of spiritual culture must use time well. No moment in time is useless. The important thing is to know what God wants us to do with it. One helpful suggestion is to live in a continual dependence on the Spirit of God. There will be time for the affairs of daily life, social contacts, business, and much beside, even recreation. Vigilance is required by the Christian so that his time is wisely used and invested to meet the demands of the kingdom of God.

To return to Winston Churchill, it has been said that his life was the story of "how an underesteemed boy of genius, of noble character, and daring spirit seized and created a hundred opportunities to rise in the world and add glory by his own merit and audacity to a name already famous." When Churchill was a boy, his father was too busy with politics to give him the attention he needed. The young lad had to struggle on his own (with occasional encouragement from his mother), only to find that in preparatory school he was near the bottom of the class. His work in English was so poor that he was placed in a special course to do it over again. In his reminiscences he notes that in spite of this early failure he did learn to write an English sentence and eventually became proficient in English composition. While judgment differs as to how much Churchill learned at school (he attended several), he himself disclosed that his boyhood education along with his reading habits in India as a young officer in the British Army developed his writing skills.

In 1949 Churchill was honored for the first two volumes of his war memoirs. In accepting a gold medal and a monetary award from the *London Times* he delighted an audience of admirers with a series of observations on the burdens and rewards of authorship and on the use of the English language. His formula for effective writing and speaking was *rational simplicity*. His thoughts on the subject are worth passing on:

> Writing a book is an adventure. To begin with, it is a joy and an amusement. Then it becomes a mistress. And then it becomes a master. Then it becomes a tyrant and in the last phase, when you are reconciled to your servitude, you kill the monster. . . .
>
> Broadly speaking the short words are the best and the old words the best of all. It is by being lovers of the English language in all its strength and purity that we shall not only improve and preserve our literature but make ourselves more effective members of the great English-speaking world. . . .
>
> We must preserve our language and see that it is not unduly damaged by modern slang and adoption.

Churchill urged everyone to read the great books, recommending that they be enjoyed in one's years of maturity rather than in youth.

As we scan the many titles on our bookshelves, there are moments when we are not sure where to begin. We are faced with the weekly stint of study, sermon preparation, Bible classes, and perhaps an occasional publication as that wider ministry opens for us. We cannot wait for inspiration or some afflatus to come like a wind to blow away the cobwebs of dullness and move us to begin. We may find that the discipline of appointed hours and a schedule will bring its own reward. Diligence and not genius explains the secret of those who have accomplished much. It is not good fortune, but regular concentration at a predetermined hour and a weekly output.

There is the temptation to excuse self in the belief that others have an innate superiority or a greater capacity to achieve what is termed "success." But there is ample and undeniable evidence that only unceasing labor and plodding can bring a measure of fruitful result. Isaac Newton confessed that it was only a habit of patient thinking which distinguished him from other men.

James Boswell once asked Samuel Johnson whether one should

wait for the favorable moment before beginning to write. "No, sir," said Johnson, "he should sit down doggedly." And that is how all the best work has been and always will be done. There are no short cuts.

There is no easy way to write. Some authors appear to have a facility which does not require labor and toil. But these are the exceptions, even among those who have made writing their profession and attained eminence. Because the minister's priority is the service of the church, writing can be only his avocation, something beyond his basic calling. The minister has sufficient to keep him busy full time. He writes not for "livery" but for "love," as a Puritan expressed his idea of service. Although there is nothing wrong in the financial benefits gained from the pen, the minister's main thrust should be a desire to express his beliefs and share his convictions in a wider ministry than the spoken word. At the same time there is a self-discipline in just putting one's thoughts down on paper and tucking the sheets away in a drawer without thought of publication. The writing is the discipline.

John Buchan described the writer's mind as being ready to explode with ideas and freshly minted words. Something of that spirit is a must. Buchan said: "The truth is that any man, whose business it is to portray life in action and who is caught up in the white heat of his task, is certain at times to take the first phrase that comes into his head, and jar the ear and the taste of the fastidious reader."

The theologian John Oman counseled: "No aim should be so central in writing as exactness. Yet this requires discrimination of the kind of exactness to be desired."

When John Wesley was engaged in the work of the Evangelical Revival in England during the eighteenth century, he found himself compelled to intervene in the public discussion which the movement inspired. Certain topics required his attention. In defending his position, he wrote *A Further Appeal to Men of Reason and Religion*. About the subjects calling for explanation he wrote: "These partly relate to the *doctrines* I teach, partly to the *manner* of teaching them, and partly to the *effects* which are supposed to follow from teaching these doctrines in this manner." Thus he began to produce apologetic literature.

Wesley was a prolific though reluctant author. He harbored no literary ambitions. Other activities had a prior claim on his time and strength. His journal, letters, notes, and published sermons were written at intervals stolen from his primary task of evangelism. His early training and education at Oxford helped him develop clear thinking and a lucid style. He was widely read; but writing extemporaneously as he crisscrossed England on horseback or by coach, he did not have access to libraries. The extreme busyness of Wesley's life is implied in Samuel Johnson's criticism that the evangelist was in such a hurry to move on to witness to others that he had not time for social visits.

Just as Wesley's writing bore the marks of his God-filled life and work, so every writer is stamped in some particular way. There is a distillation of the spirit of the writer. There is an emphasis on what is uppermost in his life and mind. This is especially characteristic of contemporary novelists, who in recent years have become obsessed with the dark side of human nature and have graphically portrayed wills enslaved to evil pursuits. Christian writers have here an opportunity to interpret evil in the light of the Scriptures. They can diagnose the problems of the modern world and at the same time point to the remedy in the Evangel.

The minister is a sinful man ever needing the grace of God. Is that why Alexander Whyte was moved to preach and write that he himself knew the depths of sin and had personal consciousness of the need of divine mercy? He was criticized for what was deemed an overemphasis upon the darkness of sin. He wrote incessantly that he kept company with the greatest sinner in the city of Edinburgh—Alexander Whyte. His many books emphasized that the personification of many sins described and denounced in the Bible could be seen walking the streets of contemporary Edinburgh. This characteristic of Whyte's spirit and style of writing came from a disciplined mind.

W. Robertson Nicoll, who knew Whyte intimately and wrote about him in *Princes of the Church* (1923), relates a personal anecdote still worth pondering. One day when Whyte was walking in The Highlands of Scotland, he received a message from God that urged him to go on in his evangelical strain:

Go on and flinch not! Go back and boldly finish the work that
has been given you to do. Speak out and fear not. Make them,
at any cost, to see themselves in God's holy law as in a glass.
Do you that, for no one else will do it. No one else will so risk
his life and his reputation as to do it. *And you have not much
of either left to risk. . . .*

This episode did not occur at the close of his ministry but at the
beginning, shortly after he was touched by the spirit of the revival which moved the northeast of Scotland in his youthful years.
Alexander Whyte's stress on the fact of sin is so overwhelming
that after fifty years his writings still touch the conscience. We
see in them reflections of persons of our own day and generation.

Every author's writing is colored by his background. John H.
Jowett both in his preaching and in his books constantly emphasized grace. Running through his writings is that note of
comfort and strength. It is like the red strand at the center of the
rope used by the British Navy. Cut through the rope at any point
and there is the red string to identify the ownership. Take the
writings of Jowett and at the center you will find the red symbol
of blood, the sacrifice of God in Christ which speaks of "grace
upon grace."

Another influence on the writer is the context in which he lives
and serves. If a writer is a confessed follower of Jesus Christ as
Savior and Lord, he gathers with those who remember Him in
regular services of worship. Worship is the highest act of man as
he bows in awe and reverence before that blazing throne of light
ineffable. The hours of worship and devotion shape and mold
the minds of writers whose supreme aim is "to glorify God and
to enjoy him for ever."

When Arturo Toscanini, the eminent symphony conductor, re-
hearsed, he steeped himself in the music. If workmen happened
to enter the auditorium to adjust some fixtures, he would stop
them and rebuke them for lack of respect. Once he knocked off
the hat of the foreman and said: "Ignorante! Take off the hat;
this is a church! Where there is music there is a church!" Whoever develops similar respect for the glorious hour of worship before God will discover a rich source of inspiration for writing.

Hebrews 12:18-29 has a sweep and an ascendancy of purpose

which sometimes are overlooked when a congregation gathers to worship. There are those who speak merely of the number counted in the sanctuary. God's arithmetic is different from that of man. When we gather to worship God in Christ by the Holy Spirit, then the living Lord of glory is present in the midst of His people. He is the Head of the church, His body, and brings with Him the entire church of all the ages. Where Christ is present, *there* is the church; and when we gather, the whole church is present in and with Him. Who can estimate the number of the worshiping throng? How thrilling and revolutionary to our thought to be caught up with this concept of worship. Read afresh the text.

Critics have suggested there should be less preaching in the hour of worship. Evidently they do not understand the true nature of preaching and its significance as an act of worship. Daniel Jenkins in his book *The Nature of Catholicity* has said:

> Preaching is to be taken seriously as proclamation of the living Word of the regnant Christ. . . . In its essence it is nothing less than an eschatological event, an act in which, for a moment, the kingly rule of Christ stands revealed among men, and He is shown forth before them as indeed *Christus Victor*. It is an act whereby we see, as in a mystery, Satan falling like lightning from heaven and the Son of Man crowned with glory and honour. . . . Something happens in Church proclamation. It is not merely a meditation or a commentary upon the sacred history, but a continuation of the sacred history, a further step in the reduction of the strongholds wherein "every high thing exalted against the knowledge of God entrenches itself." . . . It is altogether proper to speak of the pulpit as the throne of the Word of God and of the sermon as the "Monstrance of the Evangel."

The showing forth, the proclamation, the unveiling of the gospel was effective, according to the apostle Paul, when the "treasure [was seen] in earthen vessels, that the excellency of the power may be of God, and not of us" (II Cor. 4:7).

This quality of preaching is not reached by all. Those who minister weekly and steadfastly across the years do so in the consciousness of a call to so minister. Unsung and unpublicized pastors are to be found in all lands and in a great diversity of ministries. Those who place the preparation and preaching of the sermon as their main priority have the satisfaction of knowing they are carrying out the command and commission of their Lord. Yet some of the finest preaching is done by those who have commitments in business, education, and other walks of life.

Writing is a task which never ends. Day by day and week by week there is a learning process which never ceases. In *The Degrees of Knowledge* (New York: Charles Scribner's Sons, 1959), Jacques Maritain interprets the medieval classic *St. John of the Cross.* He defines with clarity and exactness the difference between the poetical language of the mystic and the scientific language of the theologian. We cannot confuse these in our writing.

Working with the Bible offers rewards to the diligent reader, day after day. We begin to discern the various genres in what is a library of literature in diverse forms. Used as a tool of learning (apart from its devotional and spiritual purpose), the Bible is a rich source of information for the aspiring writer.

There is *narrative* in the Bible. Consider the stories of the creation and the flood; the stories of Abraham, Jacob, Joseph, Moses and the burning bush, the Passover, and the giving of the law. After the heroic adventures of Joshua and Samson we come to the idyllic tale of Ruth and Naomi, the call of Samuel, the downfall of Saul and the rise of David, followed by the story of Solomon. The books of Kings, Nehemiah, Daniel, and Jonah lead on to the stories of our Lord's birth, temptation, teaching, trial, death, resurrection, walk to Emmaus, and ascension. What drama there is in Saul's conversion. The Gospels and Acts are descriptive prose at its finest.

If *poetry* is what we seek, recall Deborah's song in Judges, David's lament over Saul, and David's psalm of thanksgiving (II Sam. 22). There are majestic poetry and music in Isaiah's messianic prophecies: "Unto us a child is born . . ." (9:6); "a little child shall lead them" (11:6); "comfort ye, my people . . ." (40:1); the "Man of Sorrows" (ch. 53). For more poetry turn to selections from the Hebrew hymnbook of the Psalms or to the vision of the valley of dry bones (Ezek. 37). On to the New Testament for Mary's *Magnificat* (Luke 1:46-55) and Simeon's *Nunc Dimittis* (Luke 2:29-32). We are thrilled by Paul's poems on love (I Cor. 13) and on love without dissimulation (Rom. 12). The

Book of Revelation offers visions of the Christ and then the new heaven and new earth.

In the area of *letters*, consider the epistles which Paul wrote both to whole congregations and to individuals. Or think of the letters of Peter and John. They brought cheer and hope to people in despair or under persecution.

For *maxims, proverbs,* and *wise sayings,* look to Proverbs, Ecclesiastes, and the sayings of Christ.

What about *drama* and *dialogue?* What could be better than the Book of Job with its account of the challenges of Satan, the discussions Job had with his friends and comforters, and God's divine intervention to clarify the drama of suffering?

The art and discipline of writing can be aided as we study, read aloud, or recite from memory the majestic language of the classic of our Christian faith. Apart from moral and spiritual value, much of the Bible is worth our attention simply for its structure and the design of its writing.

When we do not read beyond our immediate duty, that is, the pressure of the demands of one sermon each week (as seems the norm for many), we may slip back in what we aspire to be and do. Is the minister growing or stagnating? One indicator might be the titles on his bookshelf.

"Peter Parson" of the *British Weekly* said that "the minister is not a special kind of Christian, but every Christian is a special kind of minister." The pastor has a special ministry whereas all the members of the body of Christ also have their ministries. The ideal is that the servant of God who is set apart to be pastor-teacher should equip all in the congregation to fulfill their role as *ministers* of God.

To find time to write demands discipline on the part of the busy person. However, it can be done by setting apart a special weeknight (for the one whose secular toil demands the daytime) or certain designated hours each week. The pastor who is given the weekday mornings for the purpose of study and preparation has a rare opportunity to use paper and pen every day. Samuel M. Zwemer, John R. Mott, and Robert E. Speer were world travelers in the interests of the missionary movement. They were constantly giving addresses and sermons as well as lectures. Yet they also wrote constantly, even when in travel. Each produced some fifty volumes. Annually they tried to meet to compare notes on what they had read during the past year. How exciting that must have been!

We learn to write by reading. Reading the works of others will stimulate and encourage a would-be writer. A few might find a mood of discouragement sweeping over their spirit when they read and hear of those whose writings are published. Perhaps the minister needs to write just to express his thoughts and ideas. Initially he has no intention of putting them into print for others to read. Our desks should have a drawer into which we put those effusions of mind and thought. There they can rest a while as in a depository for safekeeping. Periodically we can take them out. Rereading them will furnish a measuring rod by which we can judge whether we have slipped back or have advanced in skill and maturity. This may be the spur to try again and go further. There are those who have found assistance by enrolling in a writer's conference and workshop. Here at Warner Pacific College in Portland, Oregon, we have hundreds coming annually to seek help.

In his discussion "What a Book Is" (from *Sesame and Lilies* [Reading, MA: Allen & Unwin, 1919]) John Ruskin said:

> It is essentially not a talking thing, but a written thing; and written, not with a view of mere communication, but of permanence. . . . The author has something to say which he perceives to be true and useful, or helpfully beautiful. So far as he knows, no one has yet said it; so far as he knows, no one else can say it. He is bound to say it, clearly and melodiously if he may; clearly at all events. In the sum of his life he finds this to be the thing, manifest to him. He would fain set it down for ever; engrave it on rock, if he could; saying, "This is the best of me; for the rest I ate, and drank, and slept, lived. This I saw and knew; this, if anything of mine, is worth your memory."
> That is his "writing"; it, in his small human way, and with whatever degree of true inspiration is in him, is his inscription, or scripture. That is a *"Book."*

We can never tell when a new book is to be written. The diarists of earlier centuries kept their day-to-day accounts of the trivial and historical events around them, but little did they anticipate that people in the twentieth century would read them! We might mention, for example, Samuel Pepys or John Evelyn.

As sailors keep their ship's log, so poets and writers and ministers as well as businessmen and government servants have found some time each day to record their reactions and understanding of what took place around them. Our day is also filled with events. We who are the heirs of the past find we are not looking upon life from a balcony; we are on the roadway of experience and we are involved in the history of our times. Opportunities are all about us to write concerning life, nature, family, country. In fact we can write about any avenue that leads us to pluck a few flowers here or there. When Matthew the tax-gatherer left all to follow Christ, he evidently took his skill in writing with him. How grateful we are! Let us rise up and write.

12

The Minting of Words

"A word fitly spoken is like apples of gold in a setting of silver." (PROV. 25:11, RSV)

"The Lord God hath given me the tongue of the learned, that I should know how to speak a word in season to him that is weary." (ISA. 50:4)

"Let the words of my mouth, and the meditation of my heart, be acceptable in thy sight, O Lord, my strength, and my redeemer." (PS. 19:14)

"The words that I speak unto you, they are spirit, and they are life." (JOHN 6:63)

"Take with you words. . . ." (HOS. 14:2)

IF WORDS ARE to be on target, the minister must become sensitive to language, grammar, style, vocabulary, spelling, and correct application. This can be of both personal and practical benefit. A dictionary and thesaurus should be at hand each time he writes. A choice of dictionaries must be made. Perhaps *Webster's* is all that is necessary for desk use; if it becomes a daily companion, there will be growth and progress in the knowledge of words and their meanings. For others the *Oxford English Dictionary* will be the selection. In this large and exhaustive dictionary of thirteen volumes, words are traced from their roots through successive ages to our modern era. The two-volume shorter edition also has much to commend it. *Roget's Thesaurus* has long been in use. R. I. Rodale's *The Synonym Finder* (Emmaus, PA: Rodale Press, 1961) has come to be a worthy competitor.

The helps provided for our learning are legion. The minister who seeks will find assistance in a diversity of books: the golden words of Jeremy Taylor, Archbishop Trench's *On the Study of*

Words (Philadelphia: Richard West, 1878), Shakespeare, John
Bunyan, William Hazlitt's essays, and H. W. Fowler's *Dictionary of Modern English Usage* (New York: Oxford University
Press, 1965).

Modern language is part of our culture and here we need to be
alert to what is good and what is bad. Radio and television,
novels and magazines, provide a brainwashing for millions who
are prone to accept and copy thought forms and modes of
speech now current. There is a tendency on the part of the
preacher to absorb this and find himself lowering the standard
of speech. The pulpit has always been a guide and high standard
in word and speech and must so continue. But there are dangers
to be faced.

The apostle James speaks to the subject of words. "If any man
among you seem to be religious, and bridleth not his tongue, but
deceiveth his own heart, this man's religion is vain" (1:26). "If
any man offend not in word, the same is a perfect man, and able
also to bridle the whole body" (3:2). "Out of the same mouth
proceedeth blessing and cursing. My brethren, these things ought
not so to be" (3:10).

Slang and current idiomatic speech lead to the obscene and
the profane. The Third Commandment says: "Thou shalt not
take the name of the Lord thy God in vain; for the Lord will not
hold him guiltless that taketh his name in vain" (Exod. 20:7).
Our Lord endorsed the law and in the Sermon on the Mount
said many things to remind us of the sacredness of work and
word.

We assume that the preacher will not use curse words or
words tending to be suggestive, obscene, or profane. Yet there
are those who advocate we try to reach the non-Christian by using the language of the gutter. Time will tell whether this new
form of outreach will achieve results. Conversion and rebirth in
a new creation tend to purify the speech as well as the thinking
of the convert who grows in grace and in knowledge.

The chief danger to the minister lies in use of slang or careless
and casual speech. Professing Christians are not free from some
of the following: "goodness gracious," "gee," "for heaven sake,"
"darn it," "gosh," "golly," and so on. Dictionaries indicate that
such expressions, which involve the prostitution of good and

pure words either by ignorance or by carelessness, are substandard. When there are thousands of words to choose from, the minister must maintain a standard of excellence. The Word is conveyed by the words he uses. The classics of prose and poetry exhibit an economy of style and use of simple Anglo-Saxon words.

Our speech and our written words should follow the counsel of Paul, "Let your speech [words] be always with grace, seasoned with salt . . ." (Col. 4:6). Paul was himself brought to judgment in Corinth over a matter of words (Acts 18:12-15). He was accused of acting contrary to the law when he persuaded people to worship God! Gallio dismissed the charges with the comment that it seemed to him to be "a question of *words* and names" and he would not become involved in such controversy!

In today's current speech and in preaching and teaching, there are similar problems and questions. The words we use have come to us from previous centuries and from contexts foreign to most of our contemporary life and culture. How then does the servant of God mint and send forth new words to convey the eternal meaning? That is his task and he must work at it without fail.

Fortunately we have many helps at our side to assist us in our ministry of proclamation. We have the ancient words of the Bible with their theological uses. Among the more familiar are: Redeemer, Savior, salvation, substitution, satisfaction, ransom, love, grace, eternal life. What they mean to us is dependent on our knowledge of the Scriptures and our Christian experience with our Lord and Master. Is it possible to convey to our age the background and meaning of these words? Why not try to write out what we believe each means and then remint them for others who may be unaware of their signification?

"Redeemer" suggests someone paying a price in order to buy back something which has been lost or is under another's control. The idea is that the divine Redeemer entered the marketplace of our world and found people lost and under sin's control. He gave Himself in death to pay the price of removing us from sin's control, thus making us His own.

"Savior" suggests seeking out and rescuing something which is lost or in great danger. A drowning person is saved by a lifeguard. Another engulfed in a house on fire is saved by the action of a fireman. Hundreds in ill health are rescued from death by the judgment and action of a doctor. No one objects to the statement: "I was saved from death by that doctor." Then why do we hesitate to speak of the Lord who saved us from sin and spiritual death?

"Salvation" is the general term for the total work of God in seeking those of His creation who are lost and away from Him. He would reconcile them to Himself and give them peace. Note that it is not the lost one, but God Himself, who takes the initiative.

"Substitution" means taking the place of another. Modern life is shot through with this idea. One person assumes responsibility for another. This may involve payment of a debt or standing in for a friend unable to work. An athlete takes the place of another who is injured in a game. In like manner God through Christ has taken the sinner's place. By dying on man's behalf God has become the substitute.

In medieval times, when two individuals had a difference or a quarrel, the offended party would seek "satisfaction" from the other. This could involve either a challenge to a duel or a demand for an apology. Thus satisfaction came to the honor impugned. Man rebelled against God and insulted Him by rejecting His love. But God has gone beyond any act of man. He satisfied His honor and reconciled the offender to Himself by the death and resurrection of Jesus Christ, His Son. Justice in a moral universe is satisfied and the offender is now acceptable in God's sight.

In considering the word *ransom*, recall that in New Testament times the Romans enslaved conquered people. These slaves had no free life and were at the disposal of their master. But as slaves they could be bought and sold in the marketplace. A price (ransom) could be paid for the slave. The new master could set free the slave. God in like manner entered the marketplace, where He paid in Christ the price to set free enslaved man. Not with earthly money, but with His own lifeblood! Given the large number of hijackings and kidnapings with demands for money to free the captives, moderns should have little difficulty in understanding the word *ransom*.

"Love" is a word which encompasses many types of human relations. We need to distinguish the several kinds: (1) erotic and romantic love; (2) benevolent love, which involves liking something or someone; and (3) the love of devotion which never changes because it is based upon principle. This last type of love suggests sacrifice even unto death, and God's divine love. "God so loved the world, that he gave his only begotten Son . . ." (John 3:16). Such love is expressed in giving, giving in sacrifice. This sacrifice can lead to death, even the death of the cross.

"Grace" is a beautiful word. It suggests God's outreach toward the unlovely and ungracious, even an enemy and rebel. Grace is greater than sin, just as beauty is more wonderful than the ugly or the distorted. Grace is allied to truth and these together express the divine reality. Grace mellows truth and truth strengthens grace. This is of the essence of the nature and perfect balance of the person of Jesus Christ. Grace is like the tide coming in; though wave after wave has arrived, there are unlimited waves still coming. Grace has no limits, and no barriers stop its flow.

"Eternal life" tells of a quality of life which complements our biological life. Everyone born into the world has biological life—"that which is born of the flesh is flesh." But "that which is born of the Spirit is spirit" (John 3:6). This is spiritual birth, new birth, second birth, birth from above. One who is a disciple of Christ and is given this new life is different from those who do not have eternal life. The natural man cannot understand the things of the Spirit. The spiritual man understands because the Holy Spirit has brought the indwelling Christ to him. Though death comes, the Christian life continues. There is an eternal leaving behind of the natural and the biological.

These few words are examples taken at random. They demonstrate how we can remint words for contemporary understanding. By delving into the historical meaning of Hebrew and Greek words, we can enrich our understanding of their English equivalents.

In *The Word and the Words* (Nashville: Abingdon, 1975) Colin Morris, a Methodist minister from London, elaborates the thesis that God has been pleased to give the title of *The Word (Logos)* to our Lord Jesus Christ. He is the Word of God and we are the agents of communicating that Word. We do this by *words.* Our age is captivated with ideas and agencies of communication. But just to communicate better might not be enough to solve our difficulties. How easy it is to be misunderstood and for others to misunderstand us! Native ability to speak is a good thing, but we must also study the art of communication by words. The hearers may not be in a receptive mood or we not in the best frame of mind and spirit when we try to speak the words of life.

More is involved than just using words. Until the Spirit of God touches the hearer (he requires that lightning touch), he cannot begin to see or to know what is the saving Word. Our words and what we do are not sufficient. We may prepare well, but until the divine Word in sovereign grace imparts His wisdom through our spoken word we are limited in speech. The intangible and secret things belong to God alone; hence our commitment to the Word and our dedication of our words to His service. He takes the things of the Spirit and enlightens us as well as our hearers. The glory of the lighted mind is certain when the divine Word is working through the human word. The results rest with God and His sovereignty and grace.

Among the goals of the preacher who is concerned with words is a clear and gracious style. Without such a style we will fail instead of serving as channels of the Word. A man's language may be the final lens through which the light of the gospel is conveyed. T. S. Eliot spoke of "having had twenty years—trying to learn to use words." We cannot afford to neglect this demanding art.

One of the best aids toward achieving this goal is *Reader over Your Shoulder* by Robert Graves and Alan Hodge (New York: Macmillan, 1961). Principles concerned with clarity of statement and grace of expression are set forth. From this useful handbook we learn that accuracy is very important in citing facts and numbers. The reader must not be left guessing. The Scriptures are clear in this matter. For example, in the Book of Acts the numbers of converts are precisely recorded. Our writing and speech should avoid exaggeration when we report attendances or converts from crusades! We must beware of generalizations.

It is often helpful to present truth in figurative or *pictorial* language. Our Lord's example in this is obvious. His parables are verbal pictures of deeper truths. Even in His sober warnings there are elements which we can see as well as hear. It is vital that the connections between words and sentences be clear. Good writing means clarity of meaning. Unfamiliar ideas and concepts need to be explained. Ideas set forth in theological and psychological jargon should be communicated instead in contemporary idiom and expressed simply. This is difficult for those who have come directly from college or seminary and whose speech is full of technical words and terms.

However, there are always some in church groups who do understand technical terms and language and would not object to a weighty discussion. Scripture has its own language which has come down to us through the centuries. Just as law, medicine, and music have special words understood by the initiated, so in the Christian church there are informed disciples who are able to understand and to share in the deeper values of biblical-theological study. However, as a general rule, it is sound counsel to remint words and ideas whenever we try to reach those who lack that background.

Another duty incumbent on the preacher and writer is a clear and interesting style. Only when there is understanding can the truths which are being expounded be applied to everyday life. Good writing should be seen as a moral matter. We will be judged by our words. Jesus said: "I say unto you, That every idle word that men shall speak, they shall give account thereof in the day of judgment. For by thy words thou shalt be justified, and by thy words thou shalt be condemned" (Matt. 12:36, 37).

In an article entitled "Theology and the English Language" *(The Christian Century*, July 17, 1974) Virginia Owens incisively punctures ministerial complacency and indolence in the use of *words.* More precision and clarity are needed in the writing of theology—along with a more careful examination of why and for whom it is being written. Books and articles on theology are written for the most part for theologians. If such works are to have any meaning for the layman, they must first be translated into understandable English. In rewriting something into simpler language we must, of course, be on guard against distorting the timeless truth. From George Orwell's *Politics and the English*

Language (1945) Owens borrows a method of criticism of the slovenly use of words. She also commends Orwell's basic rules for writers of English. Though Orwell is no spokesman for the church or Christianity, he does call for "theological responsibility" in guarding the powers of language.

Upon induction into office, the pastor-preacher is granted a hearing as one who is a minister of the Word of God. That Word is communicated by words. Our age is noted for its specialization; each area has its own vocabulary. There is an increasing difficulty for one person to be understood by another. How can the scientist be understood by the philosopher? the poet by the theologian? the historian by the politician?

Discussing the preacher's pitfalls, "Peter Parson" (W. B. J. Martin) has called attention to the danger of using worn-out words and of saying things so clumsily that no impression is made. Four vices of the pulpit are pomposity, woolliness, circumlocution, and wordiness. Time spent with dictionaries and thesauruses will repay dividends in speech and in writing. Any help we can find to enrich our vocabulary, grammar, mechanics, and style is worthwhile. To be saved from errors in word use is cause for thanksgiving. We should emulate the Puritans who preached in the *plain style.*

For those who deal in words, consulting the dictionary is mandatory. Our spelling and our punctuation require vigilance and attention every day. No one is without shortcomings; we must ever strive for excellence to be as correct as possible.

When Alexander Whyte went to Aberdeen University he was inadequately prepared; his schooling in the little town of Kirriemuir had been intermittent. He also confessed to having an atrocious memory. Nevertheless, although, as he related, "in God's providence I was born in a poor rank of life," he struggled on and persevered. His inability to remember fact and detail, which had troubled his childhood and caused his failure in the chemistry examination at King's College, remained a handicap throughout life. He used to complain that he had the worst memory in Edinburgh, and to tell his students and friends, "No one knows the labour that my memory has cost me!" He gave as his counsel, "Always read with your pencil in your hand." That he accomplished so much is a testament to his industry.

Another Scottish preacher, who later became the editor of the *British Weekly*, John A. Hutton, advised the student and pastor: "Never read without taking notes. All other reading is self-indulgence and an occasion for sleep." Such counsel is sound in that we err so easily in the way of casual and desultory reading.

Samuel Chadwick, Methodist preacher and principal of Cliff College in England, told of his discipline in an editorial in *Joyful News* entitled "The Words of My Mouth":

> The ear tries words, as the palate tastes meat. Ever since I began to study anything I have been a student of words. For many years I worked steadily through the dictionary word by word, page after page, and in this way I have gone through *Chamber's Dictionary* at least five times. The result is nothing to boast of, but it has given me an ear that tries words. The misuse of a word jars upon me, as a discord does in the ears of a musician. I ought to have been a better student of literature than I am, but I have studied the dictionary more than the classics, and even in the study of words I have not been so patient and exact as Newman or Jowett. [The biographer of John Henry Newman says that he would spend hours, and even days, searching for the correct word.]
>
> John Henry Jowett was the most skilled master of words I have known. Every utterance was prepared with the utmost care. On one occasion I spoke with him at a meeting in the Birmingham Town Hall. He only spoke seven minutes, but it was an epoch-making speech. At the close, three men waited upon him for a meeting in a neighboring town. They pleaded with him, and in the course of their persuasion they said that they were not asking for anything that would tax his strength—a speech of six or seven minutes such as he had given that night was all they asked. A curious look of pained amusement came over his face as he replied: "That is all you ask! You will probably not believe me, when I say that behind those seven minutes there were seventy hours of the hardest work I ever did." That is the price Dr. Jowett paid for the simplicity and perfection, charm and power, of his pellucid English.

We may say that "style is the man." When we have read widely in an author, we come to recognize him by his use of words. We get to know certain characteristics, his turn of a sentence or phrase. Once we become so well acquainted with an author that we recognize his style, we will receive an extra measure of insight and inspiration as we read.

Art—whether in words or music or on canvas—is an extremely effective avenue of communication. The author uses words, the musician sound, the artist paint to produce art. Art is the making public of something that is private. The message is the sole consideration until we come to take into account the delivery and how we communicate what we see or feel. Then we are dealing with both craft and art. The relation of form to content is one of the problems of every author and preacher. "An artist must be a craftsman, but a craftsman need not be an artist" (David Daiches). A writer is a craftsman rather than an artist if he first thinks of a subject and then puts it into clear expository prose. This is the basic approach of most preachers. But some rare persons have an extra quality, the artist's touch. Of course, God is the ultimate Artist, as we are reminded by Sir Thomas Browne (*Religio Medici* I.xvi): "Nature hath made one World, and Art another. In brief, all things are artificial, for Nature is the Art of God."

To aid us in preaching and teaching there is the contribution of the poets. Poetry is a means of grace. The rich legacy of centuries of poetry awaits the person who will but take the time to acquaint himself with it. One of the best ways to study words is to read aloud what the poets have expressed. Every culture has its own representatives. Hymns are written in poetical style and with the aid of music we can sing them aloud or even inwardly to ourselves. Individuals will have their own prejudices and preferences. Every pastor should add to his library volumes like the *Oxford Book of English Verse*. This anthology ranges from the thirteenth century onward. Browse at will and discover the variety of poems with their imagery and metaphor bringing to us thoughts sometimes forgotten. Rudyard Kipling's "Recessional" (1897) is dated, but in every year of national crisis or international anarchy its somber and warning notes are well worth rereading:

> God of our fathers, known of old—
> Lord of our far-flung battle-line—
> Beneath whose awful Hand we hold
> Dominion over palm and pine—

Lord God of Hosts, be with us yet,
Lest we forget, lest we forget!

The tumult and the shouting dies—
The captains and the kings depart—
Still stands Thine ancient sacrifice,
An humble and a contrite heart.
Lord God of Hosts, be with us yet,
Lest we forget, lest we forget!

Though written within the historical context of the British Empire, "Recessional" has something to say to the modern world. When nations and rulers forget God and become "drunk with sight of power" and put their trust in "reeking tube and iron shard," the faithful must pray, "Thy mercy on Thy people, Lord!"

Poets have often ministered to the preacher, reviving discouraged and despondent minds. Among the ministries of the poets has been vivid restatement of truth when more prosaic forms would sound mechanical. They reinterpret biblical and Christian teaching in art forms which penetrate many a mind which would be closed to more conventional presentations. From the poets the preacher learns anew the value of imagination and how to cultivate its strength and vitality. Some of our contemporary poets have sensed the dilemma of unbelief and man's restless, rootless life in the modern jungle. The demonic forces which erode the inner life of modern man have made the task of the preacher more difficult in this alienated and frustrated age. Here the poets come to our aid. They feed our minds, and we in turn can use their words to reach this lost generation.

Robert Browning has already been mentioned for his virile views of character and life. Alfred, Lord Tennyson, produced poetry whose message was well attuned to the Victorian age. We treasure Francis Thompson's "The Hound of Heaven," profound and direct in its insistence that the divine Spirit pursues and catches up with the one fleeing from God. Gilbert K. Chesterton found a unique place as an apologist of the spiritual life. John Masefield showed how God acts in dealing with the wayward and the brutish man who defies Him. "The Everlasting Mercy" bears witness to the transformation of one who has been reborn and finds a new world because he himself is changed. The pres-

ent poet laureate of Great Britain, John Betjeman, has insights
reflecting a Christian background. W. H. Auden in "The Age of
Anxiety" grapples with our generation of despair, while Robert
Bridges points to faith and hope and love in "The Testament of
Beauty." We are indebted to T. S. Eliot for his perceptive treat-
ment of the reality of sin in such works as "The Cocktail Party,"
"The Waste Land," and "Four Quartets."

A modern-day prodigal son, Edwin Muir returned to the
Christian faith of his Scottish boyhood. In poetry of high standard he shared his inner struggles and set forth the truths he believed. In his view the incarnation of God in Christ was fundamental. In Him there came together a "harmony of body and
soul, imagination and reason," indeed the true divine image and
likeness:

> How could our race betray
> The Image, and the Incarnate One unmake
> Who chose this form and fashion for our sake?

Other doctrines Muir dealt with include the creation and fall of
man, the transfiguration, and the second advent. In a period
when skeptics questioned many biblical truths, Edwin Muir patterned his life in the Christian way.

These, and many other English poets, have lifted the preacher
to a higher dimension, which is evident in the message he sends
forth. American poets have also made a rich contribution. Especially noteworthy is John Greenleaf Whittier (1807-1892), a New
England Quaker. With little formal education, he was stimulated by the poems of Robert Burns "to see through familiar
things, the romance underlying." Nature, history, and home inspired him. His poems "Immortal Love, Forever Full" and
"Dear Lord and Father of Mankind" have become standard
hymns. Lesser known poets are breaking through the outer wall
of indifference to speak the language of our contemporary life.
They are bringing fresh and exciting views of Christian truths.

It is obvious by now that we need not be restricted to a few
favorites. There is an embarrassment of riches; selections must
be made within the limits of time. A pastor with a regular study
schedule might well pursue a course in the poets in addition to
what is labeled "theology." Reading only theology and philosophy could tend to make a preacher heavy, even dull. Culti-

vating the muse of poetry will bring a lighter touch and lilt in the speech as well as fire the imagination. Although most pastors may not have the gift or ability to write poetry, they can appreciate and enjoy the poetry of others. Anthologies are legion and we should select with care. There is great wealth awaiting the preacher who keeps on reading poetry as a means of grace for his own spirit, for God also speaks in that music.

Alongside of the poets there are the hymn writers. Their contribution covers the history of the Christian church. When the Christian faith is to be expounded, the preacher stands to proclaim in words alone; but when the multitudes would express their trust in God, they join together in outburst of song, combining words and music. This is a foretaste of that universal choir foretold in the Book of Revelation. Music will be the one language of that eternal state!

Significantly, there are a number of preachers who are remembered for their hymns rather than for their sermons. A partial list would include: George Matheson ("O Love That Wilt Not Let Me Go"); Phillips Brooks ("O Little Town of Bethlehem"); Isaac Watts ("Joy to the World"); Henry Francis Lyte ("Abide with Me"); Franz Gruber ("Silent Night! Holy Night!"); Philip Doddridge ("O God of Bethel, by Whose Hand"); John Fawcett ("Blest Be the Tie That Binds"); John Newton ("Amazing Grace"); Horatius Bonar ("Here, O My Lord, I See Thee Face to Face"); Cleland Boyd McAfee ("There Is a Place of Quiet Rest"); Washington Gladden ("O Master, Let Me Walk with Thee"); Sabine Baring-Gould ("Onward, Christian Soldiers"); William Young Fullerton ("I Cannot Tell"); Hugh Thomson Kerr ("God of Our Life, Through All the Circling Years"); and Walter Chalmers Smith ("Immortal, Invisible, God Only Wise").

To be on target in choosing words to communicate the various moods of the soul is a lifelong task. The pastor in preparation for public worship is never free from the haunting thought that he might fail at the crucial moment. What then? I recall preaching a sermon in which I had need to use the word *aesthetic*. My tongue twisted and I said *anesthetic!* Fortunately, I did not try to correct myself although the moment seemed much longer than it actually was. I went on. At the close of the sermon I noticed a nurse at the rear of the sanctuary. When I went to the narthex I greeted her first of all. Had she noticed anything unusual in the sermon? She smiled and said that she had, but doubted that anyone else noticed the mistake! A nurse would notice *anesthetic.* Perhaps by a kind providence that morning the rest of the congregation were affected by the anesthetic and had not yet awakened to the beauty of the aesthetic! Words may sound alike, but they are not the same in meaning. The apparent is not always the actual.

We close this chapter with a few quotations on the subject of the *word:*

> A word is dead
> When it is said,
>   Some say.
> I say it just
> Begins to live
>   That day.
>   (Emily Dickinson)

> A knack of words you have, some fancy too;
> But have you sound judgment, think you, to review?
> Treasure this maxim in your thoughts for ever:
> A critic must be just as well as clever.
>   (Sir Alexander Boswell)

> If language is not correct, then what is said
> is not what is meant;
> if what is said is not what is meant, then
> what ought to be done remains undone.
>   (Confucius)

The preacher sought to find out acceptable words: and that which was written was upright, even words of truth. The words of the wise are as goads, and as nails fastened by the masters of assemblies, which are given from one shepherd.
        (Eccles. 12:10, 11)

Remember the words of the Lord Jesus.
        (Acts 20:35)

13

The Audacity of Authorship

"I . . . was in the isle *that is called Patmos, for the word of God, and for the testimony of Jesus Christ. I was in the Spirit on the Lord's day, and heard behind me a great voice, as of a trumpet, saying, I am Alpha and Omega, the first and the last: and, What thou seest,* write in a book, *and send it unto the seven churches. . . .* (REV. 1:9-11)

OUR FAMILIARITY with the Bible may blind us to the story behind the stories found in that library. The writers were reporters of divine and human events which made history. Sometimes they were aware that God was pleased to use them as channels of revelation. At other times the authors did not know that their words would get into print and become public.

When the full revelation of God's person and work of redemption was completed with the writing of the Book of Revelation, that book was sent to the seven churches. God's blessing was upon those who heard the reading of and obeyed that word. There was also a blessing upon the reader chosen to read the book as part of public worship. But the primary honor and commendation from God lay upon the one chosen to be the author, in this case the apostle John, now in the climax of his years and looking back over a long and full life. He is *"in the isle"* as a prisoner, but he is also *"in the Spirit."* Authorship depends upon the inspiration of the moment under God.

John's experience sets forth certain principles we would do well to keep in mind. The would-be writer should begin just where he is. The Spirit of God will come to inspire and enlighten him. The author should make a point of being a keen observer and listener before he writes. In one sense it is an audacity for some of us to imagine we will become authors. In another sense it seems impossible in view of our limitations and handicaps. I did not set out to become an author, but by a strange providence this has come to pass. Looking back I cannot help but wonder and give thanksgiving in a spirit of humility. The credit is not mine, but God's.

We could add to John's experience the Old Testament story of Jeremiah (ch. 36), who used Baruch, a professional scribe. Whether the prophet himself wrote notes is not clear, but certainly he dictated his recollections and the words of God to Baruch. "Baruch wrote from the mouth of Jeremiah all the words of the Lord, which he had spoken unto him, upon a roll of a book" (36:4). Later, when Baruch carried out his commission and read from the scroll to the court of Judah, he was asked to explain how these writings had come into existence. He explained, "He [Jeremiah] pronounced all these words unto me with his mouth, and I wrote them with ink in the book" (36:18). The king quickly commanded that the scroll be cut with a penknife, and cast into the fire where it was consumed. The word of the Lord came to Jeremiah again: "Take thee again another roll, and write in it *all the former words* that were in the first roll, which Jehoiakim the king of Judah hath burned" (36:28). "Then took Jeremiah another roll, and gave it to Baruch the scribe . . . who wrote therein from the mouth of Jeremiah all the words of the book which Jehoiakim the king of Judah had burned in the fire: *and there were added besides unto them many like words*" (36:32). The burning of the roll did not destroy the oracles, but led to yet more.

Like the apostle Paul, who often dictated to a helper, so Jeremiah dictated his message to Baruch. The inspiration of the Holy Spirit covered not only the words of the prophet, but also the dictation to the scribe.

The prophet Jeremiah had the help of a professional scribe. Other authors at crucial moments have had assistance from publishers, their staffs, and some unexpected sources. The story of the English Bible is a thrilling one. Perhaps no episode is more exciting than William Tyndale's translation of the New Testament into the English of that age. In 1526 copies imported to London were seized by Cuthbert Tunstall, bishop of London, and burned at St. Paul's Cross, for new versions were strictly forbidden. The bishop bought up copies on the Continent in a further attempt to stop the new translation. The profits realized from this transaction found their way to Tyndale, who used them to improve his work and ship even larger quantities of the life-giving Word of God to England.

We who live under benevolent governments pledged to freedom of speech, worship, assembly, and press rejoice that this includes the *freedom to write* and publish. There are publishers who deal in trash and pornography and are bent on degrading the minds of the public. But there are also publishers of religious books. The Christian writer, once his manuscript is accepted, edited, and published, can reach a far wider audience than can the pastor whose ministry is confined to preaching in a building. Like the launching of a ship from the shipyards, no one can predict how far or how long a book, launched off the presses and undergirded by providence, will travel.

My first major undertaking in writing came unsought and unexpected. A few sermon digests and outlines of Bible studies had been printed in church magazines. Then, a visit to Chicago led to a dinner meeting with William R. Barbour, president of the Fleming H. Revell Company of New Jersey. Unbeknownst to me he had read a few of these publications and asked me for sermon manuscripts which might be considered for publication in book form. I sent some and the fifteen which were selected were published in a book entitled *This Business of Being Converted* (1942). Two printings were issued, and I learned much from the fact that even in wartime people were interested in the gospel.

When on a Sunday evening Samuel Chadwick (1860-1932), an outstanding Methodist preacher in England, was asked by a friend why he did not publish some of his sermons, he replied that he had never considered the possibility but would give the matter some thought. *Next day* the post brought an unsolicited letter from Hodder and Stoughton, asking Chadwick to submit a manuscript! The publishers and Chadwick had had no previous contact! From then on, publication of Samuel Chadwick's works was assured.

After my first major venture into writing, Will Barbour asked me to write the annual *The Gist of the Lesson*, a concise exposition of the International Bible Lessons. These had been originated by R. A. Torrey. After his death his material was rewritten by John W. Bradbury, editor of the *Watchman-Examiner*. Since I had no material of Torrey from which to work, I had to do some highly disciplined study in order to provide exegesis, exposition, and homiletical outlines of the Scripture selections decided upon by the Division of Christian Education of the National Council of the Churches of Christ. It was imperative that I write one lesson each week and have the manuscript in the hands of the publisher fifteen months in advance. This was done for six years (1954-1959) and afforded me the *opportunity to write because of an assignment.* This project was a useful adjunct and complement to the other demands of preparation for preaching sermons and teaching an adult Bible class.

A similar assignment came when the Baker Book House of Grand Rapids gave me the opportunity to undertake the *Bible Companion Series for Lesson and Sermon Preparation* for five years (1963-1967). The format was a paperback issued four times each year. I found it necessary to turn to my typewriter almost daily. This writing brought to me its own reward in the accumulation of material far beyond my immediate requirements and also in the demand to read, study, exegete, and expound all parts of the Bible. Binding the four quarterlies into an annual volume produced a book of about four hundred pages.

Another phase of my writing ministry lay in a more personal aspect of the pastor's life and work. A pastor finds he shares in the "confessions" of those who seek him and who trust the integrity of his character. Like the Roman Church priest, the evangelical pastor finds he must carry the secrets of many lives. In addition to those of his congregation some brothers in the ministry seek help. Some confided their needs and problems to me over many years. In reflection I discovered their needs were not unlike my own! The crucial problems of the ministry are not in the machinery, the organization, the programs and committees of the church. The true area of conflict lies in the *inner life* of the minister. Thus emerged the manuscript *A Minister's Obstacles* (1946; revised and enlarged in 1964).

The confidences of my congregation and fellow pastors reminded me of similar tests and trials which I had read about in many biographies and autobiographies. Problems which had plagued churchmen in other periods of history were still a factor in contemporary life. So I began to scribble notes. Then it was that a good friend and mentor, Samuel M. Zwemer (1867-1952), whose renown lay in establishing a beachhead for the gospel in the Moslem world, approached me. He had been a missionary for forty years and wrote fifty books, including a serious study on *The Origin of Religion.* He inquired about my writing; I told him that what was being compiled was of too intimate a nature for public reading. However, he asked to read a sample and had a chapter sent to an editor he knew. It was published in a theological journal. Evidently, those who read this religious quarterly found something touching a need. More chapters were requested and written; then the publishers ventured to send the material out in book form—but not before three other friends and critics were asked to examine the manuscript. Having passed that test, the book was on its way. Some thirty years later *A Minister's Obstacles* has been printed in several editions. Five more chapters were added as my knowledge of the temptations and tests facing ministers multiplied. That the present volume is offered as a sequel points up the grace of God poured out on behalf of a pastor who has lived through the experiences which others now face.

Another opportunity involved serving as editor of *Baker's Dictionary of Practical Theology* (1967). My pastoral experience indicated a need for a handy desk-volume to cover the major areas of the work of the minister. The format was conceived and a sampling of a section offered. On receiving encouragement from the publishers, I contacted those who might write the essays within the ten different sections. Unlike the regular dictionary where words are given a short definition and perhaps a paragraph of exposition, *Baker's Dictionary of Practical Theology* aimed at presenting a number of major contributions (ideally ten) within the framework of every division. Thus each subject had a full treatment, including a separate bibliography. The major divisions of the dictionary included preaching, homiletics, hermeneutics, evangelism-missions, counseling, administration, pastoral, stewardship, worship, and education. The dictionary has already gone through six printings in the United States and two printings in England.

Another excursion into writing involved sermons based on the New Testament. As a pastor I had preached a series on the Book of Acts. Having determined the style and form of this new undertaking, I sent out invitations to selected preachers to share the insights of their study. There emerged the fifteen-volume set *Proclaiming the New Testament* (1961). A later edition was issued in five volumes.

It was a pleasant assignment for me to edit *If I Had Only One Sermon to Preach* (1966) and *Evangelism Now* (1972). The former is a collection of sermons submitted by friends in the ministry. The latter is not a "how to" book in methodology, but rather emphasizes the spirit and purpose of evangelism. To each of these books the editor contributed one chapter to illustrate the method and manner of the whole.

Other doors to writing were opened as I prepared the regular weekly sermons. In my years in the pastorate two sermons were expected each week. In addition there was a special shorter message on radio each Sunday as well as a midweek service and also a Sunday Bible class. All of this demanded study and writing. My notes accumulated. The net result was several volumes: *Triumph in Christ*—twelve radio addresses (1945); *The Promise unto You: The Book of Acts*—five Bible studies (1948); *The Seven Words from the Cross* (1956); *Sermon Substance*—104 messages for a year of preaching (1958); *The Pathway to the Cross* (1959); *Personalities of the New Testament*—thirteen biographical studies (1960); *Personalities of the New Testament*—thirteen biographical studies (1964); *At the Lord's Table*—twenty-one communion meditations (1967); *The Book of Nehemiah*—ten Bible studies (1968); *Profile of the Son of Man*—thirteen Christological studies (1969). Each of these books had the advantage of being proclaimed from the pulpit before the final form was published.

Two major projects presented themselves as a result of my background of academic and theological studies in university and in seminary. The publication of *Jonathan Edwards the Preacher* (1958) was the fruit of research at Princeton Theological Seminary and at Yale University. It was also my great privilege to produce the third and final volume of *Dargan's History of Preaching* (1974). Before his death Edwin Charles Dargan (1852-1930), professor of homiletics at Southern Baptist Theological Seminary in Louisville, had published the first two monumental volumes of a proposed trilogy: *From the Apostolic Fathers to the Great Reformation (A.D. 70-1572)* and *From the Close of the Reformation Period to the End of the Nineteenth Century (1572-1900)*. Several years of research allowed me to produce the proposed third volume: *From the Close of the Nineteenth Century to the Middle of the Twentieth Century*. For a pastor in the midst of a ministry which did not lessen with the years, the task of completing the trilogy was a difficult but most worthwhile undertaking.

When I arrived in the United States from Scotland, I became particularly interested in the Puritans and Jonathan Edwards. I had a burning desire to know more about American preaching, of which I was now a part. Invited to deliver the American Heritage Lectures at Fuller Theological Seminary in 1964, I developed the overall subject "Preaching and Our Society and Culture." In the W. H. Smith Memorial Lectures of the United Church of Canada, which were given at Union Theological College in Vancouver, I dealt with "The Preacher's Task in the Contemporary World." I also lectured at pastors' conferences of the Presbyterian Church in Canada; the Reformed Church (at Western Theological Seminary in Holland, Michigan); the Christian Reformed Church (at Calvin Theological Seminary in Grand Rapids, Michigan); the Free Methodist Church (at Seattle Pacific University); and the Evangelical Lutheran Church (Minnesota Synod). In addition to other lectures at Presbyterian seminaries and at the General Assembly Conference on Evangelism, I have taught at Western Theological Seminary in Pittsburgh, at Seattle Pacific University, and at Warner Pacific College. With so many opportunities the discipline of writing and rewriting always placed heavy demands upon my time and energy.

From these and other excursions into the realm of practical theology and the history of preaching came the publication of *The Preacher's Heritage, Task, and Resources* (1968). This provided marvelous background material for the larger work *A History of Preaching* (1974). A secret of good writing is that if one cumulatively gathers all kinds of material (even what might seem unimportant at the moment), new levels of thought and expression will eventually emerge. Robert Browning said:

    Who keeps one end in view,
    Makes all things serve.

All previous notes and writing attempts need not be destroyed; they can become the gathered sticks from which a larger fire may be kindled.

Another series of books attempts to keep alive the memory of some outstanding preachers and writers. While the major works of some of them are still in print, there are other items not so well known and now out of print. It seemed a good idea to select samples of their best work and compile them in a *Treasury*. The results are: *Treasury of Alexander Whyte, Treasury of Andrew Murray, Treasury of Dwight L. Moody, Treasury of G. Campbell Morgan*, and *Treasury of W. Graham Scroggie*. I hope someday to present a volume of Samuel Chadwick. I have spent many pleasing hours in rereading older favorites whose life and work encouraged me in earlier years. Of course I did not hear Alexander Whyte, Andrew Murray, or Dwight L. Moody; but I recall hearing and meeting Morgan and Chadwick, and I personally knew Scroggie.

Another prime interest of mine is the reissuing of books long out of print. Because of the secondhand scarcity publishers have been prompted to bring them back into circulation. For some of these, including Yale Lectures and Warrack Lectures, I have had the privilege of providing the introductions. These volumes bear the titles *Notable Books on Preaching* and *Notable Books on Theology*. Beyond that I have had the privilege of reading and critically judging manuscripts submitted to publishers for possible publication. In addition to occasional book reviews, I have written articles for religious periodicals. Looking back upon the years of service, I am surprised at what has been "scribbled" in the midst of prior commitments to the ministry and the church. At the Christian Writers' Conferences at Warner Pacific College in Portland, I have sensed there are goals still to be attained. Yet I am humbly thankful for what has been attempted and the measure of benefits already realized. We are still learning to write and the best is yet to be, God willing.

Among the periodicals for which I have written articles is the *Union Seminary Review* of Richmond. Some of these articles were "The Evasions of Preaching," "The Meridian Test of the

Minister," "John Henry Jowett: A Preacher and His Sermons for Days of War and Reconstruction," "The Christology of Paul," and "The Ascension in Paul's Christology." When that quarterly became *Interpretation*, I was asked to write an article on "Jonathan Edwards—Bible Interpreter." *Theology Today* of Princeton Seminary carried an article entitled "The Pathway to the Cross," and the *Evangelical Quarterly* of London carried "Jonathan Edwards: A Voice for God."

Trial runs of my articles brought reactions which enabled me to understand what subjects had interest and perhaps should be studied and expounded in the future. These experiments in authorship were the precursors of later days when longer articles were written and eventually submitted as book-length manuscripts. Nothing was lost by these endeavors. Every experience fostered my growth in the art and craft of writing with the end in view that publishers might someday think kindly about still another manuscript!

When *A Minister's Obstacles* was ready to be published, the *Pulpit Digest* serialized the fifteen chapters over a period of twelve months. This brought the new book valuable publicity.

It is axiomatic that would-be authors need publishers and publishers need authors with fresh material. They should forge a close working relationship. Consider the example of Sir Walter Scott. He was a friend and business partner of a publisher named James Ballantyne. When Ballantyne fell into financial difficulty, Scott took personal responsibility for all of Ballantyne's debts and began to write as never before. This was writing under tremendous pressure. During the later years of Scott's life and work he was able to write the twenty-five *Waverly Novels*, a prodigious accomplishment.

Robert Louis Stevenson was another novelist who was able to draw on the rich lore of Scottish history. He, too, had "heard voices and seen visions" as ill health continuously dogged him. As a result, he developed a deep sympathy for and keen perception of the human condition. He owed much to books. Not only did they provide invaluable background for his novels, but they helped him develop his own literary style. Books also had a profound impact on his personal philosophy. Stevenson tells how in a crisis he stumbled upon and was deeply moved by William

Penn's *Fruits of Solitude*. Then came John Bunyan's *Pilgrim's Progress*, which, he said, "breathes of every beautiful and valuable emotion."

Authors are indebted to many sources for the best material in their books. We cannot afford to despise memories of our early years. Family, environment, culture, national background—these and much beside provide a foundation for writing in our years of maturity.

Over the centuries men have put down their thoughts in writing and endeavored to get them into circulation. Many works written during the era of the Roman Empire are known today thanks to the untold efforts of anonymous scribes and the facilities of libraries.

Even during the long night of the Dark Ages books were in circulation. The Anglo-Saxon world had literary centers in Canterbury, Jarrow, and York in England. Unfortunately ecclesiastical bans were commonplace; authorities of church and state often rejected the writings of men like John Wycliffe or later William Tyndale. Centers of learning like Oxford and Cambridge universities served as official agents with power to approve or forbid publication of specific manuscripts.

With the advent of the printing press, there was extraordinary expansion in the availability of books. The publishing business has become one of the major industries of modern times. When the Pilgrim Fathers in 1620 crossed the Atlantic Ocean for their holy experiment in New England, they took with them very few possessions. But they made sure to take a printing press. Their earliest books included the *Bay Psalm Book* (1640) and the *New England Primer*. Many manuscripts were sent back to England to be printed there. Only slowly did the publishing service become established in the New World.

Cotton Mather's *Magnalia Christi Americana: Or the Ecclesiastical History of New England* was first published in London in 1702. That three quarters of a century after the landing of the *Mayflower* it was necessary to seek a publisher in England speaks of the severe limitations of printing in America at this time. It was not until 1820 that the first American publication of Mather's book took place.

The trials and stresses of finding a publisher is vividly demonstrated by the great difficulties faced by women authors in England during the nineteenth century. Only books written by men were accepted for publication. However, George Eliot and the Bronte sisters submitted their manuscripts to the London publishers Smith and Elder.

In sending a manuscript to London, Charlotte Bronte used the pseudonym "Currer Bell." The publishers assumed this to be the name of a man. Several companies had already rejected the manuscript when it came to Smith and Elder in a brown paper parcel. On the parcel were the names of other publishers to whom the manuscript had been sent, not obliterated, but simply scored through. In Elizabeth C. Gaskell's *Life of Charlotte Bronte* (New York: Oxford University Press, 1975) we have a copy of the letter which accompanied the parcel.

> July 15th, 1847
>
> Gentlemen,
>
> I beg to submit to your consideration the accompanying manuscript. I should be glad to learn whether it be such as you approve, and would undertake to publish at as early a period as possible. Address, Mr. Currer Bell, under cover to Miss Bronte, Haworth, Bradford, Yorkshire.

Some time elapsed before an answer was forthcoming. The work was turned down, but in the rejection lay some grounds for encouragement. On August 24th another letter was sent to the firm:

> I now send you per rail a MS. entitled "Jane Eyre," a novel in three volumes, by Currer Bell.
>
> Respectfully,
> C. Bell

After the publication of *Jane Eyre*, the identity of Currer Bell was eagerly sought. Even the publishers did not know whether Currer Bell was a real or an assumed name, whether it belonged to a man or a woman. It was not until August, 1848, that two of the Bronte sisters, Charlotte and Anne, finally visited the publishing house in London and revealed the identity of Currer Bell.

Fortunately, those days of prejudice are past in the English-speaking world; today be it man or woman, young or old, no matter the cultural or educational background, there is an open door to publishers' offices if a would-be author has something to communicate. Though some authors may have their manuscripts

rejected at the first and have to go the rounds of a few publishers, no one with something really worth saying should be
discouraged in looking for a publisher!

Does it seem impossible that you who are reading this book
might become an author? Does it seem too audacious to imagine? Consider the example of Leigh Hunt, who found great romance in the world of books:

> Sitting last winter among my books, and walled around with
> all the comfort and protection which they and my fireside
> could afford me—to wit, a table of higher piled books at my
> back, my writing desk on one side of me, some shelves on the
> other, and the feeling of the warm fire at my feet—I began to
> consider how I loved the authors of those books.

Hunt himself was later to become a most prolific author.

The rewards which may come to an author are many and
varied: royalties, encouraging reviews of his work (although
there are critical reviews also), fame and influence. There are
some, of course, who will never reap these benefits. But they will
continue to write from their sheer love of expressing their
thoughts in written form. That is reward sufficient for an
author. In the case of a Christian whose writing has influenced
others to faith in Christ, there is supreme reward in the knowledge he has helped to advance the kingdom of God.

I owe special thanks and gratitude to Herman Baker, who has
been friend and colleague as well as publisher. Who but he
would risk the foibles and faults of this would-be author?

14

The Worth of a Library

"There are also many other things which Jesus did, the which, if they should be written every one, I suppose that even the world itself could not contain the books that should be written." (JOHN 21:25)

"Lover and friend hast thou put far from me, and mine acquaintance into darkness." (PS. 88:18)

THE PRIVILEGED PEOPLE of earlier, less hurried days, without the competition of the distractions of automobile, airplane, radio, and television, were able to gather treasures unlimited by building up personal libraries. The opportunity is still before us to secure such treasures for ourselves, though some personal sacrifices may be involved.

The quotation from Psalm 88 reminds us that there are three positive attitudes (taken out of context!) we may adopt toward specific books:

There are the books we *love*. These are our favorites and we read them repeatedly. We learn to live with an author and we find joy and inspiration over the years.

There are the books we see as *friends*. They serve our immediate purposes and needs. As life moves on, we discover we have many books which speak to our individual situation.

There are the books which are like *acquaintances*. These are read on special occasions for reference and information. Though we do not feel as close to them as to the others, they do have a place.

The books which we treasure tell much about our personality and character. There is a story of a woman who, when asked if she would like a book as a present, replied, "No thanks, I have one." This would be a highly improper attitude for one seeking to prepare and serve in a Christian ministry. The question may well be asked: "Why collect books? Is there any particular reason? After all, there are libraries where I can borrow what I wish to read." True. Yet the servant of God believes that he should collect books (within reason) because he needs tools to use and he requires sources to feed his mind and heart if he is to be a worthy follower of his Lord and Master.

Some people collect books as an investment. They know that certain books will increase in value and after years can be sold for profit, but that is not the primary reason for the minister to acquire books.

Other people collect books because of the lure of the hunt. Yes, there are those who instinctively enjoy a sale or an auction where books can be bought, who seek to acquire certain books just for the thrill of saying, "This is mine!"

Still others collect simply because they love reading. Borrowing has its limits. Possessing a book of one's own allows the reader to use it without time limit and to make notes in the margin.

A library is a minister's workshop, the place where he prepares for work, and the place where he dreams dreams and sees visions of his ideas being transmuted into acts and enterprises of unlimited force by his congregation.

There is a little town in Scotland named Ruthwell. It nestles in the southwest corner near the Solway Firth. Not much could happen there we imagine. Yet in 1810 the Presbyterian pastor, Henry Duncan, began to take in the savings of his parishioners and to pay them interest on it. All these transactions took place in a cottage which became known as the Friendly Society Hall and which today is a museum. This was the *first* savings bank of its kind. We cannot help but marvel at how much has transpired since that small beginning, when we think of the world's savings banks in modern times!

Another son of Ruthwell is worthy of mention. Born to a poor tailor, James Murray (1837--1915) was a young prodigy and self-taught polymath. In youth and early manhood he came to know twenty-five languages; he made an intense study of words and their interpretation. He went on to London and then to Oxford, where he became the chief editor of the *Oxford English Dictionary*. Here is a man who devoted all his waking hours to one passion—lexicography. Servants of God will forever be in his debt as they read the Bible and study its language. This interest will carry over into reading books of every description. Language is vital and alive, and the preacher-teacher must ever find new words and uses of speech. Great profit in this area can be derived from the studies of men like Murray.

In *A Minister's Obstacles* reference was made to W. Robertson Nicoll's tribute *My Father*, a small volume informing us how his father with modest salary and house served as minister of a country church at Lumsden, near Aberdeen. Harry Nicoll's chief distinction was a library of 17,000 books. This library was balanced in that it contained volumes covering every conceivable field of interest. Robertson Nicoll never criticized his father, nor did he ever complain that his youth was deprived of opportunities and material things. However, we are not to imagine that a collection of books is all that matters for the ministry. The selection of books in the collection is vital.

The man who has the reputation of having been the world's greatest book collector is Sir Thomas Phillipps (1792-1872). His biographer A. N. L. Munby has reported that the aim of Phillipps was "to have one copy of every book in the world." This was before book collecting had become a professional business. Of course, no one should attempt this impossible task! Phillipps lacked taste and discretion as a bibliophile, so absorbing was the passion which curtailed ordinary human relations. Whatever was printed and could be bought, he sought to buy and price was no consideration!

The American counterpart to Phillipps was A. S. W. Rosenbach (1876-1952) of Philadelphia, whose private collection was outstanding, but whose chief interest was professional buying and selling. In his volume *Books and Bidders* (1927) he shares with his readers some of the discoveries he made in his search for rare volumes. According to his biographers John F. Fleming and Edwin Wolf *(Rosenbach: A Biography* [Cleveland: World Publishing, 1960]) he led an extremely exciting life. He acquired treasures for the Folger Library (Washington, D.C.), the Huntington Library (San Marino, California), the J. P. Morgan collection (New York), the Widener Library (Harvard University), and the William Andrews Clark Library (University of California at Los Angeles). What a priceless legacy he gave to those libraries for the use of students who desire to read and research in the heritage of the ages.

Naturally, the minister who is pastor-teacher and shepherd of a congregation has not the resources to build an enormous library. However, within the limits of purse and interest, he may select what is a working library suited to his vocation and needs.

A minister's library does not need to be large to be functional. An ordinary room with shelves along each wall and space for desk, chair, and filing cabinet would suffice. This is the minister's workshop as well as an oratory for his soul. He must make effective use of the tools of learning. The Bible should be his major text both for devotion and for study. Personally I prefer an edition without notes or markings so that in meditation the eye and heart may receive firsthand impressions without other men's thoughts intruding.

A well-used library can help correct any impediment of mind which might overtake the minister. A few may coast along without reading and study—for a while—but judgment day will surely come for the man who is thus deceiving himself if no one else! The books in a library must not be only for show. It is ridiculous to be a bibliomaniac or a theorist who has no knowledge of the contents and the wise use of the riches between the covers. Paul bade young Timothy: "Study to shew thyself ... *a workman* that needeth not to be ashamed, rightly dividing the truth" (II Tim. 2:15). Without a time clock to be punched, the man of God must be honest as he labors in his library before God.

John H. Jowett said: "If the study becomes a lounge, the pulpit becomes an impertinence." Those who speak to us from the shelves become our judges and encouragers in times of crisis.

Once again I wish to mention *Baker's Dictionary of Practical Theology* (Grand Rapids: Baker Book House, 1967). This volume offers guidance in the ten major areas of a pastor's work: preaching, homiletics, hermeneutics, evangelism-missions, counseling, administration, pastoral, stewardship, worship, and education. Each section within the dictionary was written by men who were knowledgeable in that particular field of experience. Bibliographies were supplied in each section. It is important for our present purpose to note that these bibliographies can serve as a springboard to selecting basic books for a sound theological library. It was the hope of the editor and compiler that the dictionary would serve a practical purpose for at least ten years. More than ten years have now passed, and the volume is still being used and reprinted as it meets a need for those in the ministries of the church.

With this volume in hand, a pastor could then add other reference works—dictionaries and an encyclopedia—which cover general and theological-biblical requirements. There should be separate sections in the library for theology, philosophy, church history, general history, Christological studies, science and Christianity, Pauline studies, commentaries, biographies and autobiographies, and devotional manuals which emphasize prayer, the life of holiness, and the ministry of the Holy Spirit. There should also be Christian classics, for example, studies of the Wesleys, the roots of Puritanism, and American Puritan influence. Using these suggestions as a model, any pastor can build his library with selectivity and yet allow for his own major interest and field. Special areas should be reserved for the relationship between Christ and culture, and for American and English literature as background material for our ministries.

Throughout my service on behalf of the gospel, I was indebted to the books which were read and studied in preparation for the ministry. Other pastors and teachers as well as professors played their part. Sometimes as a young man I was able to borrow several books each month from a well-stocked library which belonged to an outstanding minister who had given his friendship and encouragement. Notes taken while reading those books became the seed of my more mature ideas and writing. What a treasure they are after many years!

During the Depression in the 1930s, when my income was uncertain and continued education necessary while I was away from college and university, God's provision lay in another direction. Dr. Williams' Library in London, which had been founded in the Puritan era and enriched over the centuries, was a treasury of theological, philosophical, and historical works. The trustees offered to loan me four books each month. The only condition was that I pay the postage on the parcel. Even a Scot seeking to be thrifty or economical could not object to that! Again, I was able to take notes from books which I could not afford and which because of the Depression seemed impossible to acquire. (Incidentally, as my income became more steady in later life, I was able to purchase many of these volumes, which have now become indispensable to me.)

Across the decades many titles still speak to us. Some still are being read and reread as books which have profoundly influenced the course of theological thought. Karl Barth of Switzerland threw a bombshell into the complacency of theological thought when he published his *Commentary on Romans* in 1919. It was discovered once more that any true renewal of the church would come by preaching the theology of that explosive epistle. What was true for Martin Luther and the Reformation of the sixteenth century reopened the Bible for the people of our generation.

An invaluable publication of the twentieth century is Kittel's *Theological Dictionary of the New Testament* (Grand Rapids: Eerdmans, 1964-1976), a ten-volume set which weds philology to theology in the interpretation of the New Testament revelation. Hermeneutics revived in an awareness that the New Testament must be seen in the light of the Old Testament. An example is found in A. G. Herbert's *Throne of David* (Naperville, IL: Alec R. Allenson, Inc., 1941). New insights began to break forth with regularity.

More and more, Bible study and preaching regarded the centrality of our Lord Jesus Christ as the key to Scripture. Christology became the prime focus of theology. After the night of uncertainty when critical research divided the Bible into separate parts and strands of revelation, the morning returned. The Bible was again seen as a unity and each part of the literature was regarded as providentially given and having its unique part in the whole. Regarding the Bible as a unity emphasized once again the genuineness and potency of the authority of Scripture. In *A Man in Christ* (New York: Harper and Row, 1935) James S. Stewart stood amid the swirling currents of change to declare the essential, abiding truth that "in Christ" the preacher-teacher can remain at the center while his mind ranges liberally without limit and restriction in spelling out the eternal message in contemporary idiom. With Christ at the center of doctrine and theology, the minister can proclaim with vitality and grace.

With the publication of C. H. Dodd's *Apostolic Preaching* (New York: Harper and Row, 1936), another disturbing truth came home to the contemporary ministry. Dodd pointed out that the emphasis in pulpit and in classroom was on the *teaching* of Jesus *(didache)*. Dodd's interpretation of New Testament passages cried out against this one-sided emphasis. The gospel was proclaimed by *preaching (kerygma)* the facts of our Lord's redeeming death and resurrection. Dodd called for both/and instead of either/or. Our Lord's ministry was characterized by both teaching and evangelism, and the pastor-teacher-preacher must keep this supreme model before him.

Biblical preaching to have integrity must emphasize the twin facets of *kerygma* and *didache*. The preacher proclaims the facts of the gospel and then instructs those who have become disciples of the Lord and Master, who is both Savior and Teacher. To help us achieve this goal, rich deposits of counsel and example are our inheritance. The whole church has been engaged in this dual task of declaration and teaching. The New Testament, literature of church history, and more specialized instruction concerning our task all serve to equip the pastor-teacher for this work of ministry.

The opportunity which confronts the preacher-teacher in the modern era is of profound significance for the gospel. Modern man is disillusioned, discouraged, defeated as he sets his sights upon the state of his world. The world scene is not encouraging, despite all the scientific advances which have made life simpler and better for many. On the contrary, there are hungry, homeless, shelterless millions living on the edge of despair and doom. The civilized nations and their powers of technology are widely mistrusted—they may wreak worldwide destruction with their deadly weapons. The advanced Western world with its heritage of the Bible and Christian standards is caught in the anarchy of permissiveness in morals; the menace of indulging in drugs and alcohol affects the total person. The church of the redeemed lives within this culture as a remnant of hope.

Those who were among the first to spread the gospel of Christ are worthy of our emulation. As James S. Stewart testified in his *A Faith to Proclaim* (New York: Charles Scribner's Sons, 1953): "In the apostolic age, the very act of proclaiming the good news was caught up into the context of the truth proclaimed and itself became part of the Gospel. I mean that *these men, risen with Christ, were themselves part of the message of the Resurrection.*" Their example should encourage us to engage in a lifelong quest for the highest and the best. Of course, not everyone reaches the heights (or else we would not need to seek assistance from those whose books we have quoted); but we should not be discouraged with our more limited endeavors as we look at summits still to be scaled and won. Our brethren who have gone ahead would encourage us to toil on, ever expecting we can be better ministers and deliver the fruit of godly character under the divine Taskmaster's eye.

Among the aids providentially afforded to us are countless devotional books bequeathed by the universal church of all ages. They speak to our heart and spirit. Preaching depends upon character and the character of the preacher can with profit feed on the devotional classics as well as on the Sacred Scriptures.

I well recall my introduction to the writings of Alexander Whyte. I was particularly impressed by his six-volume study of Bible characters and four-volume study of the characters of John Bunyan. The day when I had finally saved enough to buy those books in a secondhand book store will be remembered forever. A new world opened for me.

A list of the favorites I gathered and read would not be unlike lists of books compiled by others on the pilgrim way: Augustine, John Bunyan, Miguel de Molinos, Lancelot Andrewes, Richard Baxter, Samuel Rutherford, David Brainerd, and William Law. Later in life and after much searching, I added Henry Scougal's *Life of God in the Soul of Man.* This work was so influential in John Wesley's spiritual development that he published an edition of it, and reprinted a number of Scougal's sermons. I once came across a reference to the publication of Scougal's book. In the *Scots Magazine* of 1739 (vol. I, p. 192) appears an advertisement for Scougal's book at a price of "6d." (say, 10 cents?). The volume is still a rarity and would be worth much more to anyone fortunate enough to find a copy.

Alongside of specifically religious works there are many others which can help us in our quest for better things. The highway of reading brings many discoveries. Among them are *On the Art of*

Writing (Philadelphia: Richard West, 1916) and *On the Art of Reading* (Philadelphia: Richard West, 1920) by Arthur Quiller-Couch (1863-1944). Among the roles he filled were professor of English literature at Cambridge University, editor of the *Oxford Book of English Prose*, poet, lecturer, and inspirer of youth. The two small books mentioned abound in wise counsel and excellent examples to ponder. He stressed that in reading we would do well to go to the fountainhead of all truth and knowledge: the English Bible will give an awareness of the literary and spiritual heritage which is ours.

A. W. Tozer of the Christian and Missionary Alliance Church left a legacy of books and editorials to the universal company of the saints. His distinctive messages deliver a rapier thrust to the Christian conscience whenever it is lethargic and anemic. His *The Knowledge of the Holy* (New York: Harper and Row, 1975) is a profound interpretation of the nature and attributes of God. It owes something to Rudolf Otto's *The Idea of the Holy* and concept of the numinous in worship and life.

R. Newton Flew's *Idea of Perfection in Christian Theology* (Atlantic Highlands, NJ: Humanities Press, 1968 reprint) surveys a crucial area of the church's life. How much can we expect God to do for us as individuals in the fellowship of the body of Christ? In his investigation, Flew read widely on the subject. Footnotes are abundant, yet the style flows easily. The word *perfection* is used to describe the Christian ideal. The Methodist scholar moves within the orbit of John Wesley's thought. Others have worked in this field since, but Flew's book is the most noteworthy.

Note also Kenneth E. Kirk, bishop of Oxford, whose *The Vision of God* (Greenwood, SC: Attic Press, 1978 edition) has a similar sweep and surge. We move from the New Testament through the history of the church with the teachers who have explained and taught what the *summum bonum* is. Kirk, too, regards the goal not as merely conversion nor a life of service, but perfection, or "perfect love." Christ's promise that "the pure in heart shall see God" is for this life as well as for the eternal state.

As the minister builds his library, many books will find a place. The process of collecting books may in the early years seem almost casual and haphazard. However, in time the minister will take stock and decide to build with a plan and purpose. It is essential to acquire dictionaries, an encyclopedia, and basic reference books for language research and theological interpretation. We should collect books on the various aspects of the ministry, thus avoiding excessive concentration on a single classification. Then we will be able to cull the best for our endeavor in the ministry.

One of life's privileges is to visit large libraries, to see collections of rare and valuable items which have been gathered from all parts of the world. The Folger Library in Washington, D.C., houses a rare collection of William Shakespeare. If you would study the manuscripts of Robert Browning, then go to the Baylor University Library in Texas—not to England! At the William Andrews Clark Memorial Library in Los Angeles there is an extensive Dryden collection. The Huntington Library in southern California has similar collections of rare books. In the East are to be found the major libraries of Harvard University, Yale University, Princeton University, and the attendant theological seminary libraries. These house treasures dating back to the founding of the United States, treasures which are part of our national heritage. This reflects the fact that these universities were founded to train youth for the ministry.

When I came here from Scotland, I sought to understand more of the fascinating character of Jonathan Edwards. I am greatly indebted to the librarians of the above-mentioned libraries as well as of various historical societies. One of the richest reservoirs of Puritan literature is to be found in the McAlpin Puritan collection at Union Theological Seminary in New York.

The privilege of visiting another city or country where there is a library with rich holdings of theological books is becoming more and more accessible. Travel these days can wing a pastor overnight to another part of the world. In a short time and for a relatively modest investment his ministry can be stimulated by contact with God's servants of centuries past.

The passion for books can be encouraged and fanned into a flame. The fire of inquiry need not die but can continue to blaze upon the roadway of our Christian service for years to come. Some believe that all that is needed is to believe that if "we open our mouth, God will fill it"; and possibly He will in an emergency! But I believe there is another maxim to follow, "Fill your mind and God will set it on fire!" Preparation is the way to power.

When we cannot buy books in quantity (and I grant that with inflation books are becoming more and more costly), the paperback market is a means of putting major books within the reach of more people than ever. However, even paperbacks are assuming inflationary status. Should a minister's budget be limited, he can visit libraries, borrowing wherever possible or spending a day to read and take notes. In this way the minister will become familiar with major titles and from time to time might find a bargain in a secondhand catalog.

"How can I find the time to read?" is a question frequently asked. The answer is that we should take time to read. Each of us has twenty-four hours every day, and discipleship implies that in the midst of all the other demands upon our time we are sufficiently disciplined to set a priority upon reading. Then arises the question, "Where do I begin to read?" Lawrence Clark Powell, librarian at the University of California at Los Angeles and director of the William Andrews Clark Memorial Library, is also a book collector and author. He began with no specific reading program but simply followed the trail of his interest. He read with pencil and paper in hand to note his reactions and findings. This is a good model for the busy minister to follow.

Naturally, when it comes to reading, everyone has his own personal interests and capabilities. We work at different speeds and with different goals. The slow and the late maturing take longer, but they can learn just as much.

Books are my life; books are my love. Give me a good book (especially the Bible) and time passes quickly, without any strain or stress. There is no reason for boredom when a book never read or handled before comes our way. This is an open door to adventure!

"God so loved the world, that he gave his only begotten Son, that whosoever believeth in him should not perish, but have everlasting life" (John 3:16). This is the Golden Text of the Bible. Notice "God . . . world . . . whosoever." In like manner the minister who loves his library does not think of the total number of books in it. Rather, in loving the world of books he loves each separate book in an individual way. He cherishes each volume singly.

In the cathedral of the town of Hereford, located on the border of Wales, there is a library at the top of a winding stair. The books in this library are *chained*. Books were so rare and costly in the Middle Ages that they had to be chained. What if the books in our modern libraries were chained? Or the Bible was chained to the pillars of our churches and cathedrals, and we had to stand around while an educated man read to us?

Amid all the tools of learning we never can find a substitute for the Book of books, the Bible. Its message can heighten our sense of devotion, our discipline, our thoughts, and inspire our ministry. The measure to which we obey its commands will determine our character as servants of God.

The aim of scientific language is to provide exactly defined and unambiguous statements *about* reality; that of poetic language is to communicate *reality* itself, as experienced, by means of imagery, tone, and symbol. That is not to say that poetic language is nebulous, vague, uncertain; on the contrary, the cutting edge of great poetry is sharper and digs deeper than any prose. But we shall never hear what the mystic (or the poet or the musician) has to tell us if we are listening on the wrong wavelength.

Our library can be both the oratory of the soul and the workshop where we sharpen our tools and use them. The books on our shelves can minister to us as we would minister to others. A small library, growing larger every year, is not a luxury, but one of the necessaries of a minister's life.

15

The Mind of the Interpreter

"Who is as the wise man? and who knoweth the interpretation of a thing?" (ECCLES. 8:1)

"There is a spirit in man: and the inspiration of the Almighty giveth them understanding." (JOB 32:8)

"If there be a messenger with him, an interpreter, one among a thousand. . . ." (JOB 33:23)

"Rabbi . . . being interpreted, Master. . . ." (JOHN 1:38)

"Messias, which is, being interpreted, the Christ [Anointed]." (JOHN 1:41)

"Understandest thou what thou readest? . . . How can I, except some man should guide me?" (ACTS 8:30, 31)

IN THEOLOGICAL STUDY we have become accustomed to the word *hermeneutics.* It was assumed that both the layman and the preacher would have knowledge of what it means. However, the postwar years have disclosed that the meaning of the word is obscure. The basic meaning is the art of interpretation, and that is the meaning we adopt in the present chapter. We in evangelical circles can take heart that the *spirit of interpretation* is alive and potent. That is part of the opportunity for those who minister eternal truth in our time.

As we investigate the opportunity to become interpreters of biblical truth, we find that there are scores of articles available, written from different points of view and by a variety of competent scholars. Among the best is the article in the fifteenth edition of the *Encyclopaedia Britannica* entitled "Exegesis and Hermeneutics, Biblical." This outstanding contribution was written by F. F. Bruce, professor of biblical criticism and exegesis at

Victoria University in Manchester, England. No one today is more highly esteemed by biblical scholars than F. F. Bruce, whose intellectual acumen is wedded to a devout and committed Christian view of God and the world. His article will open new vistas of knowledge to the receptive mind. The guide is trustworthy and objective as he weighs the facts of divine revelation.

In all our studies the Bible is to be central and have priority. We are called to be men of the Book. With all our university or seminary education, the one subject about which we are expected to know more than any other is the Bible. In this connection John Wesley stated specifically that he wished to be a man of one book and that book was the Bible! When Sir Walter Scott was near the end of his life, he bade his son-in-law, "Bring me the book." The son-in-law, looking toward the library, puzzled, "Which book?" Scott replied, "There is but one, the Bible." The well-used book was brought and opened to the familiar words of strength and hope in John 14.

To study is ever to encounter new interpretations. As John Robinson said to the Pilgrims departing from Europe to the New World, "There is yet more light and truth to break forth from God's holy Word." The concepts of interpretation and interpreters appear in the Bible. For example, in Job 33:23 there is a cry for "an interpreter, one among a thousand." In John 1:38, 42, 43; 9:7; and Hebrews 7:2 we meet forms of the Greek word *hermeneuo*, from which comes our term *hermeneutics*, the science of interpretation. Hermeneutics is an indispensable section of any theological library.

John Bunyan, in *Pilgrim's Progress*, tells of Pilgrim's meeting with the Interpreter:

> Pilgrim went on till he came to the house of the Interpreter, where he knocked over and over; at last one came to the door, and asked who was there. "Christian, Sir, a traveller. . . . I would speak with the master of the house. . . . I was told . . . that if I called here you would shew me excellent things, such as would be helpful to me in my journey." Then said the Interpreter: "Come in; I will shew thee that which will be profitable to thee."

The Interpreter is none other than the Holy Spirit, promised by the Lord in the upper room (e.g., John 14:16, 17; 16:7-14).

When the Holy Spirit was given at Pentecost, His work was to bring to mind the teaching of our Lord, to show the apostles things to come, and to interpret what was at first only in embryo and awaiting development. He who inspired the writers of the Scriptures is the same Spirit who has promised to illumine our minds as we read and study the Scriptures. Thus the church is led into all truth.

The ideal ministry therefore is a *Bible ministry*. This is not in any narrow, restricted sense, for all knowledge and all experience of life may be encompassed by the ministry. The man of the Book can harness all books to his task. The Bible demands patient, persistent reading and rereading until we begin to grasp its main revelation. Let us not imagine it is an easy book to understand; rather it demands our best efforts and thoughts in order to begin to wrest its secrets and its unsearchable riches of truth.

The field of hermeneutics gives the pastor a unique opportunity to use the tools of learning. Some ministers after attaining their diploma sell their textbooks. Others put reference works on an inaccessible shelf as if they are relieved not to have to handle them again! But no pastor can communicate the wealth of biblical knowledge unless he continues to be an interpreter. The joy of discovery, the excitement in following clues to open locked treasure stores, is something far beyond material satisfaction. The late A. M. Fairbairn of Mansfield College (Oxford) said, "No man can be a theologian who is not a philologian. He who is no grammarian, is no divine."

This holds not only for the professor of theology, but also for the working pastor. As one studies words, social customs, history, geography, archaeology, and a host of other closely related items, there emerges the interpreter. "Therefore every scribe which is instructed unto the kingdom of heaven is like unto a man that is an householder, which bringeth forth out of his treasure things new and old" (Matt. 13:52).

How to read and study the Bible has always been an integral part of the training of those who are preachers and teachers in the ministry of the church. Among the best guides to this end are those who have shown how to master the English Bible.

James M. Gray (1881-1935), a pastor of the Reformed Episcopal Church in America, wrote *How to Master the English Bible* (Chicago: Moody Press, 1904), a small book packed with generous suggestions on how to read and then how to interpret. Later, when president of the Moody Bible Institute of Chicago, he authored *Synthetic Bible Studies* (Old Tappan, NJ: Fleming H. Revell, 1974 reprint) and *The Christian Workers' Commentary on the Whole Bible* (Old Tappan, NJ: Fleming H. Revell, 1971 reprint). These volumes demonstrate his method. In essence his principles are as follows: *Read* the Scripture; read it *continuously*; read it *repeatedly*; read it *independently*; and read it *prayerfully*. The lasting values are there. The means are at hand for any pastor or Christian servant to discover and apply those values.

G. Campbell Morgan (1863-1945) achieved influence on both sides of the Atlantic by his application of a similar method. He testified that he would read a book of the Bible some fifty times before he felt a strong enough grasp to expound upon it. His *Living Messages of the Books of the Bible* (Old Tappan, NJ: Fleming H. Revell, 1960) and *The Analyzed Bible* (Old Tappan, NJ: Fleming H. Revell, 1964) offer rich interpretations. His commentaries on selected books are built on a solid exegetical foundation. His volumes on the Four Gospels and Acts reflect considerable reading and rereading.

W. Graham Scroggie likewise was noted for the strength and beauty of his logical unfolding of Scripture. He pursued methods of Bible mastery similar to those of Gray and Morgan. In studying any part of the Bible he followed the pattern of reader, exegete, and then interpreter. He was ever aware of the message of the whole. Every text has its context; each context is part of a whole book; each book should be seen against the background of the whole Bible.

Richard G. Moulton (1849-1924), professor of literary theory and interpretation at the University of Chicago, was convinced that without a study of the Bible a student's knowledge of literature was woefully inadequate. Study of Shakespeare and other eminent authors was to be supplemented by study of the English Bible. Moulton edited *The Modern Reader's Bible* (Philadelphia: Richard West, 1925), which was set out in the various literary forms. In *The Literary Study of the Bible* (Saint Clair Shores,

MI: Scholarly Press, 1898) Moulton expounded his theory of study, encouraging the reader to steep his mind in the poetry, drama, rhapsody, parable, dialogue, narrative, history, essay, allegory, and sermons of the Bible. This will lay a solid foundation for exegesis and exposition. A small volume entitled *The Bible at a Single View* (1919) brought into focus what Moulton was aiming at in studying the Bible as literature:

> Not a compendium of theology or religious truth founded on the Bible. That is a separate matter. First that which is natural, afterward that which is spiritual. First, certainly, in order of time: the natural sense of the text, read in the full light of its literary setting, must precede any deductions to be inferred from it.

In Moulton's view, literature (especially the Bible) studied in this way "is the most powerful medium for the spiritual."

In my youth the first half-hour of the classroom day was spent in reading and memorizing parts of the King James Version of the Bible. This brought lasting results. Just to know the way through the library of the Bible and become familiar with its different books was worthwhile. What was stored in the mind later became alive as my understanding of the biblical message matured. That is why the King James Version (known as the Authorized Version to British readers) has a special place in my life.

One reason why people still turn to the King James Version of the Bible is its sheer simplicity and clarity, which produce beauty beyond compare. To read aloud and with understanding will bring an aliveness to both its prose and poetry. The preacher finds new interpretations in the more contemporary translations and versions in his study. Yet there remains a special glory in the words, the images evoked, and the thoughts kindled, when one reads the majestic cadences of the King James.

Testimonies to the significance of this lasting version are many. Arthur T. Quiller-Couch (18863-1944), professor of English at Cambridge University, taught courses on the Bible as literature. In his lectures, which were later published as *On the Art of Reading* (Philadelphia: Richard West, 1920), he said:

> The Authorised Version of the Holy Bible is, as a literary achievement, one of the greatest in our language; nay, with the

possible exception of the complete Works of Shakespeare, the very greatest. You will certainly not deny this. As little, or less, will you deny that more deeply than any other book—more deeply even than all the writings of Shakespeare—far more deeply it has influenced our literature. . . . It has cadences homely and sublime, yet so harmonises them that the voice is always one. Simple men—homely and humble men of heart like Izaak Walton and Bunyan—have their lips touched and speak to the homelier tune. Proud men, scholars—Milton, Sir Thomas Browne—practice the rolling Latin sentences; but upon the rhythms of our Bible they, too, fall back. The precise man Addison cannot excel one parable in brevity or in heavenly clarity. The Bible controls its enemy Gibbon as surely as it haunts the curious music of a light sentence of Thackeray's. "It is in everything we see, hear, feel, because it is in us, in our blood!". . .

These cadences, these phrases have for three hundred years exercised a most powerful effect . . . by association of ideas, by the accreted memories of a word or a name. . . . You cannot get away from these connotations. . . . If that be true, or less than gravely overstated; if the English Bible holds this unique place in our literature; if it be at once a monument, an example and (best of all) a well of English undefiled, no stagnant water, but quick, running, curative, refreshing, vivifying, may we not agree to require the weightiest reason why our instructors should continue to hedge in the temple and pipe the fountain off in professional conduits, forbidding it to irrigate freely our ground of study?

Such a eulogy from men of letters is not unusual. W. Macneile Dixon (1866-1945), professor of English literature at Glasgow University, expressed similar convictions in lectures entitled *The Englishman* (Philadelphia: Richard West, 1931) given at University College in London:

To go about an interpretation of English life and character without mention of the Bible would be sheer stupidity. As well might we, in speaking of the Greeks, forget Homer. As well might one write the history of philosophy, and omit Plato. . . . Like a painter's canvas the Bible forms the entire background not merely of our religious and moral, but of our literary history. . . .

No attempt to estimate its influence upon English character or English language can ever be wholly successful. A book

which has been read by millions where other books have been
read only by hundreds or thousands of readers, a book which
for generations was almost the only book possessed by innumerable households, which was read aloud in churches,
throughout the whole country week after week for centuries,
necessarily sank deep into the national mind, saturated and
coloured all its thoughts, wove itself into daily conversation,
and shaped in every region of activity the country's history.

The literary influence of the Bible is profound. To estimate
its scope we should have to recall and pass in review all our
literature, verse and prose. We should have to recall the mass
of books and sermons directly based upon it, the pamphlets
and commentaries and discourses beyond enumeration enforc-
ing its moral doctrine and view of life.

When British Prime Minister Stanley Baldwin (1867-1947)
spoke at the annual meeting of the British and Foreign Bible Society in 1928, he paid tribute to the Bible. He said that it was
not only the greatest literature in the world, but above and beyond all that, it is, and always has been, of

the nature of a high explosive in the world. It works in strange
ways; and no living man can tell or know how that Book in its
journeyings through the world has startled the individual in
ten thousand different places into a new life, a new world, a
new belief, a new conception, and a new faith. These things
are hidden until some man, some people, is touched beyond all
others by the divine fire. Then the result is one of those great
revivals of religion which repeatedly, through the centuries,
have startled the world and stimulated mankind; and which, as
sure as we are meeting in this room, will recur again.

Ministers of the gospel have an exceptional opportunity to become well-versed in the Bible. From childhood some of us have
had the privilege of knowing the Scriptures which are able to
make us wise unto salvation (II Tim. 3:15)—a privilege of which
young Timothy was reminded by the apostle Paul. In II Timothy
1:5, 6, Paul noted that his young friend's knowledge of the
Scriptures begin with his grandmother as well as his mother.
These two women, Lois and Eunice, are on the roster of those
who have contributed to the moral and spiritual strength of a
minister-in-the-making. Paul also made an investment in
Timothy. In the two letters to Timothy there are numerous hints
as to the characteristics of an ideal pastor. The minister should

exhibit a "love which springs from a pure heart, a good conscience, and a genuine faith" (I Tim. 1:5). Whoever sets out to be a teacher of the moral law must thoroughly understand the subject. Since the office of bishop is an honorable position, he who aspires to it must be above reproach, faithful to his wife, sober, temperate, courteous, hospitable, and a good teacher (I Tim. 3:1-7). The New English Bible has an excellent rendering here: "He must moreover have a good reputation with the non-Christian public." There are even words of counsel about physical and bodily fitness. While physical fitness has a certain value, spiritual fitness is essential (I Tim. 4:8). The young pastor should not be looked down upon but should make himself an example to believers in speech and behavior, in love, fidelity, and purity (I Tim. 4:12).

In regard to the worship of the congregation Paul advises the pastor: "Devote your attention to the *public reading* of the scriptures, to exhortation, and to teaching" (I Tim. 4:13, NEB). Generally, the Greek word *anagnosei* in I Timothy 4:13 has been interpreted as a man's private reading. But the original refers to the lectionary, prescribed Scripture readings at the worship service. This procedure was followed by the early Christians, who adopted much of the Hebrew practice at first.

After retiring from the pastorate and worshiping from the angle of the pew in a variety of churches, I found a casual procedure developing. In an effort to be free and not bound by ritual, the service degenerates into a pattern ordained by the whim and mood of the leader. In many services without the liturgy or lectionary and pericope, Scripture reading is often limited to a few verses read by the pastor just before preaching. The heritage of prescribed readings in the Bible has been discontinued. Paul advised Timothy to pay "attention to the *public reading* of the scriptures." One of today's needs is to lead a congregation in this crucial act of worship.

Constant reading of the Scriptures will familiarize the congregation with the total library of divine revelation. A beginning can be made by selecting one Old Testament lesson and one New Testament lesson for each service. One of these should be a basic text for the message to be taught and preached. The other might serve to prepare the congregation to hear the Word of

God. The people could be invited to join in a responsive reading; they might be asked to stand to read as an act of worship. When the congregation is permitted to sit, the result is usually a few garbled sounds from a small percentage of those present. Standing, the group will gradually learn to read together! The music of the rustle of the leaves and the waves of sound will gain in emphasis and volume as from every pew families are reading together. It is an idea to have an elder or deacon or someone else from the congregation lead in this act of public reading. But let no one on the spur of the moment stand up to read—preparation beforehand is necessary if we are to achieve our highest and best.

A dividend in spiritual worship comes immediately from the public reading of the Scriptures. The passage read becomes fundamental to the forthcoming exhortation. It is tragic if a preacher "exhorts" without a basis in Scripture or endeavors to "teach" what is unrelated to the authority of Scripture. This is a constant peril in our age of activism. The desire to be successful results in stress on "how-to" programs. In the process the relationship of the Scriptures to life and character is often neglected.

Those who have achieved the greatest influence for God in public ministries are those who are saturated in the Scriptures. Strange that preachers can be so casual about the Bible, while others openly offer thanksgiving for the influence of the Bible on their lives. After a public reading of literature which included selections from the Bible, Charles Laughton the actor told me that he owed much to that source of knowledge and inspiration.

The Welsh poet Dylan Thomas (1914-1953) was asked about the dominant influences which shaped his thought and words. In addition to Joyce and Freud, whose works he regarded as direct influences, the Bible was paramount.

> Its great stories of Noah, Jonah, Lot, Moses, Jacob, David, Solomon and a thousand more, I had, of course, known from very early youth; the great rhythms had rolled over me from the *Welsh pulpits*; and I read, for myself, from Job and Ecclesiastes; and the story of *the New Testament is part of my life.* But I have never sat down and studied the Bible, never consciously echoed its language, and am, in reality, as ignorant of

it as most brought-up Christians. All of the Bible that I use in my work is remembered from childhood, and is the common property of all who were brought up in the English-speaking communities. Nowhere, indeed, in all my writing, do I use any knowledge which is not commonplace to any literate person. I *have* used a few difficult words in early poems, but they are easily looked up and were, in any case, thrown into the poems in a kind of adolescent showing-off which I hope I have now discarded.

Whatever our judgment concerning the life and work of Dylan Thomas, he does testify that he was deeply influenced by the reading of the Scriptures. There is a special quality of word and depth of meaning in the language of Scripture. In its original form the Bible was written in the language of the common people of those far-off days. Translations have endeavored to match that language. Is there a secret which defies analysis when scriptural language is discussed? What strength beyond the ordinary lies within it? Far beyond Shakespeare and the other great writers of the centuries the Bible possesses an age-abiding power. We rightly speak of it as the Word of God. God speaks. Man listens. As Samuel Coleridge said, "It finds us!"

The opportunity which the pastor-preacher has to receive blessing is overwhelming. Think of the beauty of the architecture of our sanctuaries with their stone, brick, wood, and glass. Yet, even though the building may be plain or simple, when worship takes place, we are caught up in its beauty and we "worship in the beauty of holiness" (Ps. 29:2). Consider also the music provided by those who sing or play the organ, piano, or other instruments. The singing of a congregation bound together as worshipers before God can lift the ordinary hour to one of sublime majesty and sheer joy. The soaring songs of the Psalms are filled with utter joy. In the area of art the Spirit of God gives creativity to select people. Their imagination and skill afford us rich experiences of beauty.

We receive our basic training in the art of interpretation from the university. It is the university's function to introduce us to the work which has already been done in hermeneutics and to equip us with the tools to make further advances in this area on our own. John Buchan (1875-1940) touched on this theme in his installation address as chancellor of the University of Edinburgh in 1938. In "The Interpreter's House" he discussed *the meaning of a university*. As the son of a Scottish manse, it is not surprisng that he drew from the familiar language of John Bunyan, who in turn drank at the undefiled well of the prose of the English Bible. Buchan said:

> A university is not a mere Wicket Gate where the journey began; and which, once passed, is no more thought of; it is something which should influence every stage of our life. So, adopting Bunyan's language, I think of it as the Interpreter's House where we receive our *viaticum* for the road. . . . A university has two plain duties. It has to transmit knowledge, and has to advance knowledge.

As we work in the field of hermeneutics, we must beware of uncritically accepting the prejudices and biases of other preachers as accurate reflections of the meaning of Scripture. Constant awareness and vigilance are required as we study and exegete texts. Ian Pitt-Watson, professor of practical theology at King's College in Aberdeen, in a recent series of Warrack Lectures under the title *A Kind of Folly* (1977), discusses Paul's familiar reference to the "foolishness of preaching" (I Cor. 1:21-25). Pitt-Watson reasons that "part of the foolishness of the Gospel is the foolishness of preaching." He interprets this passage to mean that preaching in itself is something foolish. It may well be—at least to Greeks of old and some contemporary listeners and critics—but we prefer the translation of James Moffatt in rendering the crucial text as "the 'sheer folly' of the Christian message." What was deemed foolish in the first century was the heart and content of the gospel: God in Christ would reconcile an alienated world through the death of the cross. Pitt-Watson is most perceptive when he gives samples of what the sermon can be. His stress is that *theology is for preaching*. His book is a timely exhortation for our generation, and reminiscent of some historic figures of the past.

We might mention Jonathan Edwards, who found himself writing "Resolutions" to guide him in preparation and preaching. For example, "To study the Sciptures so steadily, constantly and frequently, so that I may find, and plainly perceive myself to grow in, the knowledge of the same." He testified, "I had then and at other times, the greatest delight in the holy Scriptures, of any book whatsoever."

Though the years may take their toll in strength and spirit, there is the abiding conviction that no other calling is as worthwhile as that of the minister. Ministering to *people*, the pastor finds a strength given when he is insufficient in himself; he finds an open door into the confidences of people in trouble and in need. There are a lilt and a glow in his personality, for he knows that "being a minister today is the most exciting, challenging work in the world. It is exhausting. It can be frustrating; it is filled with harassments and distractions. But I wouldn't swap places with any other man, and there is no work in which I could be half so happy." So witnessed Silas Kessler of Hastings, Nebraska, Presbyterian pastor and former moderator of the General Assembly of the United Presbyterian Church in the United States.

The results achieved by the interpreter cannot be measured by us in our lifetime. They are far-reaching in the ongoing stream of the church's influence and mission. F. W. Dillistone's biography of C. H. Dodd ((1884-1973) is entitled simply *C. H. Dodd: Interpreter of the New Testament* (Grand Rapids: William B. Eerdmans, 1977). Dodd was scholar, preacher, professor; yet with all his erudition and knowledge poured into more than a score of books he preferred to be known simply as an "interpreter." He sought to equip himself with the best possible tools of historical and linguistic disciplines in order that he might use them efficiently for the better communicating of the Christian faith to the world of the twentieth century. To be known as an "interpreter" is a crowning accolade for any pastor-preacher-teacher.

Baker's Dictionary of Practical Theology (Grand Rapids: Baker Book House, 1967) has a rich section on hermeneutics which develops many themes. (1) Beginning with the principles of biblical interpretation as defined in the New Testament, the reader is led step by step through the various facets of this craft. (2) It is fascinating to trace our Lord's method of teaching by means of parables and to discover how Hebrew life and customs provided background for seemingly commonplace stories which have great meaning even for us today. (3) Quotations from the

Old Testament found in the New Testament require careful study. This is basic for any would-be preacher intending to expound the Scriptures. (4) Archaeology opens up new interpretations of the history and geography of the ancient world. (5) When the Dead Sea Scrolls were discovered, there was an eruption of new knowledge and still the task of deciphering continues. Our knowledge of the original text of Scripture has been improved as a result. (6) At the time of the Reformation a new method of interpretation was employed. The Reformers insisted that Scripture should be interpreted by Scripture. No longer was the clergy or an institution the final arbiter. With the opening of the Bible to the people, the new hermeneutics came into flower. The Word of God was itself the authority under the enlightenment of the Holy Spirit. (7) Prophecy is a fascinating subject which always requires care in interpreting how the past and the future intertwine. Guidelines are set forth for the study of the messianic predictions fulfilled in the Christ.

This special dictionary also has other articles and relevant bibliographies which will enlarge the ministry of anyone who uses it. Bernard L. Ramm, for example, has written about the "new hermeneutic," which originated in Europe and has now spread to America. It is necessary to be informed about this avenue of new theories. Finally, the tools of the interpreter are discussed by an acknowledged expert, James P. Martin, now principal of the Vancouver School of Theology at the University of British Columbia. As to the bibliographies, many books should be added. Nothing stands still in the work of the interpretation of the Bible.

The evangelical ministry has always accepted the Bible as the inspired Word of God. To it the preacher and teacher turns for light and truth. Immediately he must interpret what he reads. This he does with the aid of the tools available to him. Paul told Timothy that he should *handle rightly* the word of truth (II Tim. 2:15). The Greek word *orthotomeo* means to cut a straight line. Timothy is being advised, then, to guide the word of truth along a straight line. There is peril in reading into the text instead of leading out from the text. Paul warns against the sin of corrupting the text, for in this process the truth of the Scriptures is adulerated (II Cor. 2:17).

Happy is the person whose days of preparation for preaching and teaching are filled with Bible study. We dare not imagine that what we know individually and set forth alone is final and unchanging as if we had all knowledge! We should keep an open mind, checking and rechecking the writings of those who have shared their insights with the universal church. By the Holy Spirit's guidance, we ever find new light breaking forth from God's holy Word.

16

The Vision of the Ministry

"Him we proclaim, warning every man and teaching every man in all wisdom, that we may present every man mature in Christ. For this I toil, striving with all the energy which he mightily inspires within me. (COL. 1:28, 29 RSV)

"Go therefore and make disciples of all nations, baptizing them in the name of the Father and of the Son and of the Holy Spirit, teaching them to observe all that I have commanded you; and lo, I am with you always, to the close of the age." (MATT. 28:19, 20, RSV)

"O come, let us worship and bow down; let us kneel before the Lord our maker." (PS. 95:6)

THOSE WHO ARE CALLED and equipped to serve "under orders" discover that the work to which they are appointed has certain basic aims clearly outlined. The New Testament church at the first realized its unity in Christ and the gifts to be exercised by members of Christ's body. The functions of the pastoral leadership included oversight of the members; hence the concept of the shepherd-bishop. As pastor-teacher the minister instructed and as presbyter-elder ruled the congregation. The work of the servant of God, then, was manifold and demanded a variety of gifts. Administrator, counselor, missionary, evangelist, educator, pastor, preacher—the minister has many images to project to the congregation. Each of these involves several special goals and tasks which are part of our commission.

The Great Commission of our Lord in His marching orders to the apostles directed them to make disciples. What an opportunity! The Bible has much to teach about this subject. To make disciples is to aim at the conversion of our hearers. Revealing God's role in history and in personal experience, the Word of God encourages submission to the divine mind and will. Conversion is an overall word to describe the transformation of people who have been touched by the Holy Spirit and convinced that Christ is the Lord of life. Our Lord spoke to Nicodemus in terms of being "born again" (John 3:3-5). Here the mysterious process of change and turning is related to being born from above, in contrast to our physical birth below. The natural birth is not sufficient for citizenship in the kingdom of God—there is need for supernatural birth. Charles Wesley in his Christmas hymn "Hark! The Herald Angels Sing" noted that Christ was "born to give them *second birth*." One of the aims of the pastor-preacher is to present the truth of the gospel and expect the Holy Spirit to make disciples by its application to individual hearts in the mystery and power of divine energy. The church, therefore, is not to be a religious club with membership standards and initiation fees: it is the church of the living God, and He alone decides who are members and sharers in the divine life.

John and Charles Wesley found that religious formalism and good works, even pious devotion and service to others, lacked what they later came to call the inwardness of true religion. Their friend George Whitefield likewise spoke of transformation in the new creation described by the apostle Paul. These three men of God witnessed in love to thousands who as a result entered into eternal life and the kingdom of God. At the same time, in New England Jonathan Edwards believed profoundly that the sermon was the agency of conversion. Others might stress the ordinances or sacraments as a means of conversion in a period of spiritual decline and formalism. Edwards restored the sermon to its primacy in the act of worship. He believed that the sacraments were for the elect, for those already committed in faith; but through the sermon could come renewal of life when man encountered God and the crisis of the gospel. This was in keeping with good Puritan doctrine and practice. When New England was in danger of forgetting its heritage, Edwards saw many conversions as a result of his message. "It was through a sermon that nine out of ten of the elect caught the first hints of their vocation, and by continued listening to good preaching they made their calling sure." The sermon was the way of new life to many. They saw the miracle of grace take place through "the sound of faithful words."

John Henry Newman, though poles apart from Jonathan Ed-

wards, also affirmed that the sermon is a divine agency of conversion. In his book *Idea of a University* (New York: Oxford
University Press, 1976) he stated:

> Definiteness is the life of preaching. A definite hearer, not the
> whole world; a definite topic, not the whole evangelical tradi-
> tion; and in like manner, a definite speaker. Nothing that is
> anonymous will preach; nothing that is dead and gone; nothing
> even which is of yesterday, however religious in itself and use-
> ful. Thought and word are one in the Eternal Logos, and must
> not be separate in those who are His shadows on earth. They
> must issue fresh; as from the preacher's mouth, so from his
> breast, if they are to be "spirit and life" to the hearts of his
> hearers.

The universal church over the centuries has had as its primary
aim and goal the proclamation of the Good News and the conversion of sinners.

The minister also has opportunity to bring healing and health.
Our age is one of anxiety and frustration as well as of loneliness.
Alienation is everywhere in human society. Not only are nations
in tension with each other, but groups and families as well as individuals are in need of reconciliation. Medical science, psychology, and psychiatry unveil the deep-seated wounds of the
soul and the body. Studies tell us of the psychosomatic interac-
tion of the mind and body in the stress and strain of modern life.
How can people be healed of their sickness of mind? How can
we deal with the alcoholic who is no longer spoken of as a
drunkard, but only as sick and not sinful? Then there is the
homosexual with his disordered life, and many waste away their
lives with drugs.

In every metropolitan area the submerged and forgotten eke
out an existence. The needs of millions in our world of dimin-
ishing resources and in the Third World in convulsion tug at the
heartstrings of the Christian and cry for help. What can we do?
Surely we can help to heal and make whole the person in need.
We can serve through the ministry of the gospel. Physical ills
can be remedied through medicine, faith, and prayer; we can
help counsel those who are sick and afflicted. Even as our Lord
went about preaching, teaching, and healing (Matt. 4:23), God's
servants can follow in His steps.

John Henry Jowett, an outstanding Congregational pastor and preacher of another generation, related that certain limitations of health prevented him from carrying out a program of regular pastoral visitation. He preferred to meditate and study to produce the sermons of grace and beauty he delivered. It was a custom for him to go to the church during the week and sit in different pews. As he sat in a specific pew, he would recall the name of the family that sat there on Sunday. Then he would pray and intercede for the members of that family. People testified that through his preaching on Sunday they were touched and helped in unusual ways to find strength to meet the struggles of life. His sermons had a therapeutic power which reached his hearers in worship. Truly, as the spiritual says, "There is a balm in Gilead, to heal the sin-sick soul."

Another opportunity presented the minister is nurture of the faithful. After faith in and commitment to Christ have been publicly expressed, there is a danger that people will be left on their own. Further development is essential for growth in the Christian life. Nurture of the faith of the new disciple is crucial; otherwise there is the risk of stunted growth instead of steady progress. The one who enrols in the school of Christ is still a novice. Peter counsels such to "grow in grace and in the knowledge of . . . Christ" (II Peter 3:18). A snowball gets bigger and bigger but does not grow within; it increases in size by accretion from without. Real growth in life is the result of an inner, silent process from conception to maturity. Christian nurture is most necessary for new disciples.

From the Reformation it has been emphasized that the church must have a teaching ministry. From Martin Luther, John Calvin, and John Knox, through John Wesley, and on to our day, the teaching function has been stressed. An educated ministry leads to an educated people. When the Pilgrim Fathers settled in New England, continuing their godly experiment, they sacrificed to have an educated people. Most of the oldest universities in the United States were established for the purpose of training ministers.

The agency of the Sunday school arose in addition to the teaching offered in catechism and confirmation classes. All denominations have developed youth societies and programs.

Francis E. Clark (1851-1927) was the founder of the Christian Endeavor Society, which now enrols millions of young people across the world. The pastor of a Congregational church in Portland, Maine, Clark organized the first society on February 2, 1881, to train and activate his young people. His organization became the first worldwide Protestant youth movement, crossing church lines, national borders, and cultural barriers. Its secret lay in its witness to and nurture of young people.

Since the separation of church and state in America now rules out Bible teaching in public schools, there is urgent need for more and better Christian education. Only the Christian church can attend to this business. Her measure of success in this matter will determine the strength (or the weakness) of the members of Christ's body in facing the future. Catechisms and creeds and confessions of faith are vital methods for the instruction of youth. Memorization of outstanding biblical passages will so fill and feed the youthful mind as to repay dividends in later life. The rise of false cults and religions across the world should alert us who are in the Christian church to teach our youth "what we believe" and "why we are Christ's."

Educating disciples in the faith is associated with our Lord's injunction to love God with our *mind*, as well as with our soul, heart, and strength (Mark 12:30). Some pastor-preachers will have the privilege of teaching a Bible class as well as preaching in the services of worship. Dialogue in class is excellent preparation for young and old who will then join in worship under the leadership of the same pastor. The apostle Paul wrote most of his letters to new disciples. In them he stressed the doctrines to be believed and then the duties to be carried out in moral and ethical situations. His balanced teaching also answered the questions these new saints asked concerning how to live in a world of idolatry and lawlessness.

We can do some teaching within the context of our preaching if we follow the Christian year or the church calendar. This is not a rigid or mechanical procedure, for there will be weeks when other truths can be considered. One value, however, in following a schedule adhering to the major emphases of the Christian year is that our preaching-teaching will likely include all of the vital doctrines and counsel of God. To follow a casual procedure ("What shall I preach on Sunday?") produces a personal calendar which risks omitting major vital doctrines and leaving a congregation impoverished and sometimes ignorant.

The teaching ministry wears well over the years of a pastorate. Exposition of the Bible and the regular unfolding of its books and doctrines, commandments and parables, will build up the pastor's own knowledge and character—and then do the same for his people. Springing from a pastor's serious study, sermons of this kind and quality shed biblical and theological light on the deepest needs of a congregation.

I once showed my Shorter Catechism to Samuel M. Zwemer. He found great humor in the fact that the multiplication tables were printed on the back cover. This to him was a typical example of Scottish thrift: printing such tables in a religious booklet. I informed him that on this occasion he had missed the point. The boys and girls who memorized the questions and answers about biblical doctrine were also to learn that doctrine should have its expression in ethical and moral standards. The presence of the multiplication tables taught that the Christian faith should be applied to correct handling of money and figures in business. In a practical way the booklet was stressing honesty and integrity. In all teaching of the church, the truths of the gospel should be regarded as norms of moral, social, and economic life.

The minister also has the opportunity to worship with the congregation. The pastor-preacher is to worship even as he leads in worship. The guidance of the Holy Spirit has been promised. When people gather from all walks of life and with differing levels of intellectual and spiritual experience, one of our aims is to lead them as part of the universal church of God. This is a most responsible task and requires much preparation on the part of those who lead. There are many acts of worship: the reading of Scripture, the prayers, the praises of congregation and choir, the tithes and offerings, and then there is still the sermon. The message of the hour should not be downgraded or dispensed with: it is the Word of God proclaimed!

Why is it that some leave a service of worship without having sensed the presence of God? We may find a greater sense of reverence at a symphony concert than in a church service. Is it because our worship is bleak and bare? Is it lacking in vitality and spirit? Form, ritual, and ceremony are aids; but what if the heart has gone out of them? Ritual is no substitute for reality. Ceremony cannot displace consecration. Form is less than genuine faith. If worship is the *response* of the Christian church to the revelation of God in Christ, then what happens in worship when we preach? Our preaching is the sacrament of the Word; we are the servants of the Word. When John Wesley went to Newcastle-on-Tyne in the northeast of England he wrote in his journal: "I did offer them Christ." Do we? Preaching is vital for it must expound the very heart of the Word of God. The bleakness in worship lies, too often, in the neglect of that Word.

To solve the problem of bleakness we must concentrate on the truth as it breaks forth from the Word. Symbols are not essential (although there is a place for symbols in church architecture and in our sacraments or ordinances). They do not overcome the darkness, because the darkness is an absence of the Spirit-inspired Word of God. It was not that the Reformers were willing to settle for something less than symbols and drama; it was that they had found something so much more that symbols looked pale and sick beside the living fact of the Word of God. The bleakness, then, was in the symbols, not in true evangelical worship. We can recover true worship through biblical exposition.

In the highest act of the soul we worship God. We give Him His due. How fitting that in the sermon itself is an act of such worship. It is an offering up to God of the truth proclaimed in His name. Protestant confessions claim to be no more than subordinate standards, subordinate to and reformable by the supreme standard, which is the Word of God. John Calvin is known chiefly as the author of the *Institutes of the Christian Religion*, but in his own view he was above everything else an expositor of the Scriptures. The *Institutes* is an abstract and systematic outline of biblical doctrine. Theology is an exposition of the truths in the Word of God. It is the preacher's function to make them clear to the church and to the people.

It is essential that the sermon be given a prominent place in worship. No service is complete without a sermon. Early Protestantism may have stressed the Word above the sacraments. And perhaps rightly so, in reaction against the abuses of the Middle

Ages. But Protestant preaching may be said to have a sacramental aspect. In Scotland, the large Bible is carried to the pulpit by an officer who walks in front of the pastor. Then the pastor-preacher stands behind the sacred desk. This underscores that he stands behind that book, the Bible, to expound it; he finds his message in it and nowhere else. Many attributed to the reading and especially the preaching of the Word of God an efficacy for salvation. The worshiping congregation looked up and expected to hear from that pulpit Bible what God the Lord had to say to them. They eagerly awaited that moment.

What opportunities the minister has as an interpreter of truth! At first this may seem presumptuous. Today's critic might regard the minister as irrelevant in this regard. We may not be needed now, for other commentators have arisen on radio, on television, and in the press. The dramatist and novelist also claim a hearing. We do not deny certain prerogatives to these "would-be preachers" who now compete with the church. They do bring news—but it is generally bad news, sad, tragic. They rarely carry good news and seldom the gospel. They tell what events have taken place; they analyze and comment upon the outward actions. But they cannot explain *why* human nature acts for good or ill; they have no insight into basic motivation. Time looms large in their thought, but eternity is missing.

In worship the whole church is gathered to learn of the divine view of life. Week by week we expound the eternal truths with relevancy for the contemporary scene. Our task is not eisegesis but exegesis. Our people are engrossed with demands in the workaday world. They have given us exemption from that involvement (except in rare instances) in order that we might spend valuable hours in preparation to bring to them in worship some of the unsearchable riches of Christ. They ask to be fed with the Bread of life even as they must work for the bread that perishes.

To grasp our opportunities and clarify our aims and be effective witnesses and shepherds, *we must get rid of our complacency.* It is perilous to assume that because we are in this privileged position we will have people eager to hear our latest pronouncement. We are not so important in the eyes of the world around. Perhaps only a minority will support us and hear us. We must earn the right to be heard. We dare not enter the pulpit casually or carelessly. If we have serious purpose, a burning passion, and a definite aim, we will be ready for a fresh enduement of the divine Spirit to aid us.

We must engage in a teaching ministry. We cannot take for granted that those who worship or share our services are at the highest level of Christian intelligence. Their "I.Q." in biblical, doctrinal, and experiential Christianity may be much less than we assume. Therefore teaching-evangelism is not to be overlooked. With the toil and temptation of the secular world facing them, the people will look up and expect that which will strengthen them in the struggles of life.

We must break up the fallow ground. The prophet Hosea cried out that revival might come to his nation. Our Lord spoke of the sower, the seed, and the different kinds of soil. The response of the soil to the seed sown varies. Rocky soil and thorny soil can be reworked into good soil so that the seed will be able to take root. The hard economic realities of contemporary life cause man to think of the gospel of getting on in the world and succeeding materially and financially. We must not give him in worship the gospel of trying harder, the gospel of self-effort. We must bring the gospel of the Good News, of grace, of forgiveness, of holy love, of recoverability, and transformation of life and character. God aims to reach the individuals for whom Christ died and we are honored to be agencies in the process of redemption. We are promised a harvest from the sowing of the seed. If this be our aim, blessed are we.

The opportunity to share the rich deposits of truth mined each week and over many years is one of the highlights of systematic preaching to the same congregation. The best preaching and the moments of highest intensity are found during the routine duties of a long pastorate, not on special occasions. There is an empathy born of close association with people in their daily lives, during times of joy and especially at the crucial hours of sorrow, suffering, death.

John A. Hutton, one-time editor of the *British Weekly*, a prestigious paper of religious and social impact, drew deeply from his background as a Presbyterian minister. He found refreshment in the works of Robert Browning and other poets. In *Guidance from Robert Browning in Matters of Faith* (Philadelphia: Richard West, 1930) and *Pilgrims in the Region of Faith* (Philadelphia: Richard West, 1973 reprint), which is a discussion of Amiel, Tolstoy, Pater, and Newman, Hutton shows how difficult faith is for introspective, self-analyzing minds in an unsettled, all-questioning age. His interpretations in the light of Scripture are penetrating.

I have heard Hutton preach. I recall one memorable sermon in connection with the British Association for the Advancement of Science. He had read Psalm 90. His sermon expounded its major thrusts and probing words. War had recently broken out. Having lost a son in battle, the preacher became impassioned. He was like a volcano with lava erupting from its depths! The pathos of the preacher was echoed by the congregation; we were melted and moved. The anguish of the preacher penetrated to the very depths of our souls. Preaching in this manner is the highest art known, more vivid than architecture, more intimate than music, more persuasive than poetry, more dramatic than drama—for here is the greatest drama ever staged, as we think of that lonely cross outside a city wall!

In 1921 Hutton gave the first of the Warrack Lectures, which he entitled *That the Ministry Be Not Blamed.* He preferred to call them "Conversations." This volume's ample use of literary resources results in unusual insights and expressions. Hutton's love of Robert Browning and other poets is everywhere evident. The preacher was also steeped in Russian literature, especially the novels of Dostoevsky. Unforgettable is his delineation of the spirit of the Antichrist, incarnated in the figure of the Grand Inquisitor face to face with our Lord Jesus Christ *(The Brothers Karamazov).* The pastor who would develop an imaginative style in preaching should follow Hutton's example by saturating himself with the poetry of the Bible and feeling the surge of clear, flowing music as mediated through the beauty and fragrance of the Scriptures. Then, he should become thoroughly acquainted with a large number of outstanding poets.

The ministry is the most rewarding of all vocations. Essentially it is a vocation or calling and not a profession. Our modern society has a tendency to speak of it as one of many professions, and there are not wanting religious writers who use the term with respect to the ministry. In the modern sense "profession" refers to a specialized field of skills and abilities, but the Christian ministry is more than that. As a calling or vocation, it takes all that a man possesses in dedication of body, mind, and spirit. A man of God has opportunities to live and serve surpassing all others. To enter the sacred vocation one must have *a sense of what is vital.* Without this we may excel in mechanics and fail in dynamics. Before we can achieve the highest end of the ministry, there are three vital areas to be considered—personal knowledge of Christ, experience of new life, and a sense of mission.

First, we must have personal knowledge of Christ. As the sun is to the solar system, so is Christ to the preacher. Before we can be transmitters of divine truth, we should be certain that we are not merely like phonographs grinding out an oft-repeated tale instead of being a living voice for God.

No one should enter the sacred calling apart from divine grace. The call of God may come in a variety of ways, but the fact should be beyond doubt. A person without conviction concerning this is unfit for the task. Moses at the burning bush, Gideon on the farm, Amos on the hillside, Isaiah at worship in the temple, Paul on the Damacus road, Apollos at the university, and Timothy in his childhood home—these illustrate the variety of the Holy Spirit's call. But to be "in Christ" before entering the ministry is indispensable.

Second, we must experience new life. Beyond knowledge of Christ as Savior and Lord the Holy Spirit must indwell our being. There is an experience of God *beyond* conversion, known in our confessional language as holiness or sanctification. Many testify to that deeper work of "the life of God in the soul of man." Henry Scougal wrote a small book with that very title in 1677. A copy came into the hands of Susanna Wesley, and she sent it to her sons John and Charles, who were at Lincoln College in Oxford. She requested them to read it, thinking the answer to all that they were seeking was there.

Witness the story of Sherwood Eddy (1871-1963), who told of a day when he felt that "rivers of living water were flowing through him" (cf. John 7:37, 38) to reach and enrich the student world of his generation. The result was a lifetime of service to the Y.M.C.A. E. Stanley Jones (1884-1973) likewise testified to an hour of spiritual illumination when as a missionary, discouraged and in ill health, he became the flaming prophet and apostle who walked with the *Christ of the Indian Road.*

Third, we must have a sense of mission. There must be a total commitment of our life to the will of God. "What wilt thou have me to do, Lord?" is the question of the man of God. "Here am I; send me" (Isa. 6:8). A passionate sense of mission is necessary for our best work. Working without such vision is drudgery and reflects a lack in the inner life.

A fellow student at Edinburgh University once asked me, "Are you going in for the Kirk?" (This calls to mind members of a later generation who wonder if they should study theology to find out whether they like it. If they find they do, they consider serving in the church to improve human relations and help needy people.) I responded in such a way as to correct what I perceived to be a misapprehension on his part. Ministers do not enter a profession with comforts and cushioned pleasures, but are called to sacrificial service. They might even have to work completely on their own, without benefit of an organized institution. The Lord of the harvest thrusts out His servants into the world field.

When Arthur J. Gossip went to his first charge in the north of Scotland, Alexander Whyte preached the installation sermon. The topic was "In the Fulness of the Time" (Gal. 4:4). He traced with reverent imagination the sovereign providence of almighty God bending all history, the whole church, and Gossip's life in particular, until everything converged to that significant hour when the congregation and the new pastor were brought together. No element of chance was involved. That is a sublime faith and a not-to-be-forgotten doctrine which brings spiritual stamina and power to a minister facing the opportunities of life.

No one needs to go out without this grand assurance. We may even seek to heal others when we need to be healed. Urging others to run the race, we may walk with heavy steps. There is no room for self-pity. The Holy Spirit will incline our mind and heart away from our own problems to take up the challenge of extraordinary opportunities to do God's work. We must serve the Master without reservation. We should emulate the slave of another age, who, when offered freedom, replied, "I love my master; I will not be free." We may not have our ear bored through with an aul as physical evidence that we are no longer our own master (Exod. 21:6), but we know that we now serve forever the Lord Jesus Christ.

Historically the ministry has been judged a calling or vocation unlike other areas of life in that financial rewards and tangible evidences of success are not the measure of achievement. Our postwar period has witnessed a reevaluation of the ministry. Numerous books and articles have been issued on subjects like new patterns in the ministry. A key issue is whether the office should be known as a profession or nonprofession. The *Expository Times* of June, 1975, dealt with this in an article by Peter Jarvis entitled "The Ministry: Occupation, Profession or Status?"

The new age before us requires a fresh orientation toward the ministry. The New Testament makes much of the fact that all the saints are members of the body of Christ and thus are the gifts of the Spirit to that body. In turn these people have natural gifts of endowment and they are to be used as living members of the body of Christ. Here are no distinctions of laity and clergy. It is recognized, however, that those who are set apart as pastor-teachers, evangelists, and so on, are to exercise *special* ministries. All then are ministers (servants) of the church, but there are those who are called to particular offices and functions. By ordination the pastor-teacher is recognized by the whole church for his special gifts and qualifications under the call of God.

The *Saturday Evening Post* of April 24, 1965, featured "The Protestant Minister: His Ordeals and His Triumphs" by Harold H. Martin. This article focused on Paul's memorable words in Ephesians 3:

> I was made a minister, according to the gift of the grace of God. . . . Unto me, who am less than the least of all saints, is this grace given, that I should preach . . . the unsearchable riches of Christ . . . that ye, being rooted and grounded in love, may be able to comprehend with all saints what is the breadth, and length, and depth, and height; and . . . that ye might be filled with all the fulness of God. (vv. 7, 8, 17-19)

Writing with insight and understanding, Martin offers many examples from contemporary life and ministry. The pathway of duty is not without obstacles, and not all ministers are accepted with appreciation by congregations. The preaching-teaching-counseling task brings its own satisfaction for the dedicated pastor, but there are times when the tests and trials seem almost unbearable. There are people in churches who do not like what is the dynamic application of truth as it is known in Jesus Christ as the Lord of all life and culture.

Ministers find their wives and families are caught up in the matrix of tension, and the pastor finds he is truly a man like other men with obstacles and temptations confronting him. He, too, needs a counselor and often there is no one to whom he can go and no one ready to listen with empathy. Nevertheless, the vocation is still the best in all the world.

The opportunity to grasp the sacredness of this calling comes to everyone who has consciously experienced an hour of illumination when the self-knowledge came that the ministry was to be the priority of his life. No other vocation would suffice. A true friend has been W. B. J. Martin, whose "Peter Parson" column is familiar to faithful readers of the *Presbyterian Outlook* in America and the *British Weekly* in Great Britain. For many years these reflections have been meat and drink to tried and tested pastors, offering them encouragement and fresh stimulus.

In his inimitable style "Peter Parson" has recorded his musings and personal critiques on the ministry in all of its manifold manifestations. Whether commenting upon the call to the ministry, the need to study theology, the place of music, Christian worship, the insights of the poets, or the unlimited stature of character open to us, he delivers a rapier thrust and a prodding stylus to make us uncomfortable as well as unveil the steps leading to higher altitudes. Without abandoning his Congregational heritage, "Peter Parson" has achieved a catholicity with the saints of all ages and all branches of the Christian church, opening windows of light to the responsive mind. "Peter Parson" will always be gratefully remembered for his decision to put into writing for his brethren his secret ideas and moods.

The vision of the ministry cannot be set aside lightly. It is the very warp and woof of the character of the one who would obey that divine call given in the providence of God. As the years come and go, that voice may seem far away and for some not so loud. But for those who still hear that voice sounding strongly and clearly, there is nothing else. If God really wants someone to enter His service, His call will be persistent, and that one voice will be heard above all the other voices clamoring for attention.

In that case there is a special work to be done. Professor E. Gordon Rupp of Cambridge has called attention to the call of the ministry:

> At a time when we are properly exploring the meaning of the ministry of the whole church, and the ministry of the laity, we need to remember the truth of F. D. Maurice's warning that if we take away from the significance of the calling of "the" ministry, we inevitably depreciate the meaning of all other ministries in the church.

With such vision the servant dares to venture.

17

The Passion to Preach

"Take heed therefore unto yourselves, and to all the flock, over the which the Holy Spirit hath made you overseers, to feed the church of God, which he hath purchased with his own blood." (ACTS 20:28)

"Woe is unto me if I preach not the gospel." (I COR. 9:16)

"For what we preach is not ourselves, but Jesus Christ as Lord, with ourselves as your servants for Jesus' sake." (II COR. 4:5, RSV)

AT THE BEGINNING of the century a literary critic in a New York paper reviewed a book on preaching and in derogatory terms said, "It was a pity so much ability and labor was spent by men whose work was aside from the main currents of human interest."

Other voices echoed this sentiment during more recent years. George A. Buttrick in 1931 called attention to the mood of the time by asking the question, "Is there room for the preacher?" The implication was that in the opinion of many (not including Buttrick) the church in the age of skyscrapers did not do anything and the preacher was given to words only.

A magazine article asked, "Why have sermons at all? Why not worship and silence but no preacher intruding?" Another magazine article suggested that there be a moratorium on preaching. Six outstanding preachers could be selected to broadcast over the nation at the same time and local congregations would make their selection. The local minister need not preach but simply serve as pastor to his people.

Marshall McLuhan in *Understanding Media* said that "words as media for any kind of message are dead. . . . Television and radio make preaching irrelevant. Preaching is non participating, granting to an audience a minimum of freedom." He implied that preaching would not survive in the age of television.

When in 1968 psychiatrist Paul W. Pruyser was asked to deliver the Yale Lectures on preaching, he hesitated at first since he was not a pastor or preacher. He was told by the dean, "The lectures' concern is no longer with preaching!"

After three months of research a Protestant scholar in 1970 wrote in a Minneapolis newspaper: "There are good prospects for Christianity but not for the institution of the church. Sermons are on the way out. And so is the morning worship service at 11:00 o'clock. The death rattle will be long and gruesome."

Fortunately, these forecasts have not been fulfilled across the English-speaking world. The 1970s saw widespread interest in the ministries of men and women who stand to proclaim Christian truth. Christian colleges and seminaries are aware of an upsurge of interest in preparation for various ministries in teaching-preaching.

The man who delivers a pure message in sincerity will not lack for a hearing. Our restless generation ever listens for a voice of truth which will fill the dread vacuum of the mind. People cannot live by the bread that perishes; they hungrily crave for the Bread of life. The 1950s and 1960s were times of moral and spiritual depression and disbelief. But the 1970s brought signs and portents of a resurgence of evangelical belief and conduct.

The passion to preach puts one "under orders" as it were. He cannot rest unless he engages in this divine work. If unworthy forms and distortions of true preaching have misled the church and our age, then the ideal must be sought anew in the light of revelation and experience.

The counterfeit is always the enemy of the genuine. John Bunyan knew this and in *The Holy War* he tells of Diabolus seeking to set up in the town of Mansoul a pulpit which would be "popular." Diabolus had his own "popular" gospel which he desired the people of Mansoul to hear and accept. It was his last attempt to subjugate them. But Emmanuel, the young Prince of God, would have none of it. Indeed, there have been preachers who built their ministries on "the hill called error." Christianity has suffered when Satan has come in "as an angel of light."

Apart from the methods or techniques required in the preparation and delivery of the message, the spirit of the minister is most important. We do not preach by simply speaking. Rather we share the overflow of our conviction and character as we witness to the person of our Lord. Within the context of public worship or in evangelism among the unchurched we have opportunities for God to act and have encounter with others through us.

The minister is afforded the opportunity to offer significant truth. Not all truth is the gospel, but the gospel is truth. The truth we bring is to become alive and potent in others' minds. It must be seen and grasped as being significant for them. It must shape and frame their outlook and behavior. Spiritual truth must be related to their sense of values; they must take a personal interest in it. Some do not see that Christian truth has value for them. "What difference could it possibly make?" they ask.

We must make the truth relevant and immediate. The truth must be empowered to act as a lever of decision and choice. It is dangerous and futile to leave the truth in cold storage. People may nod their heads in assent when we preach, but this does not mean that the sermon has penetrated their dull or darkened minds. "My mind to me a kingdom is" may mean that it is full of Saturday's sport or Monday's television program. If the truth does not move people, if it does not change them, if it does not lead them to action or decision, then such "believing" is ineffectual. That is why we need divine aid.

The modern world is barraged by television and radio. But, in contrast, our listeners are not on the right wavelength to receive our message. (This has nothing to do with the technical transmission of sound!). We speak, but the listener does not tune in readily. His set is tuned to Channel Vanity Fair, and should he accidentally turn the knob and pick up Channel Christianity for a moment, he may switch it off at once. He may not know that he has missed the most powerful and best station of all. To us, the sounds and the language are familiar and full of meaning; to Mr. Outsider they are sound and fury, just noise without meaning—unless some word or spirit touches him.

At this point we should not dismiss the problem of vocabulary. Do we talk over people's heads? Do our own people understand our theological jargon? If the committed have trouble at times,

how much more the outsider? I believe and treasure the great
words of the Christian faith. I know they can be learned,
studied, clarified, and simplified.

What is the vocabulary of the person whose work on the assembly line is dull and uninteresting and whose mental diet is
the sports page or the entertainment world? How many words
are in his vocabulary? It might be worthwhile inquiring. Are
some religious groups wiser than we in that they speak simple
words more than we do? This is our perennial task in preaching
and teaching—to take the eternal truth in the language which is
biblical and theological and to translate it into the thought patterns and speech forms of today. What an opportunity for us to
make clear what God has said. The thoughts, feelings, and
values of many today are so dulled that they find it difficult to
receive our message, unless like the prophet Ezekiel (3:15) we sit
where they sit.

In another generation Professor William James of Harvard
talked about "the will to believe." If a truth is to come alive and
evoke dynamic response or belief, it must possess what Professor
Herbert H. Farmer of Westminister College (Cambridge) calls
"intrinsic credibility." This is what William James meant by establishing an electric connection with the mind. Without this potency, truth remains dead, that is, incapable of stirring emotion
and gearing the will to action. Evoking response depends upon
the content or substance of the truth presented.

There was a time when most people were predisposed to believe in witchcraft. Thus witchcraft had a high degree of credibility. Today this is not so. Farmer likens a truth or proposition
to a glowing splinter and a mind to a jar of oxygen. Plunge the
splinter into the jar and it bursts into a bright flame; it comes
alive. The question now is: Do Christian truths or propositions
possess this glow today? Do men's minds, in the atmosphere of
today's mass society, contain enough "oxygen" to ignite the
glowing splinter? Or do they contain some other "gas" which ex-
tinguishes the glow?

There is ample evidence that Jonathan Edwards (1703-1758)
put the principles we have just discussed into action. In a time
when the basic truths of Christianity were given mere lip service, Edwards proclaimed the gospel with ardor and accuracy.

Edwards anticipated the teaching of William James in many ways. Especially in his preaching and command of the means of communication is his power seen.

Edwards appealed to his audience's emotions. He believed that the passions were the prime movers in life, and therefore he was not afraid to appeal to the elementary instincts of self-interest and of fear. Critics have objected to this note in his preaching, but it is certainly one of the most effective elements in his method. He believed that unless a man was moved by some affections, he was by nature inactive. "Take away all love and hatred, all hope and fear, all anger, zeal, and affectionate desire, and the world would be in a great measure motionless and dead; there would be no such thing as activity among mankind or any earnest pursuit whatsoever" (cf. *Works* III.19, 20).

His defense of the Great Awakening against its critics in large part consisted of a presentation of psychological principles in harmony with the times. "As the passions are the springs of conduct, vital religion must consist in an exercise of them and the kind of religious expression which the supernatural sense bestowed by God's grace on the elect might be expected to bring forth" (cf. *Works* III.275). The element of fear, in particular, loomed large in the imprecatory sermons. The appeal to selfishness and man's hope for the hereafter was also there. No one pictured more glowingly the joys of the redeemed, the blessedness of union with Christ, and the felicities of the full knowledge of God.

We today must ask the question: Are we missing a breakthrough in communication because we hesitate to use the eschatological, to call attention to death and judgment, the climax of history and time? Consider the early Christians' emphasis on this, and the Christian hope of Christ's second advent and coming kingdom. Our age is endangered by weapons which could blast away much of global life. Communism and other totalitarian forces of false religions threaten millions with slavery and death. Are we remiss in not playing upon the fears of the present age in order to press upon man's conscience the final absolutes, the dread alternative, and the ultimate destinies in the Christian message? It is not so much that people need understanding, but that their hearts should be moved.

The minister has opportunity to preach evangelistically. During public worship the spiritual life of the minister and also of the congregation is unveiled. The same holds true when there is an outreach in witnessing to others without. Both in the order of worship and in evangelism among unchurched society the evangel is proclaimed in word and in deed. Too long has this been left to the so-called evangelist. The itinerant does have a place in the total church. But the spirit of evangelism should permeate the whole church at all times. Paul counseled young Timothy, "Do the work of an evangelist" (II Tim. 4:5). The pastor-preacher-teacher does have opportunities to lead his congregation in Christian nurture. But families and individuals in the community are also touched by his life and witness. He is God's representative on all occasions and these become opportunities of evangelism.

To be effective evangelists, we must have a special encounter with God. In 1827 at Charlottetown, Prince Edward Island, the Reverend Donald McDonald stood on the road, a thin column of smoke arising from a heap of manuscripts before him. On that morning of his spiritual resurrection he burned his old sermons. This may be an extreme example, although others have gone through a similar crisis. We assume that those who engage in the Christian ministry have had an encounter with God in Christ. In the biblical pattern there must be the sequence of "revelation, experience, mission," as in the records of Isaiah, Amos, Hosea, Jeremiah, and the apostle Paul.

In Scotland Thomas Chalmers, after some years in the ministry with barren results, had a transforming experience with God. He testified to this in his well-known sermon, "The Expulsive Power of a New Affection." Perhaps Chalmers burned some of his old sermons, but many of them were kept for a new day and transformed. The sermon born in the study can be born again in the pulpit.

In England, John Wesley and his brother Charles were both revitalized in spirit and purpose during the Whitsuntide of 1738 when within a week of each other they became conscious of a "warmed heart" through the divine Spirit. God moved upon these men in an unusual measure and the fire of God fell upon them.

It is this deeper life, this richer affluence, which brings the spirit of evangelism. By preaching evangelistically we do not mean that the sermon must follow a conventional mode with stereotyped phrases or clichés. The vital element is the *spirit* of every sermon and service. As is clear from the parable in Luke 15, God is a seeking God; and His servants must catch that compassion and feeling. The evangelical spirit can be present at all times. What deed of social action is urgent? What community problem needs attention? What new adventure of faith do we bring to our people? What concerns do we transmit in preaching? What seals and tokens do we communicate in this spiritual odyssey? If the sermon is comfortable or too easy for people, then we need to reexamine ourselves and our message. Communication of the divine love bathing our human love, the deep soundings of man's need, and the spirit which seeks and searches, woos and wins—these are vital for God's servant.

The minister's spirit must be vital. Nothing cold or inanimate will do. We are as men charged with the power of God. "Not by might, nor by power, but by my spirit, saith the Lord" (Zech. 4:6). Fervor and conviction cancel human dogmatism. Truth comes alive in us. Truth must have its advocates and God will have His witnesses. Something is mediated through our personality. Phillips Brooks affirmed, "Preaching is truth through personality." If we give the impression that we are simply reading something from a sheet of paper, that it is not very important nor urgent, and that we are not desperate about what happens, then nothing will happen. Language that is nebulous as well as cold and casual preaching means that the preacher has lost the wonder of his calling. (This is not to downgrade the use of a manuscript if that be one's method; in the hands and the voice of certain preachers it has been a mighty means of power.) Whether with or without a manuscript, with notes or without notes, whatever the mode of delivery, I am not calling for shouting in the pulpit but for intensity and compassion.

Peter at Pentecost was a man eager and excited with good news he could not contain. It burst forth in speech which was exuberant and spilled over. Some thought him drunk as others judged Paul mad. Certainly Paul was intoxicated—but with the exhilaration of the Spirit who used him as the flame of God.

When Jonathan Edwards stood in the Northampton pulpit, he hardly raised his voice as he delivered a series of expository sermons on I Corinthians 13: the love which is Christ. Yet those messages were the occasion of revival in his congregation. When he preached the well-known and much caricatured sermon, "Sinners in the Hands of an Angry God," nothing happened; the congregation left the church to talk about the usual mundane events of the parish. Later on at Enfield, where he was called upon to substitute for another, he took the manuscript from his saddle bag and changed some of the words and sentences. In a period of moral and social decadence, God's voice thundered through the pleading tones of Edwards to multitudes. Many decisions for Christ were made. In the ordinary work of the pastor-preacher there are mighty moments when the divine presence is felt and realized.

The minister must also display the heart of a shepherd. Both Old and New Testaments make much of the image of the shepherd. Our Lord and Master is spoken of as the Good Shepherd, the Chief Shepherd, and the Great Shepherd. John Bunyan has described the function of the undershepherd who is pastor of the flock. In *Pilgrim's Progress* the ideal shepherd is depicted in terms of Jeremiah 3:15: "I will give you pastors [shepherds] according to mine heart, which shall feed you with knowledge and understanding." In the geography of Bunyan's allegory the Delectable Mountains rise out of the heart of Immanuel's Land. On one side is the Celestial City, and on the other side the Plain of Destruction. On these mountains the two travelers (Faithful and Christian) met shepherds whom we should emulate.

Knowledge was a minister with talent and attainment. Think of the roster of names in church history who have exercised their brilliant minds and plodded diligently for advance in learning. Not everyone has the same natural endowments; there is the ten-talent man. But even the one-talent man can work hard and persevere to increase his knowledge.

John Bunyan himself is a luminous example of making use of one's full capacities. His unusual gift of imagination found outlet in simple, clear writing. Development in knowledge implies that we should be students all our day. We have opportunity to study. The best books are available. If we lack income to buy the latest, we can borrow from libraries. A few of the masters read and studied (including taking notes) will bring ample reward later. Bible study beckons with the latest tools of interpretation and exciting new developments in theology and correlated subjects. All kinds of literature bring rich dividends and contribute to the total ministry. Knowledge is not for itself alone. It becomes a medium of spiritual enrichment without which all else is in vain.

Experience is another of Bunyan's shepherds. He is pictured with a high forehead and a kindly (yet shrewd) eye. Worn in age, he had a readiness in bearing; all his hard-earned wisdom he evidently put to practical use. Pastors know that there is no substitute for experience. We may pass through academic halls and theological studies, but we still have everything to learn in the work of the pastor-preacher. The ministry involves growing and deepening experience in faith and devotion. "My heart had great experience," says the Preacher in Ecclesiastes 1:16. No one is exempt; even the Son of God "learned obedience by the things which he suffered" (Heb. 5:8). Amos was no college man but he was a man of God. He learned as a shepherd the deep things of God in the school of experience. There are times when people sense that our words and prayers come from experience and not from theories of life.

In this connection there is an area of concern with respect to theological education. Many seminaries and theological colleges have not provided courses in experiential religion. When we recall our own mistakes and blunders in the spiritual life, when we remember how ignorant we were of the rich devotional books and of the art of prayer and devotion, it is evident that we had great need of the shepherd Experience to assist us. It is imperative to cultivate acquaintance with the classics of the soul and with people who have "been far with God." To deepen the spiritual life is to enlarge the influence of the ministry.

Watchful must be placed alongside of these two shepherds. "Son of man, I have made thee a watchman unto the house of Israel" (Ezek. 3:17). Those who have command over you "watch over your souls" (Heb. 13:17). This is the command and counsel given to the man of God. We are to be awake and alert. The true pastor-shepherd watches for the souls of others. This concern is necessary before preaching. Remembering the needy and the forgotten involves plodding on and many lonely and weary hours.

In his farewell to the Ephesian elders Paul told how he loved them and how he taught "from house to house" (Acts 20:20). The hospital room, the family call, the special journey to sit and talk with the man of the house for an evening in seeking to win him for Christ and the church, the visit to cheer and support the aged, and the outreach to the outsider—all this requires the spirit of the watchman. Richard Baxter (1615-1691) stands out as a classic example of this practice. In *The Reformed Pastor* (Richmond: John Knox Press, 1963 reprint) the story is told of his painstaking work and toil in pastoral ministry, especially in private instruction and catechizing.

The pastoral life of Thomas Boston (1677-1732) of Ettrick, Scotland, was recalled by the writings of George H. Morrison (1866-1928) of Wellington Church in Glasgow, in whom was incarnate the same spirit. Morrison stresses Boston's love of pastoral visitation. Morrison himself made an average of a thousand visits a year among his congregation. Our generation has problems unknown to earlier centuries. Then the parish was a well-defined and stable community, with every family anticipating the pastor's visit. Now we have the mobile "cave-dweller" who lives in impersonal, high-rise flats or apartments. How to gain access is part of the problem! Blest is the pastor who is inventive in establishing contact with people so removed one from the other!

Sincere is the fourth of the shepherds. Paul wrote to young pastor Titus to show "sincerity" in all things (Titus 2:7). The word also means "gravity," a quality associated with a minister. He must be a person without guile. To love people for their own sake and accept them without prejudice will open doors of opportunity. Before one is set apart in ordination, he should be tested and examined as to motives. Over the years one is expected to grow in grace and in knowledge. His sincerity should not be in doubt. Whatever gifts may be lacking, sincerity is essential to empower the minister for the kingdom of God. Let a man's word be doubted as unreliable and let any aberrations of conduct reveal him to be out of step with the ideals he talks about—and the effect of everything he says will be nullified. No one is perfect, without fault, but the preacher must ever strive to demonstrate his love and loyalty to Christ. The ministry is the one vocation where character counts most. To be kind and tenderhearted with those who struggle with temptation and sin, and to be willing to exhaust one's strength and time for the gospel— these are the marks of the sincere pastor.

Then, because we talk more than any others (except perhaps the politician?) we are always in danger. The ministry is not generally regarded as an occupation with risks to life and limb, but surely it is a dangerous calling. The danger lies in keeping up a pretense of being what we are not. Well does the apostle Peter counsel: "Gird up the loins of your mind" (I Peter 1:13). In the ancient Near East a belt or girdle tucked in the long robe at the waist. This helped in walking and in working. Jesus girded Himself with a towel in the upper room (John 13:4), exemplifying to the Twelve the ideal of a disciplined life of service. We need to adopt this servant role lest we be tempted and fall. We must learn the grace of humility in all things. Loving Christ we are to attend to His sheep and lambs (John 21:16). Oddly enough, it is the fisherman who has the final word on the shepherd's task:

> Tend that flock of God whose shepherds you are, and do it, not under compulsion, but of your own free will, as God would have it; not for gain but out of sheer devotion; not tyrannizing over those who are allotted to your care, but setting an example to the flock. And then, when the Head Shepherd appears, you will receive for your own the unfading garland of glory. (I Peter 5:2-4, NEB)

Thus there is opportunity to serve within the context of the whole church of God. "All churches either rise or fall as the Ministry doth rise or fall—not in riches or worldly grandeur— but in knowledge, zeal, and ability for their work" (Richard Baxter).

One of the minister's basic opportunities is communication of the gospel. Among the manifold duties of the minister is that of preaching a sermon or two each week. There is a difference of judgment among pastors and preachers as to the wisdom of attempting more than one proclamation each week. However, such a man as John Wesley in the eighteenth century preached several times a day and was heard by multitudes to their profit. The modern preacher cannot be charged with too much preaching, unless he is an itinerant of some kind. The maxim, "we learn to preach by preaching," is not out of date. Preaching is a primary emphasis of the ministry and congregations still consider it a priority.

Looking back, I recall how each Sunday required a morning and an evening sermon and in addition there was a Sunday Bible class for young people or young married couples. There was also a midweek Bible study and exposition; usually a book of the Bible or a doctrine was to be interpreted. I mention this simply to indicate the regularity of preparation and the daily and weekly stint in reading and study. Such discipline brought its demand upon my time; in the process I accumulated material far beyond normal use. No one reads and studies in the Scriptures without the reward of a treasury of knowledge.

A rereading of Harry Emerson Fosdick's article "What Is the Matter with Preaching?" *(Harper's,* 1928) raises a question that is still relevant. Each generation asks a similar question. There are those who would predict the demise of Christian preaching and that speedily. The Bicentennial celebrations evoked nostalgia and thanksgiving for the past. Much has been said concerning the roots of "this nation under God" and credit given to the Founding Fathers. However, there has been neglect in acknowledging the debt we owe to those who by their religious convictions and the preaching of the sermon influenced the nation as it laid the foundations of freedom and democracy.

Fosdick sought to remove religious ideas from strictly biblical exposition and instead to begin with a need to be met or a question to be asked. His awareness of people's needs led him to this method of preparing the sermon. He grasped the advent of the radio as an instrument to disseminate his message. It was his approach that was different from ours. He emphasized the topic, the question to be answered, the practical discussion; he neglected exposition, proclamation of doctrine, tradition.

Advocates of this method would claim that Fosdick did not neglect the doctrines or the theological teaching of the Bible when he dealt with problems. This new type of "life-situation" preaching had its vogue and influenced the American pulpit for several generations. The rise of the counseling ministry was linked in no small way with it. Fosdick aimed to make this type of preaching intellectually respected, socially responsible, and generally appealing.

A new generation has arisen which takes for granted radio and television as means of communication. The words and the events bombard the listener incessantly. The new generation of the sixties and seventies is biblically illiterate and secularized by daily exposure to the second-rate and the mediocre. No longer can we assume that our youth or even the adult population has the background to appreciate the traditional message of the Christian pulpit. We have to deal with a lost generation. Certainly it is a guilt-ridden and sex-deluged age. The seeds of its own decay and destruction are obvious. If the pulpit does not proclaim with passion the eternal message for man's deliverance, the future is dark indeed. The decline in preaching passion and the new emphasis upon "know-how" programs for the faithful within the church have stultified the clear aims of the Christian faith.

A paradox of the present hour lies in the fact that when the pulpit has not dealt with the inner disease of man, others on the outside have become obsessed with the nature and actions of man in his lostness. When preaching has lost that note of conviction concerning man's sin and guilt, the novel, the drama, the film, and other forms of communication have rushed in to exploit this empty void. Recent writers like William Golding (*Lord of the Flies*) have dealt with the end of innocence. T. S. Eliot, C. S. Lewis, George Bernard Shaw, Evelyn Waugh, George Orwell, D. H. Lawrence, and others from various schools of thought have discussed the aberrations of man's nature in facing life, love, sex, pleasure, suffering, and death. These writers and their contemporaries have realistically plumbed the manifold depths of human nature apart from redemption. The idea of progress has been rejected in the light of our moral and spiritual condition. Man is a sinner because of his nature, which is sinful. Man is a rebel against the sovereignty of divine love. Man is infected with pride in his intellectual and cultural attainments. P. A. Sorokin, professor of sociology at Harvard University, spoke of modern man as infected by "demoralization, dehumanization, and brutalization." The present world is filled with pertinent evidence.

That we have the opportunity to preach as never before is obvious. There is always a hearing for the man who stands to proclaim eternal truth to this age. Across our weary and disillusioned world there are millions who worship the one true and living God, and there are faithful ministers who preach week by week. The penetration of the gospel is having results. Renewal and revival are words heard afresh. Our concern lies with those ministers who have lost their first love or have lost the passion and ardor of what is the exciting good news.

The situation of our day intimates that the world is sick. T. S. Eliot wrote of his weary generation in terms of "the hollow men . . . the stuffed men . . . and the waste land," a diagnosis confirmed by two world wars and their aftermath. Have we forgotten Hitler's holocaust? Read Solzhenitsyn's *Gulag Archipelago* crying out to the present world about the unspeakable atrocities and indignities of Communism and the threat to man's freedom. Our own home base is witness to an unparalleled increase in crime and violence, vice and immoralities, the hedonism of desire and drunkenness. Our boasted technology creates new idols. Our very success can enslave us. Our substitute religions blind us. Our wisdom and knowledge but bring us lack of moral control. The tides of secularism and godlessness advance swiftly, and the church seems anemic.

How glad we are that there is a divine solution for the dilemma in which man finds himself. Moffatt translates I Corinthians 1:21, "When the world with all its wisdom failed to know God in his wisdom, God resolved to save believers by the *'sheer folly' of the Christian message.*" There must be an awareness of the urgency of preaching for our day. In a day of mass education and abundant knowledge, the preacher comes with the wisdom of God. He must stand to proclaim the eternal Word of truth.

The opportunity to communicate the gospel is one that weighs heavily upon mind and heart in these stirring times. According to John Henry Newman in *The Idea of a University* (New York: Oxford University Press, 1976 reprint) the preacher should aim at the spiritual good of his hearers. As the marksman aims at the bull's-eye, and at nothing else, so the preacher must have a definite point before him, which he has to hit. We may ask questions about the preacher's delivery, his diction, elocution, rhetorical power, but Paul reminds us that "the kingdom of God is not in word, but in power" (I Cor. 4:20). This is not to deny the importance of gifts and their development, but rather to emphasize the concentration required of the servant of God in his preaching. "Earnestness creates earnestness in others by sympathy; and the more a preacher loses and is lost to himself, the more does he gain his brethren." Newman does not mean that a preacher must aim at earnestness, but that he must aim at his object, which is to do some spiritual good to his hearers, and which will at once make him earnest.

Newman has much to offer for our encouragement. He comments further on earnestness:

> He who has before his mental eye the *Four Last Things* will have the true earnestness. . . . His countenance, his manner, his voice, speak for him, in proportion as his view has been vivid and minute. . . . It is this earnestness, in the supernatural order, which is the eloquence of the saints, of all Christian preachers, according to the measure of their faith and love. . . . [Thus] it is the preacher's duty to aim at imparting to others, not any fortuitous, unpremeditated benefit, but some *definite* spiritual good. It is here that design and study find their place; the more exact and precise is the subject which he treats, the more impressive and practical will he be. . . . Here is the necessity of addressing himself to the intellect of men, and of convincing as well as persuading.

The scriptural phrase, "preaching the Word," implies a proposition addressed to the intellect in order to persuade the hearer. Perhaps the best description of preaching I have ever come across is that of Bernard Lord Manning: "To preach the Gospel . . . it is a manifestation of the Incarnate Word, from the Written Word, by the spoken word." That definition goes right to the heart of the matter. Not everyone knows that it was the distillation of *a layman in the ministry*. Manning was the son of a Congregational pastor whose influence was felt largely in small country pastorates in England. The son became a senior tutor at Jesus College, Cambridge, where his special subject of research and teaching lay in the social history of the medieval period. In addition to this work Manning was equally at home in preaching messages which stabbed the conscience and inspired worshipers to new levels of consecration.

In 1931 Manning was invited to address the faculty and students of Yorkshire United Independent College. His subject was "Effectual Preaching: The Reflections of One Hearer." In his acute and penetrating words he had much to say of a personal nature: "I am no preacher, but I have tried to preach enough times to begin to see the problem from your side too." He reminisced about his boyhood when he sat in the back pew and acquired a taste for hearing sermons. He shared his findings as one who had been worshiper and also the worshiping leader in proclaiming the biblical message from the pulpit.

He objected to the judgment of those who tried to distinguish between the preaching house and the place of worship, as though the one were in opposition to the other. Preaching to Manning was not set in antithesis to worship, but was itself an act of worship offered to God. It was in this context of affirmation and of conviction that he uttered in fuller measure the memorable maxim:

> To preach the Gospel, as we have received that means of grace from our fathers, is not to express the opinion of an individual, is not personal exhortation or instruction: *it is a manifestation of the Incarnate Word, from the Written Word, by the spoken word*; it is a most solemn act of worship, in which the thing given—the Gospel of the Son of God— overshadows and even transfigures the preacher by whom it is declared. In the preached word Christ Himself is set forth before us as He is set forth in the Bread and Wine of the holy Supper.

Nothing worthier is given us than to proclaim the authentic Word of God to this age.

Bernard Lord Manning was not alone in describing the heart of preaching. Bishop Phillips Brooks in his Yale Lectures noted: "Preaching is the communication of truth by man to men. It has in it two essential elements, truth and personality. Neither of those can it spare and still be preaching."

Karl Barth characterized the preaching task: "A man is concerned 'to proclaim to his fellow men what God himself has to say to them by explaining, in his own words, a passage from Scripture which concerns them personally.' "

Professor Herrick Johnson spoke of the sermon as "a religious discussion founded upon the Word of God and designed to save men."

Henry Sloane Coffin, president of Union Theological Seminary (New York), spoke of "the kindling and rekindling of the fire of piety. It is easy to fall into the professional attitude toward religion. Theology has not always been taught or studied devoutly. Thinking and talking *about* God may take the place of life *with* Him, of speech *to* Him, of thought *in His Presence*. The things of God must be examined fearlessly. But they disclose themselves only to humble, reverent and obedient souls."

The servant of God must take every advantage of the opportunity to preach and proclaim the eternal Word.

18

The Gospel in the Space Age

"For by him were all things created, that are in heaven, and that are in earth, visible and invisible, whether they be thrones, or dominions, or principalities, or powers: all things were created by him, and for him; and he is before all things, and by him all things consist [i.e., cohere in one harmonious whole." (COL. 1:16, 17)

WHATEVER THE JUDGMENT of the novelist and the historian, the minister in today's world knows the reality of tests and trials which come from the calling in which he is engaged. It is not a sheltered profession or one lived in an ivory tower (as some would state), but a life involved in the culture of our civilized society. There have been those, and some there are in this generation, who think Christ is above our culture and therefore has abandoned it to the secular forces which would destroy it. Thus in their view there is no use in seeking to evangelize and penetrate our culture, even though our Lord said that we are to be as salt and light. The Christ (who Himself lived in a culture) will transform our culture by the power of His presence and by the power of the gospel to change and renew human nature by the supernatural energy displayed in His death and resurrection.

In our age we face new levels of thought and life unknown before. We live and labor in the Space Age with its unlimited frontiers. Earth and time are now within space and eternity. New hermeneutics are demanded as we proclaim eternal truth from God. The church today must relate the Good News by symbol as well as in word and in deed. The cross is still central to a redeemed universe, created and sustained by divine energy.

Our opportunity to minister in the Space Age opens up new frontiers of knowledge and understanding. The Creator has revealed Himself in nature, and all around us is the vast universe with its storied power and the evidence of design from God's handiwork. Paul has reminded the church of this in the beginning of his Epistle to the Romans. A natural theology is developed. This is balanced by the supernatural revelation of truth recorded in the Scriptures. The one realm is separate from the other but they agree in the fact of the same Creator, who is also the Revealer and Redeemer. God revealed Himself *to* man in nature and *in* man in the form of conscience. The Space Age demands of the preacher that he be aware of its presence and power as he ministers.

Worship is an unchanging experience for the minister, who not only leads a congregation in the act but is himself a worshiper. When we enter a sanctuary to worship, there is an atmosphere of inspiration in the presence of almighty God. Offering to Him our thanksgiving in the name of our Savior and living Lord, we are inspired by the Spirit of the Eternal in praise, prayer, sermon, and offering. To engage in these forms of worship is the highest act of the spirit of man. To worship is to experience the emotion which most cleanses us from selfishness, because it is the most selfless of all emotions—adoration.

The most intense divine-human encounter occurs when we worship. William Temple (1881-1944), Archbishop of Canterbury, gave to the church a description of true worship which catches the imagination and probes the mind. To worship is

to quicken the conscience by the holiness of God,
to feed the mind by the truth of God,
to purge the imagination by the beauty of God,
to open the heart by the love of God,
to devote the will by the purpose of God.

In this light worship means

the subjection of the whole being to the object of worship,
the opening of the heart to receive the love of God,
the subjection of the conscience to be directed by God.

This particular concept is needed by contemporary people who seek a loftier outlook on the universe, such a vision of the true nature of our world as will by its splendor thrill us to worship. Alienated man in the lostness of his age of anxiety becomes weary of the whirl of wheels and the throb of engines. He needs wings, the wings of the soul to be lifted up. The preacher-teacher has opportunity to lead others to breathe an ampler, purer air, and refresh the spirit in the presence of things sublime. Christ's

relation to the universe opens into a surprising revelation of
glory, and leads us through new flights of knowledge to hitherto
unknown experiences of worship.

As man explores the edge of the universe, astronomers, physi-
cists, philosophers, scientists, and theologians with insights from
divine revelation find scriptural facts unfold with ever greater
application to our period of history. Time, space, and imagination see man set within the immensities of our larger universe
and give a new framework for the etching of the picture of the
drama of redemption. What is spoken of as eternity is not unreal
but the hallmark of destiny. The finite and the infinite are closer
than ever. In God's house—the universe—we find the secret of
their relationship. The Father's house (John 14:2) is described as
having many resting places, many abodes. Today we know there
are worlds upon worlds in galaxies and systems beyond our
comprehension. This earth is but one temporal dwelling place,
but the "Father's house" speaks of others. The Lord assured His
disciples of that certainty and experience for those who follow
Him as the true and living Way.

Just as the Christian has relationship bodily to his earthly
experience, so in the power of the resurrection body he will have
transcendent relationship to the eternal state. Thus the worshiper
is brought face to face with God, who is transcendent in majesty
and glory and power. We bow in reverence and worship in spirit
and in truth. Then when worship ends we return to the daily
round and tasks to be involved in life with its sins, sorrows, and
suffering. But we go with renewed faith and courage, sharing
love and generating hope. We carry the Good News of the redeeming God who still seeks and saves the lost. In all walks of
life and in all areas of human need we are witnesses in ministry.
Jesus Christ is Lord and to Him every knee shall bow. The end
of worship is to serve. The opportunity to declare such truths is
the most exciting privilege a minister has.

God has clothed man with a dignity that was never fully realized until the Space Age. The Space Age demands a set of revisions in our religious thinking. For one thing, we are now compelled to admit the *possibility* of life beyond this planet. Although space research has not yet confirmed the existence of life
on other orbs, there is a growing openness of mind that there

might be and that our tiny speck of dust called earth in the vastness of the universe is not the only planet with life.

Our Lord Jesus said, "Other sheep I have, which are not of this fold" (John 10:16). We have assumed that He referred to the Gentiles, who were separated from the Jews in that day, or even perhaps to aborigines whose existence was unknown until Columbus discovered the New World of the Americas. Now theologians are wondering if "other sheep I have" might refer to life on other planets yet unknown to man.

The rainbow sign of Noah's day was interpreted as God's promise that man need never again fear total inundation. But now comes the threat of total destruction by the fires of nuclear explosion or radioactive fallout. When this threat reaches its peak, a "new escape hatch" may open with manned space flight to the moon and to other planets. The symbolism has changed, but theology is still interpreting experience and revelation. The backdrop of history is enlarging our minds, and eternity seems much more real since the coming of the Space Age. In a world in which man can already outdistance the speed of sound, it is not difficult to conceive of a boundless creation that knows no limits of space or time. It is not difficult to believe in life everlasting or life eternal which is the gift of God in Christ.

J. B. Phillips's *Your God Is Too Small* (New York: Macmillan, 1953) is a reminder that the God of creation is larger and greater than we can imagine. He who fashions the universe is also the one who designs the drop of water and the infinitesimal. He is not only the tiny Babe of Christmas and the incarnation, but the transfigured Man of glory of the resurrection and the ascension.

William G. Pollard, general director of the Oak Ridge Institute of Nuclear Science, has written several books to unfold his own personal experience of God in Christ and his new awareness of the universe since then. In *Chance and Providence* (New York: Charles Scribner's Sons, 1958) and *Physicist and Christian* (New York: Seabury Press, 1962), he has united his scientific knowledge with his theological understanding of divine revelation and Christian experience. His witness in this age is clear and profound in his interpretation of truth. Pollard is an outstanding witness that the God and Father of our Lord and

Savior Jesus Christ is actively involved in the universe and has provided for man a salvation experience in and through the incarnation, a salvation experience which brings to pass a new order in the sphere of time and of space. Yes, there is a theology for the Space Age and the minister now has an exciting time in which to minister the Good News from the Eternal to the temporal.

A grandmother held upon her lap a small child. She was giving the little girl her first biblical instruction, and began by reading to her the stories of the various stages of creation recorded in the Book of Genesis. "Well, dear," said the grandmother when she had finished, "what do you think of it?" "Oh, I love it. It's so exciting," exclaimed the child. "You never know what God is going to do next!" That is precisely the mood in which we live from day to day in the Space Age. In such times of rapid change we wonder what new interpretations we will bring to our Bible and what new insights will emerge concerning God and His purposes in Christ.

Theology is always the explanation of experience. We bring our experience to the judgment of the eternal light of divine revelation written in the Scriptures. Our theology is behind and cannot keep pace with God's revelation. Experience comes first and interpretation follows. Any theology which is anchored to a static conception of knowledge restricts itself to a fractional view of God. It isn't science that outruns religion. It is God who outruns explanation!

These are thrilling days in which to live, to think, to study, to write, to work, and to minister. What opportunities open before the man of God to teach and preach as never before! How can a minister be indolent and see the hours fritter away before him when he has the allies of science and of theology begging him to get to work in Bible study several hours each day in preparation to come before his people on a Sabbath day to declare the whole counsel of God? Not that books on science can take the place of the Bible, but that they become the adjuncts of divine revelation as natural theology is wedded with dogmatic theology. In a biblically illiterate generation the minister has supreme opportunities to proclaim the unsearchable riches of Christ.

Think of all those who have written in recent decades to throw light upon our age and its baffling problems. Wise men of old were guided by the star. We can be guided and spurred on our journey in quest of truth by satellites and spaceships.

The expanding universe (Arthur S. Eddington has written a book with this title—New York: Cambridge University Press, 1933) need not frighten any Christian as science is not the enemy of religion. Only an unbelieving, non-Christian world needs to be afraid of today and of tomorrow. We as prodigals have come home to our Father's house, now in the earthly and natural dwelling and certainly later in the supernatural dwelling place. Karl Heim, German theologian, in his book *Christian Faith and Natural Science* (Magnolia, MA: Peter Smith, 1953) has discussed the supernatural and the transcendent in the context of today's thought forms. Imagery of other periods requires to be reminted for this new age. Heim's allusions led William G. Pollard to restate his belief in the biblical concepts of heaven and hell. "Reality is not so restricted to one dimension. The supernatural domains of heaven and hell, which have been so universally acknowledged in human experience, have as much claim on reality as does the restricted spacio-temporal domain which constitutes nature."

Heim made use of Edwin Abbott's *Flatland: A Romance of Many Dimensions* (New York: Barnes and Noble, 1963 edition), which deals with the principle of dimensionality. We are familiar with the tridimensional character of our experience of space. But for the moment suppose the existence of a being whose apprehension of the world is only bidimensional, who lives in what Edwin Abbott called *Flatland.* Nothing in his experience could possibly suggest to him the existence of a third dimension—that of depth.

John Baillie of Edinburgh University wrote a series of Gifford Lectures but was not privileged to deliver them. In *The Sense of the Presence of God* (New York: Charles Scribner's Sons, 1962) he left his last will and testament of faith. Naturalism does not exhaust the meaning of our human experience. Baillie refers to Pollard's *Chance and Providence* and concurs that this world is wrapped up in the providence of God. "The Christian sees the chances and accidents of history as the very warp and woof of the fabric of providence which God is ever weaving."

There are also the voices of C. A. Coulson, professor of mathematics at Oxford University, in his book *Science, Technology and the Christian* (Nashville: Abingdon, 1961), and of Alan Richardson, professor of theology at the University of Nottingham, in his book *The Bible in the Age of Science* (Philadelphia: Westminster Press, 1961). According to these competent scholars natural science developed only in the Christian ethos. According to Arnold Toynbee, the eminent historian, natural science, technology, and medicine are the gifts of Christian civilization to mankind. Discerning the hand of God in creation and history, we have evidence to refute the judgment of those people who think in terms of "chance" and "accident." The world is bound up in God's providence. God works in everything for good (cf. Rom. 8:28).

We have noted already that the Bible speaks of the Father's house (John 14:2) and "the Lamb slain from the foundation of the world [ages]" (Rev. 13:8). Three major truths emerge in relation to this Space Age in which we now minister.

First, God has created the universe. "In the beginning God created the heaven and the earth" (Gen. 1:1).

Second, God has redeemed the universe and man. "Worthy is the Lamb that was slain to receive power, and riches, and wisdom, and strength, and honour, and glory, and blessing. And every creature [all creation] which is in heaven, and on earth, and under the earth, and such as are in the sea, and all that are in them, heard I saying, Blessing, and honour, and glory, and power, be unto him that sitteth upon the throne, and unto the Lamb for ever and ever" (Rev. 5:12, 13).

Third, God upholds the universe by the word of His power. "Now Christ is the visible expression of the invisible God. He existed before creation began, for *it was through him* that everything was made, whether spiritual or material, seen or unseen. Through him, and for him, also, were created power and dominion, ownership and authority. In fact, every single thing was created through, and for, him. He is both the first principle and the upholding principle of the whole scheme of creation" (Col. 1:15-17, Phillips).

Creation, Redemption, and Providence lie at the heart of the Space Age. The servant of God must grapple with these exciting truths. Science has opened up fresh insights into the mysterious universe. How can the gospel be related to this vast and expanding universe of knowledge? How can we communicate the truth of the living Christ to new and successive generations born and living in the new age? Electronics, astrophysics, and space travel open up new vistas of discovery and thought. Our God is the God of the universe; and He thinks of and loves man through His Son, the Lord Jesus Christ. Psalms 8 and 139 as well as many other Scriptures take on new meaning in the light of the new knowledge and symbols.

The opportunity for the minister to proclaim with certitude the manifold counsel of God in this era of history is unparalleled. We are the heirs of the ages; we have been given the wealth of their heritage. Discoveries in archaeology (papyri, the Dead Sea Scrolls, the Hebrew background, the ancient world), the literature of the universal church over centuries, the new light upon translation of the Scriptures—all these servants of truth have been complemented by the discoveries of the Space Age so that this century is crowned by the creative encounter of science and "Christian existentialism." The "I-Thou" encounter between man and God receives special emphasis: natural man is without excuse if he refuses the light of divine knowledge; the Christian minister is without excuse if he fails to grasp the opportunity to learn from the new tools of learning how to restate and make clear and relevant the eternal biblical message of God in Christ.

One who anticipated the breakthrough of this new age was Alice Meynell (1847-1922) in her poem "Christ in the Universe":

> With this ambiguous earth
> His dealings have been told us. These abide:
> The signal to the maid, the human birth,
> The lesson, and the young Man crucified.
>
> But not a star of all
> The innumerable host of stars has heard
> How He administered this terrestrial ball.
> Our race have kept their Lord's entrusted Word.
>
> Of His earth-visiting feet
> None knows the secret, cherished, perilous,

The terrible, shamefast, frightened, whispered, sweet,
Heart-shattering secret of His way with us.

No planet knows that this
Our wayside planet, carrying land and wave,
Love and life multiplied, and pain and bliss,
Bears, as chief treasure, one forsaken grave.

Nor, in our little day,
May His devices with the heavens be guessed,
His pilgrimage to thread the Milky Way,
Or His bestowals there be manifest.

But in the eternities
Doubtless we shall compare together, hear
A million alien Gospels, in what guise
He trod the Pleiades, the Lyre, the Bear.

O, be prepared, my soul!
To read the inconceivable, to scan
The million forms of God those stars unroll
When, in our turn, we show to them a Man.

The opportunity to minister in this new age opens up remarkable avenues of teaching and preaching. Resources are being
provided by those who have a specialist's knowledge by reason
of their mental and spiritual equipment in the realms of science
allied to theology. One could wish for a turning back of time in
order to fashion anew and study certain tools of learning to
match the present hour. But that is the privilege of younger men
and women who will grasp the torch of truth and speed on their
way to proclaim to this new generation that God in Christ is
still the Lord of all good life and Master of His house, the universe in which we must live and move and have our being.

Thomas F. Torrance, professor of Christian dogmatics at the
University of Edinburgh, has placed us in his debt for his
thoughtful, probing words in several books in recent years. The
trilogy *Theology in Reconstruction; Space, Time and Incarnation;* and *Theology in Reconciliation* (Grand Rapids: William B.
Eerdmans, 1966-1976) deals with the interrelation of spirit and
matter and the rejection of scientific materialism. The heart of
these books is that God Himself in His own being is actually

present with us as personal Agent within the time and space of our world. The language of Scripture, hymns, and creeds is to be taken not merely as symbolical, but as an expression of truth and reality. The transcendence of God is reflected, for example, in the language of the Nicene Creed: "God the Father, Almighty, Maker of heaven and earth, and of all things visible and invisible."

The minister has a superlative opportunity to stand as a man set apart for God and for unique service in an age torn with anxiety and fear, an age in which people are alienated from God and from each other, knowing only their lostness and hopeless condition as they face the unknown future. All in all, the wise minister who is open in mind and heart to learn from those who have pioneered the new dimensions of truth interrelated with the Bible, the "impregnable rock of Scripture," will find his preaching and teaching rewarded by listening minds and responsive hearts.

New thinking in science and about science will reinforce the theology of grace as well as the doctrines of the incarnation and transcendence. God is viewed as being in partnership, or covenant, with His creation and His creatures. To open the windows toward Jerusalem (cf. Dan. 6:10) through our devotion and Bible study is not to disparage that other direction with its look toward Athens (cf. Acts 17). The question asked by Tertullian, "What has Athens to do with Jerusalem?" is answered as we reread the Scriptures in the light of the Space Age. Instead of the one being in tension with the other, we find them uniting in ever increased understanding of the place of our Lord. "Declare, O Heavens," a contemporary hymn written by Robert Lansing Edwards and sung to the tune "Lasst Uns Erfreuen," illustrates this:

> Launch forth, O man, and boldly rise;
> Beyond our planet pierce the skies;
> Boundless venture! Alleluia!
> No soaring flight can e'er outrun
> Truth God has shown us in his Son;
> Alleluia! Alleluia! Alleluia! Alleluia! Alleluia!

In the same vein is "God of Everlasting Glory," written by John W. Peterson and sung to the tune "Breton Road.":

God of everlasting glory, filling earth and sky,
Everywhere Your wonders open to our searching eye;
In our telescopic probing—light years from our world,
In the atom's theoried structure science has unfurled.

As we push man's frontier forward into outer space,
Reaching for the stars and planets, still Your hand we trace;
In the lab'ratory's silence, where Your secrets hide,
There the marvels of creation are for us supplied.

In the open book of nature faith remains unmoved—
Patterns of the Master Builder by each fact are proved;
So with rev'rent hearts we ponder all the grand design
Of the universe around us, wrought by hands divine.

Thru the course of human history has Your purpose run,
And in substance have we seen You in Your glorious Son:
He it was who came to save us and our hopes to raise—
God of everlasting glory, Your great name we praise!*

To spur on the would-be preacher, and the one who has had a
long time in service, to achieve higher goals in content and delivery of the message, there is inspiration to be found in the
poets. Read the poem by Frederic W. Myers (1843-1901) on
"Saint Paul" and catch anew the total commitment of the apostle, especially as you stand to minister and proclaim the gospel
that saves:

Oft when the word is on me to deliver,
    Lifts the illusion and truth lies bare,
Desert or throng, the city or the river,
    Melts in a lucid paradise of air.

Only like souls I see folk there under
    Bound who should conquer, slaves who should be kings;
Hearing their one hope with an empty wonder,
    Sadly content in a show of things.

Then with a rush the intolerable craving
    Shivers throughout me like a trumpet call.
Oh, to save these, to perish for their saving,
    Die for their life, be offered for them all.

Karl Menninger's *Whatever Became of Sin?* (New York: Hawthorn Books, 1973) brought into focus the basic truth of human failure and responsibility. He felt that after expounding his thesis he could then tell why he wrote it. Accordingly, at the end of the book he placed an "Epilogue: The Displaced Preface." His work had led him to the conviction that the ills of the people were being adequately handled by the psychiatric profession, but there was a conspicuous shortcoming on the part of the pulpit. Disillusioned and frustrated clergy were neglecting what to him was a supreme opportunity in this generation. The message preached from the pulpit has in it the means of preventing some of the accumulated misapprehensions and guilt which underlie late aggressive actions and mental disease. He asks, "How? Preach! Tell it like it is. Say it from the pulpit. Cry it from the housetops. What shall we cry? Cry comfort, cry repentance, cry hope. Because recognition of our part in the world transgression is the only remaining hope."

Discussing our moral history Menninger goes to the heart of what is wrong with persons in today's society and how the concept of sin seems to be disappearing today. A new social morality has arisen. Only crime is regarded as sinful wrongdoing and even that is often viewed as the collective guilt of all society. Menninger cites the seven deadly sins—and some new ones—as a basis for interpreting what sin really is. Pride, rebellion, and self-will are still with us; as a result the preacher can never be out of work.

During the Bicentennial celebrations in 1976, Warner Pacific College had several outstanding guest speakers, including Karl Menninger and Helmut Thielicke, a preacher and also chancellor of the University of Hamburg. While Menninger called for the clergyman to get down to his true business in proclamation in order to deal with the mental and emotional ills of society and bring back the reality of the meaning of sin, Thielicke demonstrated how to preach and the theological basis for such ministry. He himself has attracted thousands in his homeland. In the nihilism and emptiness of a lost generation, he has preached the eternal revelation of God through the gospel of the redeeming work of Christ. Sin has been exposed and the remedy for fallen man outlined.

The golden opportunity spoken of by Menninger has been clearly snatched by Thielicke, an intellectual giant whose sermons and addresses are able to penetrate the crust of modern indifference and unbelief. Europe has cause to stop and listen to the theologian-preacher who speaks with power and precision. The pastor-preacher in any parish and culture has a supreme opportunity to do likewise in the fight against sin.

Another factor today is the widespread means of communication now available. In addition to radio and television, there are also the local press, magazines, and books. New converts to the Christian faith have been reached in a variety of ways. C. S. Lewis is an example of how an unwilling convert was suddenly arrested by the living Savior and commissioned to go and write a word of witness. His writings now comprise a corpus of distinction to be studied by friend and foe. His apologetic approach is timely and offers the preacher down-to-earth help.

Born Again (Old Tappan, NJ: Fleming H. Revell, 1976), the confessional account of Charles Colson's role as a legal advisor to President Nixon in the Watergate scandals, has moved thousands. It is a vivid record of the grace of God. It shows how the power of God touches lives and brings home to the conscience the reality of sin, and the need to repent and be reborn.

We might also mention Malcolm Muggeridge, whose checkered career spanned the rise of Communism and Socialism. The idealism of youth and the energy of maturity were poured into an effort to find the truth of social salvation in the Russian experiment. Disillusionment followed. In the wilderness of uncertainty he assumed the editorship of *Punch*. His barbed pen cleverly manipulated words.

But suddenly Malcolm Muggeridge met the Christ of the Emmaus road; his old world fell into ruins as he found a new and better life of the Spirit and of grace. In the book *Paul, Envoy Extraordinary* (1972) Muggeridge traces the steps of the apostle Paul. With New Testament open, he testifies to the impact of the scriptural revelation concerning the apostle's cataclysmic conversion. There emerges an enlightening picture of Paul, whose message continues to be relevant after twenty centuries.

From Jerusalem to Rome would be a fitting theme for reflection as we consider this beautiful book, which was adapted for a series of television talks. Muggeridge uses the skills of humor and satire to effect a picture of a great human with all the foibles and failures common to the first century. Yet there are also flashes of insight which depict the dynamic influence of this apostle whose sole aim in life after conversion was to proclaim by word and letter the manifold spectra of the life and work of his Lord and Master. Paul became the most outstanding interpreter of Christ. Muggeridge, like Paul, is also a convert in later life, an evangelist, a missionary, a witness—and a writer!

We cannot expect Muggeridge to change his writing habits and style immediately. The caustic critic of *Punch* may still dip his pen in irony and satire. Nevertheless, his recent three-volume autobiography, *Chronicles of Wasted Time* (New York: Morrow, William & Co., 1972-1978), has tempered his style somewhat. This followed the publication of *Jesus* (New York: Harper and Row, 1971), an attempt to interpret the Life of lives. In this volume a convert without maturity of study and biblical knowledge shared early effusions of a confession of faith.

The Third Testament (Boston: Little, Brown & Co., 1976) is a compilation of television lectures. Six characters in search of God over the centuries had in common an overwhelming need to experience and express what they found to be the truth for them. Muggeridge sees them as part of the continuing testament to the reality of God. Saint Augustine, Blaise Pascal, William Blake, Sören Kierkegaard, Leo Tolstoy, and Dietrich Bonhoeffer left behind enduring writings for our generation to ponder. The pastor-preacher has the opportunity to go to these works and see how God dealt with these Christians of different centuries. There is enough to afford sound reading for many months. As each individual minister reads, the question will arise: How do I relate to God in Christ and what has been my experience? Then will unfold the desire to share these six pilgrims of eternity with our people through the lens of history, Scripture, and our own personal witness. Thus the Space Age will provide opportunity to see new unfoldings of truth eternal, yet at the same time the gospel will continue to transform individuals as in the past.

19

The Memory of Other Days

". . . Thou shalt remember all the way which the Lord thy God led thee these forty years in the wilderness, to humble thee, and to prove thee, to know what was in thine heart, whether thou wouldest keep his commandments, or no. And he humbled thee, and suffered thee to hunger, and fed thee with manna, which thou knewest not, neither did thy fathers know; that he might make thee know that man doth not live by bread only, but by every word that proceedeth out of the mouth of the Lord doth man live. . . . Thou shalt also consider in thine heart, that, as a man chasteneth his son, so the Lord thy God chasteneth thee. Therefore thou shalt keep the commandments of the Lord thy God, to walk in his ways, and to fear him. . . . Beware that thou forget not the Lord thy God, in not keeping his commandments, and his judgments, and his statutes . . . lest when thou . . . art full . . . and all that thou hast is multiplied; then thine heart be lifted up, and thou forget the Lord thy God, which brought thee forth out of the land of Egypt, from the house of bondage; who led thee . . . who fed thee . . . And thou say in thine heart, My power and the might of mine hand hath gotten me this wealth. But thou shalt remember the Lord thy God: for it is he that giveth thee power." (DEUT. 8)

THE ORATIONS of Deuteronomy bring the last words of Moses, whose leadership of the Israelites is recalled as he reminds them of the past days. The emphasis of the Book of Deuteronomy is to *remember*. We have much to learn from this part of the Word of God. Looking back over the years wherein God has led me, I recall the stress this passage of Scripture places on the principles for leadership in our day. I remember obstacles I had to overcome and opportunities I grasped. Israel, as well as every servant of God, must be proved and tested, must learn to depend upon "manna," must come to know that all power is from God and not of self.

Having retired from the pastorate (but not from the ministry), I can reminisce concerning the years that were filled with differing experiences and service. In preparation for this, God led me in various paths. Every servant of God must learn that *testing* is necessary, that the *Word of God* alone is sufficient to satisfy in personal life and in any ministry, that *strength* and *power* are not generated by self but come from God. These three aspects of the Christian life humble the mind before the divine grace; thus we remember all the way God has led us.

As a lad in Edinburgh, there were two strong influences in my life: my family with its Presbyterian background, and my experience as a chorister in an Episcopal church choir. Exposure to the majestic hymns of the ages, oratorios, anthems, and the reading of the King James Version of the Bible enriched me both spiritually and culturally. At school the first half-hour was spent in memorizing the Shorter Catechism and outstanding passages of the Bible. That foundation has stood the ravages of time.

In 1914, Dr. J. Wilbur Chapman came to our city with choir leader Charles M. Alexander to conduct a campaign for six weeks. Some six thousand people attended each night. This was the first time I had heard an American preacher. The one-thousand-voice choir sang the spiritual: "Were You There When They Crucified My Lord?" and the Presbyterian pastor-evangelist preached on "What Think Ye of Christ?" My younger brother and I committed our lives to the Savior. I still have the invitation card, based upon John 3:16, which was handed out. My name is written in the space for "whosoever." That schoolboy writing reminds me of that glorious hour which has never left me, especially when I stand to minister.

The influences which led me into the Christian ministry were several. In my boyish committal I had an impression that it might be for me to preach even as Dr. Chapman preached. My mother's prayers and encouragement no doubt assisted in that direction. Membership in the Christian Endeavor Society gave me experience in taking part in public—reading a paper, praying, and leading discussions. In addition we held open-air services which were a feature of those days. A midweek Bible class under the leadership of a budding theolog and would-be minister led to serious study and further encouragement. Meantime, I was busy in the business world and there learned for over seven years the intricacies of the manufacturing of chemical fertilizers and of selling feeding stuffs to farmers. In the process I learned both bookkeeping and how to deal with people. All this prepared me for situations I later met in the ministry.

Among the many preachers I heard at that time, Dr. W. Graham Scroggie came to the city and began his outstanding ministry, including a weekly school of Bible study and a special Christian service class. Several years of attending lectures and taking notes along with others who were definitely seeking that "extra" knowledge proved invaluable. For a number of years Scroggie guided my reading, lending me books from his library; and month by month my theological knowledge increased. Notebooks still on my shelves remind me of the spoils I gathered during those years before going on to academic degrees. The day came when others were led to suggest that I had reached the stage to consider seriously the call of God to minister. I had assumed that I could go on in business (which I enjoyed fully) and alongside that occupation render service to the church by teaching and preaching—without stipend and organizational commitments. However, the open doors of full-time service in the ministry beckoned. Thus gradually I came to see that I must give up the life of business for the business of life. Simultaneously, I learned through my mentor in Bible studies that with commitment to Christ there was also the privilege of knowing the lordship and empowering of the Holy Spirit.

I recall the special influence of other servants of God during those early years. Gipsy Rodney Smith came to preach and sing with that rich melodious voice. Robert Laws of Livingstonia and Mildred Cable of Manchuria brought the challenge of overseas missionaries. Later Samuel M. Zwemer became my personal friend and challenged me with the needs of the Moslem world.

There were prominent Bible teachers of first rank, G. Campbell Morgan, W. H. Griffith Thomas, F. B. Meyer, and Samuel Chadwick. From Australia and New Zealand came Frank Boreham with his sermon-essays, F. W. Norwood, F. C. Spurr, Henry Howard, and Lionel B. Fletcher. Several had been born in the British Isles, but had gone to the Australian lands to minister. Some returned to visit and some to stay. If no new message was proclaimed, there was the vitality of fresh voices and striking personalities.

Among those who came to the Keswick Convention to witness to the deepening of the spiritual life were J. Stuart Holden, W. Y. Fullerton, J. Russell Howden, Charles Inwood, Alexander Smellie, A. C. Dixon, and Bishop Taylor Smith. John MacBeath of Glasgow made his contribution and as he preached in prose the message seemed to be delivered as poetry. If somewhat different from Keswick, Methodism had much to offer in its emphasis of holiness and in the Wesley tradition of a crisis hour of the Spirit. Among names I recall in this area are F. Luke Wiseman, William E. Sangster, Wilfred Hannam, A. E. Whitham, and Dinsdale T. Young. Leslie D. Weatherhead broadcast messages with a psychological emphasis. Memorable times then included reading Samuel Chadwick's weekly *Joyful News* with his incisive editorials and economic style of English. Once he came to speak in the General Assembly Hall in Edinburgh, where each night for a week he expounded the major doctrines of the faith. One night he stopped suddenly and pointing to the congregation said: "If you will stop for five minutes and really *think*, you will be born from above!" A profound truth stabbed that large congregation that night.

Among the preachers who held pastorates in Edinburgh, I recall James M. Black, fiery and dramatic with a flair for the unusual approach in sermons. I recall Alexander Frazier with his shaggy head and burning sentences interrupted by humor. A. J. Gossip would begin quietly and slowly until he suddenly caught fire; then he was off at intense speed, pouring forth cascading sentences. When his wife died during his Aberdeen pastorate, the pastor who had comforted others now felt great grief himself. At that time he preached what was to become a celebrated sermon, "When Life Tumbles In—What Then?" John A. Hutton, who later became editor of the *British Weekly*, was unforgettable in his preaching as one who felt and spoke from hidden depths of suffering and knowledge.

Of theologians who also preached there were Hugh R. Mackintosh at New College and later James S. Stewart, whose winsome approach came from an inner life of devotion and dedication. His sermons in print have a timeless quality about them. Nathan Soderblom, the Swedish theologian, came to give the Gifford Lectures and contact people of Scandinavian ancestry. Likewise,

Sadhu Sunder Singh came from India as a Christian mystic who followed Christ's steps and ministered unto others. A sermon I heard him preach in an Episcopal church, "I Am the Chief of Sinners," was memorable for its simplicity and burning passion.

I recall Alexander Simpson, Christian surgeon and teacher, nephew of the discoverer of chloroform, and his influence among young men. I remember Alexander Whyte's striking figure at the Chapman-Alexander evangelistic services. When his death was announced in Edinburgh, he was referred to simply as "the last of the Puritans." Everyone knew who had ended the earthly course and triumphed gloriously.

Among the well-known preachers I was privileged to hear was George H. Morrison (1866-1928), who became a model and standard for others. He gave his mornings to study and writing and his afternoons to visiting his congregation—he left committee work to others. He preached two services on Sunday and conducted a Bible class for young people after the evening service. This was a carry-over from his having served earlier as an assistant to Alexander Whyte, who for years gave of his best to such classes. On one occasion when leading the worship at Wellington Presbyterian Church in Glasgow, Morrison just before the sermon slipped off his robe and then preached on "The Life of Drift" (Heb. 2:1-3). What a treat for the class afterward to discuss with Morrison the subject "Christ in Shakespeare"! There was a feast in that lecture and in the questions and answers following. New vistas of truth opened for those who longed to know Christ as the Lord of *all* life and thought.

Dr. Morrison was elected moderator of the General Assembly of the United Free Church (Presbyterian). At the Assembly Hall in Edinburgh I sat in the students' gallery and heard his address. His subject was "Revival in Scotland," tracing what God had done in our history up to that time. He spoke without notes. Leaving the hall we had the opportunity to buy the printed text for a small sum. In that moving address he paid tribute to the evangelism of D. L. Moody, whose ministry he believed had brought strength and vitality to the religious life of Scotland. He especially stressed that church leaders in large numbers were the converts of the Moody-Sankey campaigns.

John Henry Jowett studied at Edinburgh University after he

had studied theology in Yorkshire, England. Like many other students he worked his way through those years. He boarded just across from Meadows Park near our home. After he had become well known, he returned to preach one Sunday in St. George's Parish Church (Presbyterian). My younger brother and I found standing room in a small gallery to the right of the pulpit. He placed his manuscript on top of the open pulpit Bible, and soon we were under the spell of a master preacher. The congregation in worship was still and listened without movement as Jowett worked his way to the climax and application of his message, which was based on Isaiah 62:1: "For Zion's sake will I not hold my peace, and for Jerusalem's sake I will not rest, until the righteousness thereof go forth as brightness, and the salvation thereof as a lamp that burneth." No one was conscious that Jowett read the manuscript and turned the pages. Once he seemed to pause and hesitate, as if groping for the right word. He put up his right hand and the gesture plucked a word out of the air, like a gardener plucking a flower. The combination of pause and gesture was most effective.

Jowett was criticized on one occasion for just such a gesture, as if he were playing for effect. My brother and I concluded that he was carried away by the inspiration of the hour, and it was natural for him to pause while feeling for the right word. I left the hour of worship that day dedicated to the concept that one day, God willing, I would proclaim the everlasting gospel. Later in life I learned from a Methodist friend and servant of God, H. Cecil Pawson, that he had been at the same service and felt the same call to serve.

John Daniel Jones (1840-1930) was unlike either Morrison or Jowett. Stockily built, ruddy-faced, strong, and with a silvery voice, "J.D." (as he was known) was Welsh and had the poetry and imagination of that musical people. His lilting voice suggested the music of the hills and valleys of Wales as he proclaimed the harmonies of divine truth.

During a church anniversary I presided over a service at which J. D. Jones was to preach. Before the service began, I mentioned that he did not need to watch the clock as there would be plenty of time before the next session. "Young man," he said, as he pointed to his loose-leaf notebook, "when I have read and preached what is here I shall stop!" And stop he did, but not before he had preached a strong biblical message from Matthew 22:32, "God is not the God of the dead, but of the living." Jones prepared by writing out the sermon. His method of preaching was to read the manuscript with passion and power.

Over the years I have had the privilege of hearing outstanding preachers and in some cases of meeting them in person. The experiences of life are of divine providence and no human manipulation could contrive certain of them. Through these experiences a neophyte began to see how God uses people in diverse stations of life and molds them for particular tasks.

Andrew W. MacBeath was a close friend and companion from school days. At the University of Edinburgh he was outstanding in scholarship. Some predicted a scholar's mantle in teaching, but Andrew, like Henry Martyn of Cambridge, had heard the call to serve overseas and right loyally he gave his best years in the Congo of Africa. There revival came and he and his wife were agents of Christian faith and life to thousands. The Bolobo revival did not come easily. Later our friend served as a pastor for a while before taking up teaching at the Toronto Bible College. Finally he served as principal of the Bible Training Institute of Glasgow. Our interchange of letters and books and talks was a foretaste of the fellowship yet to come when eternity breaks.

H. Cecil Pawson of Newcastle-on-Tyne in the northeast of England is another whose witness for Christ inspired me. He became a professor of agriculture at the university in that city. In the Wesley tradition he conducted a class each week for a group of men and this class has continued to meet for forty years. My friend was what was termed a "local preacher." In Methodist circles this means he was on call to conduct services on Sundays and this he did throughout his professional life but without remuneration. His love for the soil was balanced by his love for souls. He was honored to be vice-president of the Methodist Conference in 1951-1952.

James C. Young of Jarrow and Newcastle-on-Tyne is another layman whose life and witness counted for God. He was a prominent dentist. His Christian witness inspired many a young pastor, and his gift of a good book which he had found helpful was a means of encouraging his own pastor to pursue higher goals of study and preparation for ministry. Friendship-evangelism was his means of reaching people in all walks of life. His interests were not confined to Tyneside but reached out to other lands and peoples through his support of the missionary enterprise.

That these three close friends were British does not shut out others in Canada and in the United States. Among several to whom I have been indebted for loyalty and friendship in Christ there stands out Arthur E. Simon, whom I came to know and work with at the First Presbyterian Church of Seattle in 1954. His legal work has earned for him the highest reputation in his chosen profession, and for thirty-six years he has served the church he loves as the clerk of the session. The elders of that august body recognize his worth and esteem him highly for his works' sake. When I became the pastor of that congregation, there was Arthur Simon with his background of working with other pastorates ready to strengthen and guide mine. Under God I shared his insights and counsel as befitted his eldership. He has exemplified the ideals of the Christian gentleman. Truly he is "Mr. Presbyterian" to those of us privileged to witness his spiritual acumen. In matters of civil and ecclesiastical law he has no rival as he discusses and delivers simply and clearly judgment for his brethren to follow.

Recalling to mind the variety of preachers I have heard, I must make mention of William Temple, Archbishop of York and then of Canterbury. At a united service of commemoration at Blackpool, he preached a sermon from Hebrews 11:1: "Faith is the substance of things hoped for, the evidence of things not seen." The theologian-philosopher at the zenith of his ministry stood up and one wondered how erudite he would be. There were children present and it seemed that the archbishop looked at them and then, as it were, addressed them in conversation. Philosophical and theological words were not used, but the simple speech of that day as he explained to *them* (and so to the rest of the congregation) what the Scripture being expounded meant for everyday life. In his church in London in other days Temple had taken the Gospel of John and spent two years expounding that book in detail. Those expositions became a book entitled *Readings in St. John's Gospel* (New York: St. Martin's Press, n.d.). Here in modern dress is a devotional classic indicating the simplicity and singularity of that profound message. That day as Temple discussed faith he talked to the babes in Christ and so communicated God's love. Not the philosophic erudition of his Gifford Lectures on "Nature, Man, and God," but the same truths recast in language suited to family worship.

One bright summer day at Floors Castle in Kelso I stood for several hours in the open air, waiting to listen to Winston Churchill. He was then out of high office but still active in politics, eager to find another opportunity to return to Parliament. The cost of entrance to the grounds of that famous castle was a modest sixpence. There was standing room only when it came time to listen to one of the foremost orators of that generation. I do not recall the subject of the address, but I cannot forget the thrill of seeing and hearing a speaker who had dedicated his life to bringing his country through times of strain and stress. He worked assiduously at his addresses and steeped himself in the classics of English to arouse his countrymen to stand up and be counted in the hours of civilization's peril.

The address that day lasted almost two hours and yet the spell of that lilting voice touched our spirits and gave us hope about the future. Whatever the dangers might be in preparing to defend our honor and our land, God had raised up a leader of destiny.

Worth noting is the testimony of Winston Churchill concerning the Bible. When the Book of books was criticized and its veracity and authenticity questioned, Churchill had this to say:

> We reject with scorn all those learned and laboured myths that Moses was but a legendary figure upon whom the priesthood and the people hung their essential social, moral and religious ordinances.
>
> We believe that the most scientific view, the most up-to-date and rationalistic conception, will find its fullest satisfaction in taking the Bible story literally and in identifying one of the greatest human beings with the most decisive leap forward ever discernible in the human story.
>
> We remain unmoved by the tones of Professor Gradgrind and Dr. Dryasdust. We may be sure that all these things happened just as they are set out in Holy Writ. We may believe that they happened to people not so very different from

ourselves, and that the impressions those people received were faithfully recorded and have been transmitted across the centuries with far more accuracy than many of the telegraphed accounts we read of goings on today.

In the words of a forgotten work of Mr. Gladstone we rest with assurance upon "the impregnable rock of Holy Scripture."

Let men of science and learning expand their knowledge and prise and probe with their researches every detail of the records which have been preserved for us from these dim ages. All they will do is to fortify the grand simplicity and essential accuracy of the recorded truths which have lighted so far the pilgrimage of man.

Although liberal, conservative, and evangelical views have been in tension for generations, the Scriptures are still with us and bring light and hope to millions around the world. Walter Horton, professor of systematic theology at Oberlin College, and one-time exponent of liberalism, spoke of the swinging of the pendulum in his *Contemporary English Theology* (1945):

That pre-war liberalism—call it modernism if you will—with its excessive trust in human science and human cooperative endeavour, is not able to weather the gale of the present stormy era of social change and catastrophe, I take for granted. The steady growth of conservatism since the World War I, both in England and on the Continent, foreshadows the inevitable trends of events in America, by a law which has never failed throughout our history. Divine revelation and divine grace, as the ultimate ground of all human hope, are concepts which are destined to rise to new power in our thought and life.

During his teaching career, John Baillie saw the breakdown of modern man's cult of *progress* and finally testified to the fact that two world wars had dissipated that doctrine once and for all. The human nature of man is radically tainted by sin and the bent to evil is there, so that man's boasted progress becomes an illusion in values, morals, and character, even though he claims progress in technology. In his *Invitation to Pilgrimage* (Grand Rapids: Baker Book House, 1976), Baillie recalls his journey from youth to seasoned experience, a journey on which he found evangelical conviction and the truth of Christ still aflame.

Looking back over my studies in theological colleges and in

universities where the critical light is brought to bear upon what is believed concerning God and the Scriptures, I found extremes of interpretation presented (and some not without prejudice!). In the search for truth, knowledge and faith have been tested and reexamined. I had the benefit of the steadying power of an evangelical experience as well as a personal and vital awareness that one can encounter new levels of interpretation without thereby surrendering to every wind then blowing. Allied to personal faith in the Savior and Lord of all life were my reading of the Bible and its unusual facility in "finding me" (as Samuel Taylor Coleridge expressed about Paul's Epistle to the Ephesians). That "finding" was the inner work of the Holy Spirit applying truth and bringing an equilibrium of judgment.

Robert Murray McCheyne of Dundee, Scotland, confessed that after his studies at the university he felt unclean because of the thought forms and ideas presented to his imagination by some of the Greek classics. However, there is a kindness in God's mercy; and we, too, may "forget the things behind even as we press forward" to the biblical riches. Every age has its demands upon student and preacher. In connection with religious thought there is much that may appear disturbing and not worthwhile to read or examine. Nevertheless, we are surprised at how unexpectedly we may change our minds on this score.

In student days I had the opportunity to take a course in moral philosophy at Edinburgh under Professor A. E. Taylor, one of the outstanding thinkers of the time. What was not always apparent was the fact that within that period the professors in similar chairs at Glasgow and Aberdeen universities were also showing appreciation of the Christian faith and were certainly not guilty of denigrating Christianity. Professor A. A. Bowman at Glasgow was much appreciated for his *Studies in the Philosophy of Religion* (1938); Professor J. Laird at Aberdeen recognized the divine ethic in *Morals and Western Religion* (1931), while Taylor shared penetrative insights pointing toward Christianity in *The Faith of a Moralist* (1937). A short time thereafter C. S. Lewis brought a cogent defense of the truth of the gospel to a new generation. Whenever there is a litany of jeremiads mourning for the coming demise of Christian witness, suddenly God raises up defenders of the faith.

From Bible times throughout church history and to this day and hour, God continues to call people to serve. There was John Newton (1725-1807), who, having spent four years in the slave trade, eventually became a Christian preacher. He wrote many hymns, including the still popular "Amazing Grace." In a few of his letters Newton spoke of the ministry as a choice service for God. But he pointed out the snares and difficulties associated with it. Newton noted that in Satan's temptations of and attacks on would-be ministers, there is a sifting under God. "The work of the ministry is truly honourable; but, like the post of honour in a battle, it is attended with peculiar dangers: therefore, the apostle cautions Timothy, 'Take heed to thyself, and to thy doctrine.' " Newton pointed out that "opposition will hurt you, if it should give you an idea of your own importance. . . ." He also warned that if opposition has hurt many, "popularity has wounded more."

The words of Newton are encouraging to the one who testifies he has received a call of God to the ministry. There is "a warm and earnest desire to be employed in this service." This means it is preferred to any other vocation and there is no thought of giving it up. Newton also notes that God gives "a sufficiency as to gifts, knowledge, and utterance." In other words, if the Lord of the harvest sends a man to teach others, He will furnish him with the means. The final seal of divine approval is the evidence of a proper call when "Providence, by a gradual train of circumstances, [points] out the means, the time, the place, of actually entering upon the work." This may not come with clarity at once, but gradually it is discerned.

The apostle Paul addressed Timothy as a "man of God" (I Tim. 6:11). Here we have a plumbline to judge the reality and righteousness of our ministry. Paul counsels that the man of God should "flee . . . follow . . . fight . . ." (I Tim. 6:11, 12). Who is this person according to the Scriptures? He is:

Noah, a preacher of righteousness, alone, misunderstood

Moses, a leader, legislator, bringing the divine law

Samuel, a prophet engaged in ministries of destiny for his people

Solomon, a wise man, seeing life lived without meaning "under the sun"

Elijah, a strong voice for God against idolatry, standing alone

Nehemiah, a rebuilder of devastated places and a bringer of hope

Isaiah, a patriot turned prophet with evangelical good news

Hosea, a compassionate lover of others, whose own heart suffered

Amos, a herdsman who preached in righteous tones, and without portfolio

Ezekiel, a preacher in exile who sat where others sat

Jeremiah, a youthful servant who burned for God with tears

Micah, a messenger of grace who stabbed the conscience with notions of justice and ethical obedience

Jonah, a disobedient prophet given an unattractive mission

John the Baptist, a voice for God, who worked no miracles, yet spoke truth in all he said about Jesus

Peter, a large-hearted witness, with blunt speech and yet love

Apollos, an eloquent preacher, with ardor and accuracy of message

James, a teacher of moral standards and of faith with works

Philip, an obedient servant, leaving crowds to win one man

Paul, a chosen vessel for God with profound reason and spiritual insight able to reach his world

In church history, the names are legion—Savonarola, Luther, Calvin, Wycliffe, Whitefield, Wesley, Finney, Moody, Edwards, Spurgeon, Brooks, Beecher, Bushnell, Gladden, Whyte, Bunyan, and a host of others whose names are on the divine honor roll of obedient servants as men of God.

Memories generally focus on ordinary days and events. But there are lessons to be gained from the unusual. If Winston Churchill has been mentioned a number of times, it is because he is an example of how one can rise in spite of limitations. It is not always recalled that Churchill in his days of destiny during wartime was subjected to tests and trials not unlike those facing the preacher. The statesman, the politician, the military strategist, the historian, we see clearly, but what of *the man?*

There were times when despair swept over him. He had bouts of depression, discouragement, and loneliness. These are common to multitudes of people, but in his case they were well nigh crushing in the light of his commitments and the load he carried as a wartime leader. Because he had gone through this type of experience from boyhood, he was able in his periods of leadership to bring courage and hope to others who had lost hope.

One of the ways in which Churchill forced himself to fight tendencies of gloom lay in his forced ambition. He worked hard to compensate for his lack of certain strengths and virtues. Coupled with this were his conviction that he would be preserved to long life and his constant reference to the belief that he was here for a special purpose and design. When civilization needed a leader bold and brave, a prophet, a realistic visionary, a dreamer of victory, Churchill was there. The man of God, likewise, is tested and tempted in depression, loneliness, and discouragement (and in some cases presumption). Like Churchill, who spoke of himself as a servant of the monarch, the man of God knows that he is "a servant of the Christ"; and so he rises to new levels of devotion and service without suffering defeat.

In looking back we relive our defeats and victories. The years of ministry bring discipline, experience, and a maturity. It has been suggested that John Milton (1608-1674) "lived his books and wrote himself into them. His own life was not eventful, but the times were; and of those times Milton made himself intensely a part." He had his limitations. He had much contact with men's minds in books; he had little contact with men's minds in the world; and to the end of his days Milton tended to think of man as spirit and never as mere clay. One of our dangers is that like Milton we have similar limits—our bookishness and our ivory-tower existence. Only when we get out into the street and the arena where people work and live do we find the reality of Christian ministry.

We dare not forget our background. We had nothing to do with our heritage of family, education, and endowment of nature. Some ministers begin with handicaps which plague them all their days. Others have advantages which seem to give them a running start and speed them on their way. Whatever our starting point, we can begin there and let the call of God be the spur to work and serve Him. John Buchan (Lord Tweedsmuir), man of letters and writer of a variety of books, never lost the memory of his youth. He remained the son of a happy but poor

Scottish manse. So it will be with those who have served as ministers of the Head of the church, even our Lord Jesus Christ. Truly, like the psalmist we can say, "Yea, I have a goodly heritage" (Ps. 16:6). In retrospect over past years we see an ordinary life lived by an extraordinary faith in God. Only the grace of God can explain this. It has been more wonderful than dreams have imagined it would be. We have learned from those who were not friends but critics and adversaries, and we trust we have been humble enough to acknowledge that. Our friends have overwhelmed us again and again by their trust and confidence in us. We do not deserve their love of our character and our ministries; their esteem is grace upon grace!

Our heritage determines our destiny. Every child born into the world is a fresh creation; there is a purpose transcending our earthbound ideas. We believe that there has been a plan wrought out over the years of our life and ministry and the necessary qualities of character have been supplied. The precept in Proverbs 22:6 has puzzled some: "Train up a child in the way he should go: and when he is old, he will not depart from it." The generally accepted interpretation is that if the parents bring up the child in the knowledge of God and of the Christian faith, the child will abide in it when he becomes an adult. However, I believe an entirely different meaning is possible: "Train him up at the mouth of his way," that is, "as his way requires" or "directs." *Observe his aptitudes*, and so learn the sort of work for which he is providentially designed; and whatever it be, educate him for that. It is the making of a lad when he realizes that life is a high enterprise and he has a work of his own to do in the world, and recognizes that whatever be his natural aptitudes, these are the qualities wherewith God has entrusted him, and it is with these he must find his vocation.

20

The Pilgrim in Progress

Who would true valour see,
  Let him come hither;
One here will constant be,
  Come wind, come weather;
There's no discouragement
Shall make him once relent
His first avowed intent
  To be a pilgrim.

Who so beset him round
  With dismal stories,
Do but themselves confound—
  His strength the more is.
No lion can him fright;
He'll with a giant fight,
But he will have a right
  To be a pilgrim.

Hobgoblin nor foul fiend
  Can daunt his spirit;
He knows he at the end
  Shall life inherit.
Then fancies fly away,
He'll not fear what men say,
He'll labour night and day
  To be a pilgrim.

JOHN BUNYAN (1628-1688), the author of *Pilgrim's Progress*, became poet and hymn writer when Mr. Greatheart's and Mr. Valiant-For-Truth's discussion of the dangers of the way led to the above hymn, "The Pilgrim Song." When Winston Churchill planned his own memorial service, he included this as one of the three hymns to be sung by the congregation gathered in Saint Paul's Cathedral.

John Buchan (1875-1940), Lord Tweedsmuir, Governor-General of Canada, historian, novelist, poet, and man of letters was caught in Bunyan's spell. In his major work of an autobiographical nature, he said that he had not penned reminiscences of the past but had ventured into what might be termed a *diary of a pilgrimage.* The British edition was named Memory Hold-the-Door, but the American edition has the intriguing title of *Pilgrim's Way* (New York: AMS Press, 1977 reprint). He had planned another short book in tribute to the fisherman's art and skill but left only two chapters and a tentative title *Pilgrim's Rest!*

The Pilgrim Fathers, leaving the shores of Holland and England in 1620, ventured to the American eastern seaboard with courage and faith to begin a noble experiment under God for a destiny not wholly determined then. That they, like others of biblical record (Heb. 11), were "strangers and pilgrims on the earth," and in retrospect strangers "of whom the world was not worthy," testifies to the implications of a pilgrimage journey into the unknown.

Later, the theme of a sermon preached by Samuel Danforth (1626-1674) slipped into current speech and coinage: "Errand into the Wilderness." Like a refrain in music or the motif in a literary masterwork, this became the slogan for those who followed the first pilgrims across the ocean. As they wrote their diaries, letters, and journals, the idea of pilgrimage entered into the fabric of the new order and new world.

Of Bunyan himself, there are depths yet unplumbed in interpreting much of what he has written. His interior life appears as a testing ground, a proving ground for the weapons of the evil one who wars against the soul. Shortly after Bunyan had rejoiced in the assurance that salvation is offered in Christ and that a ransomed soul is precious to the Savior even when it appears worthless to itself, diabolical temptation came to him. One temptation was to doubt the very existence of God. His heart was so hard that it startled him. He could not shed a tear nor even feel desire to shed one.

It was just then that he took the step which lifted him out of the old entanglements. He fell upon Luther's commentary on Galatians. He longed to read the experience of some godly man who had endured so that he might have company and counsel in his own lonely pilgrimage. In Luther, Bunyan found a fellow pilgrim. Thereafter Bunyan heard God's voice in the valley of the shadow.

On a memorable day, Bunyan read the words, "Thy righteousness is in heaven!" Then he wrote:

> I saw that it was not my good frame of heart that made my righteousness better, nor my bad frame which made my righteousness worse; for my righteousness was Jesus Christ Himself, the same yesterday, and today, and forever. . . . 'Twas glorious to see His exaltation and the worth and prevalency of all His benefits, and that because now I could look from myself to Him and reckon that all those graces of God were on me. . . . Now Christ was all, all my righteousness, all my sanctification, and all my redemption. Further, the Lord did also lead me into the mystery of union with the Son of God. If He and I were One, then His resurrection was mine, His victory also mine.

Thus the interior struggle of the pilgrim.

What then are the marks of a pilgrim in progress? Bunyan's writings would indicate that *no one is exempted from tests and trials by temptation.* As W. Graham Scroggie expressed it, we are tested by temptation. Bunyan confessed that he was susceptible to sullen and desperate moods against which he struggled. For example, there was a day when a voice assaulted him fiercely, saying, "Sell Christ! Sell Christ!" He resisted for a while, but at last he seemed to consent. "Now was Satan's battle won, and down fell I as a bird is shot from the top of a tree." For some hours he wandered among the fields, but a kindly voice pursued him and kept saying, "Return unto Me, for I have redeemed thee."

Another mark of the pilgrim way is that *there are varieties of Christian experience.* Bunyan had a generous and liberal mind. He did not insist that his was the only real experience under God. He was receptive to others on the same highway provided they were sincere and genuine in their faith. His temptations were different from others. Faithful never fell into the Slough of Despond; he had found sunshine in the Valley of the Shadow of Death. Christian crossed the River of Death "not without horror"; Hopeful felt the bottom all the way.

In his imaginative and economic style, Bunyan indicates that in the pilgrimage *each man's convictions are influenced by his individuality*. What we are by nature may color what we believe. Our various temperaments influence and modify our expressions of faith and belief. Bunyan's characters have an individuality and distinctiveness. Their conscience is not asleep at any time. The divine Spirit is working within the pilgrim to remake each one by faith in God.

As we struggle to find a footing in the Christian life, we are enriched by the generosity of those Christians in the past who have left a written record of their spiritual experiences. It is thus that the flaming torch of the Good News is carried from one period to another; one life passes it on to another. The great value of the Christian classics for our day is evident in the number of reprints and new editions being processed by publishers.

Another who has traveled the pathway of a pilgrim is John Baillie (1886-1960), whose works in philosophy and theology are known throughout the church. Some of us will remember him best as the author of *A Diary of Private Prayer* (New York: Charles Scribner's Sons, 1949), *A Diary of Readings* (New York: Charles Scribner's Sons, 1955), and *Invitation to Pilgrimage* (Grand Rapids: Baker Book House, 1976 reprint). These books assist the devotional life and can be used for short periods each day. The third book is of special interest—for here is another writer who viewed his life as a pilgrimage. After a youth grounded in evangelical principles, he traveled through a torturous period of intellectual growth. Finally, he experienced a renewal of faith and hope based upon the foundation of eternal truth. John Baillie's experience has much to say to us in this restless and tension-filled generation. Enduring floods of trial and suffering in mind and heart, he found the steps of faith when he touched the bottom. He generously shares with us what he endured and now invites others to pilgrimage in Christ.

A rereading of John Baillie's *Invitation to Pilgrimage* suggests to us that many who have tried various ways of seeking fullness of life have also come to experience a divine-human encounter, a choice at the fork in the road. This is reminiscent of John Bunyan's pilgrim, who has had many follow his example across the centuries. Baillie witnesses to the higher wisdom, the sounder knowledge, and the liberating truth which he found in the gospel of the Savior, who brings health and completeness of life. The strong evangelical note of his boyhood guided him through varied currents of thought. As he encountered different intellectual and philosophical systems, there was still etched on his mind and heart the lesson he learned in his youth that "man's chief end is to glorify God and enjoy Him for ever."

At the climax of his life Baillie prepared a series of erudite lectures published as *The Sense of the Presence of God* (New York: Charles Scribner's Sons, 1962). He testified to the relevance of the gospel across the years. Not only is the pilgrim endowed with Christ's righteousness through justifying grace, but he receives sanctification as God's gift. "Because sanctification means the progressive defeat of pride, it must mean gradual growth in humility." Thus the pilgrim in progress.

Two Scottish ministers, Alexander Whyte and W. Graham Scroggie, introduced me to John Bunyan. It was through Whyte that I came to appreciate the classics of devotion and to gather the nucleus of the special bookshelf which I have reserved for the quiet hour. One day, while I was returning from work, I saw the four volumes of Whyte's *Bunyan Characters* (Philadelphia: Richard West, 1973 reprint) in a bookdealer's window and purchased them a few days later. The cost was modest then. The letters "A.W." were stamped in gold on my red-cloth editions, which also contained Whyte's own inscription (Whyte had given these very volumes to a friend).

Later Scroggie, who shared with me books from his first-class library, reminded me again and again to read Bunyan and to read Whyte! As he was indebted to them, he thought that they would profit me in my pilgrimage.

John Bunyan's immortal classic of the Christian life has spoken to every age and to people in all sorts of conditions of life. His genius lay in his gift of imagination. Do not be surprised that over and over again he uses the expression "I saw." What we read or hear does not affect us as much as does what we see. No one before Bunyan saw that the Christian is a pilgrim. He taught each successive generation in the church to see it. His characters and experiences are with us still in the Christians of today and their struggles. Of course, the names of Mr. Brisk, Old Honest, Mr. Hategood, Bye-ends, Mr Ready-to-Halt, have changed a little and been modernized; but similar struggles are waged within each modern-day pilgrim.

To be a pilgrim in modern dress and habit is to keep company with a multitude who across the centuries have progressed from the City of Destruction to the Celestial City. Our contemporary world experiences convulsions and tensions because of the eruptive lava of human nature, which, left to itself, is incapable of redeeming itself. The flesh wars against the spirit. Paul's commentary in Romans 5-8 is as relevant today as when he wrote of conditions in the Roman world of the first century. Natural man must still find his way to the Wicket Gate and the Cross and the Empty Sepulchre to find release and renewal.

In our moments of well-being, when the days slip past easily and without extra demand upon our powers, we are prone to assume that we are progressing very well. However, it may be it is precisely then that we need to be on our guard lest we slip on the slope of self-sufficiency and self-love. That mood of the soul is the occasion of seduction and our undoing. The minister who dreams of plans and programs leading to "success" might well pause and discover that he is in danger. We in the ministry are special targets of evil and the fire of temptation is thrice-heated.

Reading the classics of the soul's quest, those books of devotion and spiritual insight, teaches many lessons. One of the most vital is that we are never free from attack from without and also from within. Especially the interior life requires daily scrutiny and strength.

When the Wesley brothers first read Jeremy Taylor's *Rule and Exercises of Holy Living* (Cleveland: World Publishing, 1956 reprint) and *Rule and Exercise of Holy Dying* (Cleveland: World Publishing, 1952 reprint), they did not find what they were seeking. Until they had an hour of illumination and their hearts were warmed, the texts were too advanced for them. In retrospect they came to understand and to appreciate the truths Taylor was attempting to convey to growing disciples. In one of his sermons, Taylor taught that "nature and reason alone cannot produce growth in wisdom; there must be something else. But this is to be wrought by a new principle, that is, by *the spirit of grace.*" A similar experience is the testimony of the saints of all ages who have told what God has done in and for them.

Among the perils of our lot lie sins like hypocrisy, worldliness, revenge, luxury, aversion to prayer, and disbelief even when we talk of faith. Many of the dangers and perils of our calling have been discussed in *A Minister's Obstacles*. We are never free from unexpected gusts of temptation arising without warning. We can benefit from guides in Christian living and holiness of character who have traveled the way before us. Of course, the Scriptures are always at hand. In them we find many examples of people who have fallen but been saved by the grace of God. Their testimony is genuine and still vital.

Let the moving words of Edwin Hatch rekindle our appreciation of the saints of every age (from J. Marchant, *Deeds Done for Christ* [London: P. V. Cassel & Co., 1928]):

> Saints of the early dawn of Christ,
>   Saints of Imperial Rome,
> Saints of the cloistered Middle Age,
>   Saints of the modern home;
> Saints of the soft and sunny East,
>   Saints of the frozen seas,
> Saints of the isles that wave their palms
>   In the far Antipodes;
>
> Saints of the marts and busy streets,
>   Saints of the squalid lanes,
> Saints of the silent solitudes,
>   Of the prairies and the plains;
> Saints who were wafted to the skies
>   In the torment robe of flame,
> Saints who have graven on men's thoughts
>   A monumental name;
>
> Come, from the home of holiest hope,
>   Under the altar-throne;
> Come, from the depths where the angels see
>   One Awful Face alone;
> Come from the heights where the Mount of God
>   Burns like a burnished gem;
> Come from the star-paved terraces
>   Of the new Jerusalem:
>
> Come, for our faith is waxing faint,
>   And the lamp of love burns low;

Come to these lower heavens, and shine,
    That we may see and know;
Come, for the flash of a moment's space,
    With your snowy wings outspread,
O God-lit cloud of witnesses,
    Souls of the sainted dead.

Measured by the standards of our age, a minister seems a fool,
for he might gain much more in other walks of life. But the call
of the Christ to service and to the joy of selfless discipleship is
reward enough. We belong to a great company; no other society
provides as many opportunities to give of ourselves in love as
does the Christian ministry. Francis Xavier (1506-1552) expressed this in his hymn (which should be better known):

My God, I love Thee:
    Not because I hope for heav'n thereby;
Nor yet because if I love not
    I must for ever die.

But, O my Jesus, Thou didst me
    Upon the Cross embrace;
For me didst bear the nails and spear,
    And manifold disgrace;

And griefs and torments numberless,
    And sweat of agony,
E'en death itself; and all for me
    Who was Thine enemy.

Then why, O blessed Jesus Christ,
    Should I not love Thee well?
Not for the hope of winning heaven,
    Nor of escaping hell;

Not with the hope of gaining aught;
    Nor seeking a reward;
But as Thyself hast loved me,
    O ever-loving Lord!

E'en so I love Thee, and will love,
    And in Thy praise will sing;
Solely because Thou art my God,
    And my eternal King.

In retrospect, there are many experiences which call for consideration and remembrance. Youth has its moments when at school and play we discover certain treasures which appeal to the growing mind. Looking at my bookshelf today there are a few books which still hold appeal after a long interval. Some I met in youth forecast the direction of my life. A. J. Grant's *Outlines of European History* dealt with the classical world, the Middle Ages, and the modern world. Wider horizons beckoned as I read it. E. N. Hoare's *Seeking a Country* is an account of the Pilgrim Fathers which traces the finger of providence in the course of human history. Here was the *making* of history. These two books given to me at school fed my interest in history. *Chambers's Encyclopaedia* was a constant companion. This single volume gave great stimulus to mind and spirit as I read the articles and looked at the illustrations. My knowledge of many subjects continued to grow.

William Booth's *In Darkest England and the Way Out* told me of a world outside my home, a world in which ugliness and disease and sordid environment oppressed thousands, especially in the major metropolitan areas of the land. The Industrial Revolution saw tremendous growth in the liquor traffic and slums. Who but a Christian like William Booth would dare to attack the enemy where he was entrenched? His book told of how the gospel could and did transform human nature so that conscience might be stabbed afresh and the nation alerted to what should be done to transform social and economic life. As a result of reading Booth's work, I geared my ministry to contact and serve those who needed the compassion of the Savior.

Dean F. W. Farrar's *The Life of Christ* was one of my father's treasures. The day came when I completed the reading of this 700-page volume which reflected vast research and critical studies of the text of Scripture. It set me on the road at an early age to think in terms of hermeneutics and to delve into the Hebrew background of the Life of lives.

In school I received a copy of *The Poetical Works of Sir Walter Scott*. This fanned the flame of national patriotism and as one born in The Lowlands of Scotland excited me with dreams of what might be! In "The Lay of the Last Minstrel" we find:

> Breathes there a man, with soul so dead,
> Who never to himself hath said,
>   This is my own, my native land!
> Whose heart hath ne'er within him burn'd,
> As home his footsteps he hath turn'd,
>   From wandering on a foreign strand!
> If such there be, go, mark him well;
> For him no minstrel raptures swell;
> High though his titles, proud his name,
> Boundless his wealth as wish can claim;
> Despite those titles, power, and pelf,
> The wretch, concentred all in self,
> Living, shall forfeit fair renown,
> And, doubly dying, shall go down
> To the vile dust, from whence he sprung,
> Unwept, unhonour'd, and unsung.

When later I traveled to Canada and then came to the United States to become a citizen, the foundation of my national heritage became a spur to adopt new allegiance to "this nation under God." The strength of the older birthright has but enriched the new.

There was also Scotland's national poet, Robert Burns. Around the world there are tributes to this eighteenth-century plowman. A Scottish peasant in that era would have had few books, but there would have been the Bible, some standard work of theology, and a history of Scotland. Alongside of them, almost for certain, Bunyan's *Pilgrim's Progress*. The young Burns undoubtedly had a similarly limited library, but used it well. His youth was characterized by an irregular school education as well as hard toil. Among his major themes were communion with nature and the sufferings of the poor. He became a critic of the church, but also expressed a faith often tainted by his moral lapses. His vernacular language puzzles those who come to him for the first time, but with glossary in hand they will find a fresh unfolding of truth and beauty as the poet fills the mind with sights and sounds unforgettable.

A most significant boyhood influence was my copy of Bunyan's *Pilgrim's Progress*. Given to my parents on their wedding day by the pastor who officiated at the ceremony, this volume has been treasured over the years. This is the most valuable item

I inherited from my parents. Not wealth, material possessions, or position, but the book I used to read lying on a carpet before the open fire on dark and cold days. It is not to be thought that I could ever match Charles Spurgeon, who said that he had read Bunyan one hundred times! Over the years of ministry I acquired Bunyan's other works to increase my knowledge of the intricacies of the heart.

The saying is valid that "the child is father to the man." Early days at home and in school brought certain books into my orbit. Each of these had great impact on my progress in faith and culture and service. My present library of thousands of books grew from that tiny seed of a few books and owes much to the sacrifices of my wife, whose partnership helped make possible what it has become. A true library is not "a cemetery of dead books" (as Lord Rosebery said). Nor is it a collection, but a *selection* of what is required in life and work.

In the pilgrimage of the years critics have spoken against the organized church because of its supposed failure in avoiding *social activism*. The congregation has been seen as a group of people who have separated themselves from the rest of society. Whatever the basis for that criticism (and no doubt there have been those who have given the impression of indifference to social wrongs), it is the record over the centuries that the Christian church has led the forces of social reform and political transformation. Personally, I have witnessed the outgoing, caring ministries of Christian people from local congregations.

During the Depression of the 1930s, when thousands were unemployed, a group of churchmen from the northeast of England, who were also "on the dole," rented an old mill (defunct and delapidated), cleaned and renovated it, and then invited unemployed men to come daily with any tools they might have. As a beginning, they repaired furniture; then they made toys for the coming Christmas; later they began to develop other items until after a year or so they were able to sell a variety of products to alleviate their distress. Self-respect was not lost, and skills were not destroyed as morale returned. The Christian faith had made its impact. In addition there were those who became active and involved in the political arena. When stores and shops went out of business, when shipbuilding yards had no ships to build, the outlook was dark. The church in that industrial area served as a lever to raise the fortunes of those who were hardest hit.

I will cite another example, this one from the northwest of the United States when recession came and a metropolitan area was threatened. Thousands were laid off in the airplane and related industries. At once, Christians met to share with those who were affected by the recession. Training, education, skills, experience, and character were assessed. Then the search began to find other jobs for those out of work. The church thus sponsored a massive undertaking of caring and sharing.

There are untold other ways in which Christians have been of service to their communities. Note the number of church people who are involved in programs like Head Start, Big Brothers, and the Red Cross. They visit the lonely and the forgotten in nursing and retirement homes. They provide meals, clothing, and shelter to the poor. They find homes and work for refugees. They help delinquents start anew. They enter the medical professions, provide free legal service to the destitute, teach in circumstances where there is special need. They send out relief supplies wherever disaster may strike throughout the world. Much more could be listed in detail.

There has also been frequent criticism of church building programs as unnecessary. But the money given for these projects comes from voluntary gifts of hundreds of people who have paid their taxes to the state and nation and then give over and above that for the church. There is one thing some critics have overlooked. When men and women were out of work, the building programs of Christian churches contributed to the economic life of the city, pouring millions of dollars into industry. And this involves contractors, craftsmen, carpenters, plasterers, steel workers, electricians, glass workers, carpet manufacturers, truckers, painters, utility employees, organ builders, as well as draftsmen and architects. Those so employed (at least in the case of one church which I know particularly) come from various ethnic and social and religious backgrounds without any discrimination. Of course, such contracts cannot resolve the total unemployment situation, but they do stimulate the economy.

A spiritual pilgrimage involves years of experience, a growing faith, and a joyous recollection of service rendered. Who can tell when a spiritual pilgrimage begins? While Moses was called as a mature adult, Gideon was a young man and Samuel a mere boy. Amos was taken from the fields as Elisha from the plow and David from the sheepfold. Isaiah was called when engaged in worship at the temple of Jerusalem, while of John the Baptist it is said that he was filled by the Holy Spirit even when in the womb of his mother.

Across the years of the history of the church there are reports of individuals receiving God's call to minister. We dare not be content with a human motivation to ministry. Only a living and vital faith can assure us that God has placed us in the ministry. Paul spoke of a "received ministry" (Col. 4:17), and wise teachers and interpreters of the New Testament have agreed that there is an unmistakable assurance in that call. John spoke of having "an unction from the Holy One" (I John 2:20). The eighteenth-century revivals of Christendom (the Evangelical Revival in England and the Great Awakening in New England) were launched by men with special calls. John Wesley and Jonathan Edwards were called to be an itinerant evangelist and a pastor to a congregation and community, respectively. That they had widely different theological emphases in their preaching is clear evidence that it is not the theological stress that brings the Holy Spirit's moving upon people, but the peculiar power or unction poured out upon the Word of God. That is the voice of God Himself.

To relate what is private and personal is not easy. God has His way of molding each one of us. After my baptism and dedication as a babe, there were many who prayed and believed that I would eventually be counted among the people of God and then called to be a minister. That prayer was answered when as a lad at school I experienced conversion and committed myself to discipleship. Assurance that God in Christ had accepted me came from John 5:24.

After several years in the business world, during which I acquired new knowledge of the Bible, there came the call to leave the life of business for the business of life. Further preparation in private study and classroom led to degrees in the arts and theology. My subsequent years in the ministry involved disciplined study, travel, teaching, writing, and witnessing. Of ill health, not much over the years until near retirement, when I underwent major operations and suffered a breakdown. In God's providence I was raised up and now with thanksgiving look forward to further service. I have enough strength to serve and know that there is *health for the day*. I told my surgeon, "I am ready to go but willing to stay"; so it has been to the present. In the word of a Welsh poet:

> So, take and use Thy work;
> Amend what flaws may lurk,
> What strain o' the stuff, what warpings past the aim!
> My times be in Thy hand!
> Perfect the cup as planned!
> Let age approve of youth, and death complete the same!

The minister who counts the blessings of God finds unusual opportunities to praise God. God is the Giver of every good and perfect gift, and constantly we are reminded of the benefits received. A vast number of our fellow pilgrims must toil within the confines of the assembly line with its soporific and deadening monotony. But we have a work which we enjoy to the full, and we find open doors with people everywhere because of it.

Thanks be to God then for the life and work of the minister at its noblest and best. We have been given sufficient—in depression years as well as in other decades—so that the basic needs of our family have been met. Health has been given. When sickness and operations have come, we have been brought through to serve again after trial and testing. How much we owe to those of the congregation who have prayed, to the devotion and skill of doctors and nurses, and to loved ones who have stood by during the waiting hours of crisis and recovery. Thanks for the places where we have found our homes, for a minister has no permanent dwelling place but expects to move on across the years of service. Other causes for thanksgiving include the friends who have demonstrated their love and loyalty more than we deserved.

When Clarence Edward Macartney (1879-1957) neared the end of his life, he told his friends, "My anchor still holds." He had gloried in the infinite grace of God, and this was reflected in the grandeur of his preaching. His personal faith found added strength in the singing of hymns like "Rock of Ages" and "Amazing Grace."

More and more there is a quiet confidence that the God and Father of our Lord and Savior Jesus Christ is able to guide us throughout the pilgrimage to the harvest of the years. For some that is a short period; for others it seems long. However, whatever the years granted here, there is the certainty of the continuance of eternal life beyond time. That incident called death is not to be feared as it is a transition into eternity. There will be a continuity of the life known here. There is identity of personality here and there will be hereafter. There is progress expected in the life to come. There are perfection and fullness of life hereafter. All that is best here is seen as short of what will be when we see the Christ of God and when we shall be made like unto Him. All endowments of nature and gifts of God will be transformed and enlarged in that unlimited sphere of life. No longer shall we think of the honors of this life or of the human aspirations which make people compare themselves with their peers. Then we will live in the glory of God, and the music of the spheres and of the people of God will guarantee the harmonies of life in the abundance of the new creation.

Samuel Rutherford, a Covenanter from Anwoth in the southwest of Scotland, thought of that final mode of life as a privilege:

> Oh! If one soul from Anwoth
>   Meet me at God's right hand,
> Then Heaven will be two Heavens
>   In Emmanuel's land.

And what finer epitaph could be spoken than that of John the Baptist by our Lord's followers: "John did no miracle: but all things that John spake of this man were true. And many believed on him there" (John 10:41, 42)? Or that of the psalmist: "I shall be satisfied, when I awake, with thy likeness" (Ps. 17:15)?

Lines for a Bookmark

You who read—
May you seek
As you look;
May you keep
What you need:
May you care
What you choose:
And know here
In this book
That you use,
Something strange
That is sure,
That will change
You and be yours.

(Gael L. Turnbull)